Popular Witchcraft

OTHER BOOKS BY JACK FRITSCHER

Mapplethorpe: Assault with a Deadly Camera

Some Dance to Remember: A Memoir-Novel of San Francisco, 1970–1982

The Geography of Women

What They Did to the Kid: Confessions of an Altarboy

Popular Witchcraft

Straight from the Witch's Mouth

JACK FRITSCHER

Featuring High Priest Anton LaVey

THE UNIVERSITY OF WISCONSIN PRESS / POPULAR PRESS

The University of Wisconsin Press
1930 Monroe Street
Madison, Wisconsin 53711

www.wisc.edu/wisconsinpress/

3 Henrietta Street
London WC2E 8LU, England

Library of Congress Cataloging-in-Publication Data
Fritscher, Jack.
Popular witchcraft : straight from the witch's mouth / Jack Fritscher ;
featuring Anton LaVey.—2nd ed.
p. cm.
"A Ray and Pat Browne book."
Includes bibliographical references and index.
ISBN 0-299-20300-X (hardcover : alk. paper)—
ISBN 0-299-20304-2 (pbk. : alk. paper)
1. Witchcraft. I. LaVey, Anton Szandor, 1930– II. Title.
BF1566.F75 2004
133.4′3—dc22
2004005380

For Mark Thomas Hemry,

as well as for

Anton LaVey

and for Benjamin Christensen

whose 1922 documentary film *Haxan*,

and Gerald Gardner

whose 1954 book *Witchcraft Today*

are the models and inspiration for this book

CONTENTS

How Witchcraft Saves Civilization

You have bent up the Pentagram, young man!
—MARIA OUSPENSKAYA, *The Wolf Man*

WHY I BENT UP THE PENTRAGRAM . . . TWICE!

PREFACE: TAKE ONE, 1972

San Francisco

I began this book as an unbeliever in the occult. I leave it, if not believing, then not disbelieving. What is here is not everything you need to know about witchcraft, nor everything you need to know about the selling of God, sex, and the Age of Aquarius. What is here is not the sociology or anthropology of witchcraft, nor a taxitive compendium of horror movies, sex cults, pornography, and American law. What is here is not anti-Christian or anti-God. What is here, simply, is the popular culture of American sorcery.

The first manuscript pages of this book appeared in 1969, only a few days after a British vicar's widow, Maisie Pearson, confirmed an I Ching reading. She predicted for me a long occult adventure. "You must do it," she said.

Some time later, after meeting at midnight with Anton LaVey, who is the high priest of the Church of Satan, interviewing white witches, and attending Black Masses, I asked myself, "Is this any way for an exorcist to behave?" I had been ordained an exorcist in the Catholic Church in 1963, but my exorcising days, like my Catholicism, were gone with the winds of spiritual upheaval that blew with Vatican II. Hot knees bewitched mine beneath ouija boards from New York to San Francisco; witches invited me into their confidence; reportage became adventure. This was New Journalism at its gonzo best. The reporter, like Alice through the looking glass, participated in the experience. To get at the truth of craft, velvet gloves crucified me nude in a New York art gallery, and I was dipped naked in the healing waters of the Virgin at Lourdes.

Now astrology, magic, tarot, and yin-yang macrobiotics, as well as occult psychedelia, gender magic, and phallic worship, are no more exotic to me than the philosophy of Thomas Aquinas, the theology of John Calvin, and the sadomasochistic erotica of the Inquisition. I do, however, understand why inside the table top of every altar in every Catholic church rests an altar stone containing human bones.

In the poker game of American spirituality, the witchcraft card trumps traditional religion. No longer a silent minority, witchcraft is part of the liberation movements of sex, race, and gender that are transforming American popular culture. Witchcraft labels Christianity, Judaism, and Islam as cults far less ancient than witchcraft. Most important, the U.S. Supreme Court constitutionally guarantees that witchcraft is a valid religion whose rituals are now part of the *U.S. Chaplains' Manual* for military bases.

Three hundred years after the Salem Witch Trials, witchcraft has saved civilization by leveling the playing field of spirituality. No longer can Christianity, Judaism, and Islam control American spirituality. The occult offers ancient answers to human needs repressed by these dogmatic religions that came along thousands of years after witchcraft ruled the earth. I mean this book to sound no more anti-Christian than I intend it to sound pro-occult.

Arthur Miller titled his 1953 Salem witch drama *The Crucible*. The present volume chronicles how American popular culture is shifting from crucifix to crucible. The crucifix nails religious dogma down to the four corners of a cross. A crucible is a scientific vessel for melting materials at high temperatures to analyze what they are made of. The counterculture revolution continues to test declarative faith, revealed fundamentalism, and dictated government. Liberation fronts are opening the interrogative possibilities of intellect and diversity. America works best as an experimental society when it is a crucible for progress.

In these times of fast change, necromancy seems better suited to match

the continued questing of the American character, colonial to astronauti-
cal. For in the evolution of the world, obviously enough, old maps ill serve
a new Columbus who walks on the moon, taking steps to the stars. The
space program changes everything about earthbound religions, science,
and customs. Old totems fall as fast as old taboos. We look in the last
generation of this century for a spirituality progressive enough to match
the frontiers of outer and inner space. We resensitize. We reconceptualize.
Technology demythologizes the moon. Erich von Däniken's *Chariots of the
Gods* (1968) makes the Bible a documentation of UFOs with Christ as an
extraterrestrial cosmonaut. *The Mushroom and the Cross* (1970), a best-
selling book written by John Allegro, one of the original scholars of the
Dead Sea Scrolls, rethinks Jesus into an acid hallucination.

American astronauts, covering both sides of providence, carry Bible
passages, rosaries, and occult amulets to the lunar surface. Despite
numerologists' warnings, NASA launched *Apollo 13* at 13:13 Houston time,
and carried the 12th, 13th, and 14th men to the moon. Two days later,
Apollo 13 suffered a terrible space accident on Friday, the 13th of April,
1970. *Time* magazine asks on its cover *Is God Dead? The National Enquirer*
knows Satan is alive and well.

Ralph Waldo Emerson was the revolutionary pioneer who gave America
soul—and the Over-Soul. Emerson raised the consciousness for alternative
spirituality, including witchcraft. He dared tell Harvard Divinity School
graduates (1838) that they were as divine as any Jesus. He wanted the
American intellectual to be free of European dogma. He wanted American
spirituality to be free of the kinds of Puritan theology that hated the body.
He wanted personal rights unfettered by race, sex, gender, and religion.
His transcendentalist group changed American society. They began the
women's movement with Margaret Fuller; the children's education reforms
of Elizabeth Peabody, and her sisters Mary and Sophia, of Salem; the com-
mune movement at Brook Farm; and the abolition movement set afire by
Uncle Tom's Cabin, written by Harriet Beecher Stowe, to whom Abraham
Lincoln said, "So you're the little woman who started the Civil War."

Emerson led the way for Henry David Thoreau, the conservationist
author of *Walden: Or, Life in the Woods* (1853) and *Civil Disobedience*
(1848), as much as for the very Wiccan Walt Whitman and his magic
epic *Leaves of Grass* (1855–1892) which, like witchcraft, is centered around
nature, persona, and sexual energy. Emerson changed American intellect
and spirituality by introducing the eastern mysticism of the Bhagavad
Gita, the German idealism of Immanuel Kant, and the environmental

British romanticism of Lord Byron, John Keats, Percy Bysshe Shelly, and William Wordsworth into the New World Magical Mystery Tour long before the Beatles refreshed his act.

Linear Western thought debates *to be or not to be*. Spiraling in circles, Eastern mysticism challenges global humans beyond *to be* into *to become or not to become*. Something in humankind's spiritual psyche refuses to buy our beginning with birth and our ending in a lazy eternal Elysium. Something in the way we move tells us we intersect romantically with the circles of nature, of the spheres, and of the expanding universe where no line is straight and no answer absolute. Witchcraft, like an ancient druid umbrella, covers the human existential situation.

Emerson's was the American mind that invented the self-help genre of the "power of positive thinking." He told men and women that—as "all that Adam had and all that Caesar could"—they as New World potentialities had and could also. Experience may have jerked Emerson and company up short, but as pop-culture scholar Marshall Fishwick says of the pre-electronic likes of Adam and Emerson, "Where Hannibal, Caesar, and Napoleon failed, Edison succeeded."

In short, electrical media make people real. Had Emerson guested on the TV talk shows, he could have transcended himself and become a pop star. Thoreau in *Walden* waxed skeptical about media as a vast wasteland: "The devil goes on exacting compound interest to the last for . . . our inventions. . . . We are in great haste to construct a magnetic telegraph from Maine to Texas; but Maine and Texas . . . may . . . have nothing important to communicate."

Marshall McLuhan notes that media make everything from the trivial to the important "global" in (his new term) the "Global Village." If television interviews a witch, the next morning that witch's book climbs the lists, giving astrologer Jeane Dixon a following, making British witch Sybil Leek a millionaire, and fixing Anton LaVey as the veritable face of the new Satan. No totem is so, but the media make it so.

American Zen Buddhism. Eastern postures of meditation; still popular in large urban areas, the movement achieved peak popularity in the late 1950s with the Beatniks: Jack Kerouac, Ken Kesey, and Allan Ginsberg, who wrote like William Blake on peyote.

Scientology. A Western mode of spiritual renewal founded by L. Ron Hubbard; a kind of Dale Carnegie approach to psychoanalysis through computer programming. Popular in Hollywood.

Bahai. Founded in 1864, its architecturally stunning temple stands on Chicago's North Shore; the chairs of this supremely ecumenical religion face Persia.

Gurdjieff. This dervish cult became highly visible in the streets of New York, Los Angeles, and San Francisco in the early 1970s. Saffron-robed members shave their heads, leaving a ponytail at back of crown. Meditative ritual of dance and music. Ecstatic. Founder George Gurdjieff (1874–1949) wrote his incomprehensible *All and Everything*, and supported himself by dyeing sparrows yellow and selling them as canaries.

American Theosophical Society, Rosicrucians, Spiritualist Churches. Ethel Romm's July 1970 *Penthouse* investigation of America's multiple sects notes, "The Theosophical Society studies comparative religions, ancient and modern, alchemy, Cabala, etc. Started in 1875. . . . Others of this type go in for various occult practices like spirit card reading, seances, scrying (reading images in crystal balls, crystal rocks, mirrors, glass, ink, etc.). Some feature mentalists (who read minds), clairvoyants (who see things out of sight), mediums (who speak with the dead). Many of these grew rapidly with the rise of the once-popular Flying Saucer Cult."

Church of Satan. Founded in 1966 by Anton LaVey, later the author of *The Satanic Bible* (1969); San Francisco-based, former carnival man LaVey has reinstituted a nonorgiastic Black Mass as well as Satanic baptisms, weddings, and funerals for his world membership of nearly ten thousand.

Black Magic or Demonology. Worship of the Devil as the polar opposite of the Christian God; orgiastic celebration of the body; nudity, sex, drugs, sadomasochism, sexual inversion. Purpose: to effect curses, celebrate evil; very little prescribed ritual, mostly ad-lib (and sometimes dangerous) innovations to the historic ritual of the Black Mass.

White Witchcraft or Wicca. According to anthropologist Margaret Murray, this is the world's oldest spiritual discipline. Many sects currently in schism over ritual, nudity, homosexuality, and drugs. Purpose: to undo evil curses and effect good. The late Gerald Gardner revived the term *Wicca* and promoted witchcraft as "the Old Religion" in post–World War II Britain; he attempted to restore white witchcraft to its prehistoric purity. London's Alex Sanders succeeded Gardner with the white magic of the Alexandrian tradition. New York's Raymond Buckland is America's chief Gardnerian witch. In Chicago, bisexual Pontifex Maximus Frederic de Arechaga is the chief American practitioner of the

Sabaeanist system of the Old Religion. White witchcraft covens number in the thousands in the United States.

Popular culture is by essence neophiliac: in love with what's new. Witchcraft is old enough to be new, attractive enough to be commercial. It has style, sensibility, and appeal to body and mind. It opens, in this last generation of the twentieth century, the closet door of American sex.

However, ancient witchcraft sometimes seems snagged by modern religion. Witches might claim their hereditary origins in Wicca, the Old Religion. Yet some are still caught in a kind of inquisition: they let Christianity define them. Many witches forget their purity of source. Instead of *acting*, they *react* to Christianity. Real systems of witchcraft gain little power or altitude when white witches try to be "co-Christian" or black magicians are petulantly "anti-Christian." Actual witchcraft has its own identity. Witchcraft predates all known religions; it is based on instinct, intuition, and nature. Christianity, Judaism, and Islam are revealed religions, subject to politics, cultures, and geography.

Witchcraft has always been liberal, natural, and global. No liberation movement should let spirituality, race, sex, and gender be anything less. Witchcraft is a seeing eye into the American spirit, which is about personal freedom.

Through phenomena like witchcraft, popular culture analyzes the American character. Witchcraft has always bubbled just below the radar of America's revealed religions. The founding fathers winked when they designed Masonic symbols into the seal of the thirteen (count 'em!) states, as well as the one dollar bill: the pyramid with the all-seeing eye of the god Horus, the son of Osiris, the god of the underworld. American revolutionary patriot Benjamin Franklin in 1772 joined the stylish London Hellfire Club, and designed coins with thirteen circles. Currently, rich and powerful government figures meet secretly and ritually at the Bohemian Club.

American culture is a crystal. It is the "Labrador spar" Emerson mentioned in his essay *Experience*: "A man is like a bit of Labrador spar, which has no lustre as you turn it in your hand, until you come to a particular angle; then it shows deep and beautiful colors."

That spar is the philosopher's stone. It makes us know ourselves. As we dare scry such a crystal proof-rock, we see hidden facets. The occult is one such face of the American experience. We observe witchcraft because it is there.

Preface: Take Two, 2004

San Francisco

In the thirty years since I first bent up the Pentagram and wrote this book, witchcraft has become an even more popular template of American culture, which sees Satan everywhere. Various liberation movements that were then new now drive culture. The revolution in sex, race, and gender has actually enhanced the content of this book, as has my experience in life and my education with the Silva Mind Institute, at which I have also been a postgraduate guest lecturer. In fact, thirty years' passage has revealed one principle: how a country treats its women, children, and homosexual people is how a culture truly shows its character.

It may be of interest to note that everything that rises must converge. The 1960s' liberated world of the occult—particularly the Knights Templar aspects of gay leather culture, with its rituals, costumes, and lingua franca—found its way into this book, published in 1972, as it did into William Carney's *The Real Thing* (1968), and Anne Rice's *Interview with the Vampire* (1976). Rice was then a longtime San Franciscan, living in the Castro where in coffee chops, bruncheries, and bars, the leather S&M talk was of tops complaining of hungry bottoms who were, as then defined exactly, "energy vampires." Although Anne Rice and I both lived in the Castro at the same time, soaked up the same vibes, and wrote and produced books four years apart (with strangely similar titles—hers in fiction, mine in nonfiction), neither of us knew the other. Both books nevertheless represent by genre certain insights into human truths—true at the time, and true universally in the world of the occult.

That said, witchcraft remains a perfect measure of human rights, persona, diversity, and acceptance. The principles of analysis, scholarship, and interview, as well as most of the examples cited, remain valid because most of the citations that were new to pop culture in 1970 have, like *Rosemary's Baby*, survived as classic benchmarks in witchcraft. Impressively, most of the occult books mentioned in the first edition have remained in print—and are even more popular. The teenage witch Sabrina has migrated from the pages of an *Archie* comic book to the television screen. Occult personalities who were popular (like Anton LaVey and Gerald Gardner) or notorious (like Aleister Crowley and Charles Manson) have become legendary. In fact, of all the priests I've known of any faith, Anton LaVey was one of the greatest and kindest.

This text connects the dots for the analytical modern reader. For instance, the government persecution and martyrdom of the cross-dressing Joan of Arc for sorcery in 1431 is noted as archetype for the 1990 government persecution of the gay photographer Robert Mapplethorpe for obscenity, driven by a subtext of Satanism.[1]

The new American inquisition, begun by fundamentalist religionists, reveals how deeply the personal freedoms inherent in witchcraft threaten those who refuse to separate church and state. The forever-onward-marching Christian soldiers are waging a culture war that they aggressively declared. Satan is spied behind every aspect of popular culture including high school shootings, rap and heavy metal music, goth fashions, *Harry Potter* novels, New Age lifestyles, the war on drugs, hypnotherapy, and government-funded art.

Nevertheless, the fair-minded cannot indict Christianity for the excesses of some fundamentalists or some popes anymore than one can indict witchcraft itself for the excesses of its practitioners, from Gilles de Rais to thrill-killers who call themselves Satanists.

Thirty years on, I have gently opened up my text without breaking the historicity of the original period piece.

Facts that were censored in 1970 are restored.

Facts that were secret at first publication are inserted where they would have appeared in the first edition if the people involved had been able to speak freely thirty years ago.

Brief thumbnails and dates are added to names, titles, and places, to allow modern readers instant access to arcane information that was common knowledge thirty years ago.

Within these edits, I have tried to honor the book's original 1970s voice and update its accuracy for the casual reader, the research student, and practicing witches who encouraged me to prepare this edition for the twenty-first century.

This was the first book on popular American witchcraft.

This was the first book to touch upon the women's movement and witchcraft.

This was the very first to deal with gay witchcraft, and, in that, gay men's emerging spirituality.

Thirty years have proven that Ray Browne, Marshall Fishwick, and Russell Nye were absolute visionaries when they founded the American Popular Culture Association in 1969 for the purpose of shedding the immediate light of analysis and scholarship on American culture. In 1968, as a twenty-something assistant professor at Western Michigan University, I had written such articles for their *Journal of Popular Culture* as "*Hair*: The Tribal Love–Rock Musical" (1968), "Stanley Kubrick's *2001: A Space Odyssey*: A Sleep and a Forgetting" (1968), and "Originality in Mart Crowley's *Boys in the Band*" (1970). I thank Ray Browne particularly for daring at a 1969 cocktail party to say yes to my proposal to write this book, which was first published by his Popular Press at Bowling Green State University.

Actually, the watershed year 1969 lit the pop-culture fuse on an endless litany of changes that included those in sex, witchcraft, women's liberation, gay liberation, race, space, and the antiwar movement. By 1969, seventy million baby boomers had become teenagers and young adults. That year, Richard Nixon was inaugurated. Shirley Chisholm became the first black woman to sit in the U.S. House of Representatives. Gloria Steinem wrote her first feminist article, "After Black Power, Women's Liberation." The world grew smaller with the first flights of the jumbo jet (the Boeing 747) and the supersonic Concorde. *Midnight Cowboy* was the first and only X-rated movie to win an Academy Award for best picture of the year. *Life* magazine published, every seven days, the faces of the young American soldiers killed that week in Vietnam. *Easy Rider* changed Hollywood. Woodstock delivered up live sex, drugs, and rock-and-roll. Anton LaVey, who had played the Devil the year before in *Rosemary's Baby*, published *The Satanic Bible*. Gay icon Judy Garland, who declared "I'm no witch at all" in *The Wizard of Oz*, died on June 22 and was waked by twenty-two thousand mourners at Frank Campbell's Funeral Chapel in Manhatten on June 27—the very night that her mourners at the Stonewall Bar in the Village rebelled against the New York Police Department and kick-started gay liberation. On July 20, two American astronauts stepped out onto the face of the moon. On August 9, ten days before the historic Woodstock concert, the Manson Family murders immediately changed the public idea of cult, coven, and evil. Suddenly, America believed in witchcraft. When I had begun this book in April 1969, people had thought witches existed only on Halloween cards.

In 1972, I wrote, "I began this book as an unbeliever in the occult. I leave it, if not believing, then not disbelieving." The truth is, I never left it, nor did it leave me. For thirty years, parts of this book, particularly the legendary interview with Anton LaVey, have been quoted and reprinted in other books and articles and at websites. For as many years, in the month before Halloween, universities, church groups, and radio stations have invited me to tell them the secrets of witchcraft, magic, and religion. As if I could. Or would.

Actually, since we crossed the millennium, time has revealed only one bit of wisdom.

If the Four Horsemen of the Apocalypse ride the political whirlwind of war and religious terror that blows through the world, there is a distinct human worth to blessing water, burning candles, invoking guardian angels, conjuring sex, achieving ecstasy, and worshiping something of one's own free choice.

ACKNOWLEDGMENTS

My thanks for research assistance to David Sparrow, Deanna Haney, and Maisie Pearson, and, particularly, Mark Thomas Hemry, my partner of twenty-five years. I owe special thanks to Professor Thomas R. Gorman and his wife, Eve Gorman, and the Gorman children for their support at Loyola University, Chicago; and best thanks to Professor Ray B. Browne and his wife, Pat, for first seeing this book into publication at Bowling Green State University Press.

The author was partially funded by a National Endowment for the Humanities grant, and by a grant from the State of Michigan.

Popular Witchcraft

Anton Szandor LaVey

INTRODUCTORY INTERVIEW

*H*igh *priest and founder of the Church of Satan, author of*
The Satanic Bible, *and icon of 1960s counterculture;*
San Francisco, midnight, July 29, 1971.

Anton Szandor LaVey invoked the United States Constitution on a night sacred to witches, Walpurgisnacht, April 30, 1966. That night he founded his Church of Satan on the premise that Satanism is an ancient religion protected by the Constitution. On the next morning, May Day, the pagan feast of Beltane, his was a defining act during the cultural revolution of the 1960s. At age thirty-six Anton LaVey was young enough to influence the best of the decade, and old enough not to fall prey to the worst. The media loved his invention of himself; the press named him the "Black Pope" and the "High Priest of the Church of Satan" and he appeared on many magazine covers. Director Roman Polanski cast him as the Devil in his 1968 film *Rosemary's Baby.* And in 1969 LaVey wrote his witchcraft manifesto, *The Satanic Bible,* which became an international bestseller.

His controversial religion of Satanism was a human-interest lark to the hungry media for three years, until on the night of August 9, 1969, the Manson Family, headed by Charles Manson, killed Polanski's pregnant movie-star wife Sharon Tate and several others, and changed everything in American popular culture concerning cult and coven, sex and violence. America demanded serious investigations. On the morning of August 10, 1969, the media anointed LaVey as the point man to explain the dark side of American culture.

LaVey became a lightning rod. He was feared, loved, hated, and respected. He became an icon of popular culture. He was called the "Devil Himself." Sprung from his intellect, and carried on his shoulders, the Church of Satan entered history, and will be mentioned for centuries to come.

Anton LaVey certainly looks like the archetype of the archfiend: shaved head, goatee, piercing eyes, black clothes. When he invited me to his Victorian, the Black House, at 6114 California Street, San Francisco, he insisted I arrive at midnight as July 28 became Thursday, July 29, 1971. His companion, Diane Hegarty, to whom he dedicated *The Satanic Bible*, welcomed me into their parlor, invited me to have a seat in Rasputin's sleigh chair, and left me alone while the clock chimed twelve. The black room lined with book shelves resembled a faculty professor's home, except for the huge tombstone coffee table, the animal heads, the art and scarves and candles piercing the shimmering gloom.

To my left, the front parlor was painted black, with a red ceiling. Black curtains draped the windows, through which I could not hear California Street. Against the west wall stood an altar installed over the fireplace. On its mantle, candles guttered. Shadows flickered on the wall above the altar where hung a huge painted baphomet of the traditional five-pointed star in a circle. Director Roger Corman has said that in a horror movie, a house is always a woman's body. This sanctuary perfectly reflected the centrality of women in the Church of Satan. In fact, Diane later joked that the altar was exactly sized to fit a woman—precisely, her.

As the clock chimed fifteen minutes past midnight, a bookcase opposite the chair on which I was sitting glided open. Anton LaVey appeared, all in black, wearing a Catholic priest's Roman collar and a red-lined Bela Lugosi cape. He was everything he was supposed to be. He was absolutely charming. He was every inch the assured embodiment of his proverb in *The Satanic Bible*: "Positive thinking and positive action add up to results." Our months of correspondence had paid off. We each understood the other. For two and a half hours, we talked. Our time together was purposeful conversation as much as interview, even though, from start to finish, he watched me write notes on my yellow legal pad of every word he said.

At nearly three in the morning, LaVey summoned Diane to join us. For thirty minutes, we three chatted. (It was then that she mentioned that the altar was perfect for a five-foot-three blonde woman, which, that being the message, she happened to be.) LaVey asked me if I would like to participate in a ritual. But of course! He asked Diane to bring out a baphomet amulet.

"I wish," he said, "to present you with this token." The three of us entered the front parlor. Diane stood to the side as a witness. LaVey stood on the altar. I knelt shirtless on the altar step. Ritual to a Catholic like me is universally familiar, and universally respected. LaVey spoke his invocation, and raised the red-and-black enameled amulet, embossed with the pentagram and a goat face, hanging from a silver chain above my head. Again he made an invocation. I had been blessed by many priests, and he was blessing me again.

"Hail, Satan," he said.

"Hail, Satan," Diane said.

"Hail, Satan," I said.

The earth did not open up and swallow me. The ritual blessing was repeated three times. On the third solemn pass, Anton LaVey, high priest of the Church of Satan, placed the silver chain over my head. The metal baphomet rested cold for a moment on my forehead. I felt his fingers pull at the chain, which was a perfect circle with no clasp. I had not yet told him that in 1963 the Catholic Church had ordained me as an exorcist. As his fingers struggled to fit the chain over my head, the chain broke and the baphomet fell to the altar step and rolled across the floor.

LaVey and I looked at each other.

It was one of those inquisitive moments when two people's eyes really connect.

In the way that women introduce irony to levitate seriousness, Diane said, "Oh, you're exactly like Anton. You have a big head."

We laughed.

We breathed.

We turned serious.

We hailed Satan one, twice, thrice more.

Then, successfully, LaVey worked the chain down my head and across my face. My eyes studied up close the palms of his hands. He smelled human. Finally, the baphomet rested on my naked chest.

Since that time, Anton LaVey has told people how pleased he was with the way the interview I wrote turned out.

This is the best interview Anton LaVey has given.

—Fate Magazine

This seminal interview, conducted in the fifth Satanic Year, is the first
and earliest in-depth interview given by Anton LaVey, whose *Satanic Bible*
had been published only sixteen months earlier, in 1969. He was still rather
reclusive because the Manson Family murders had threatened the public
image of the Church of Satan. Villains like Manson had, in olden days,
often been the point of ignition for witch burning. LaVey personally had
the "grace and gravitas" to help calm and correct American confusion.

Over the past thirty-four years, my interview with Anton Szandor LaVey
has entered the classic canon of Satanic literature. Certainly, the candid
conversation catches one of the most intriguing men of the twentieth century around the moment when the Swinging 1960s became the Titanic
1970s. Here is the truth of what Anton LaVey said. He himself frequently
endorsed my accuracy. This is the restored question-and-answer version
of my handwritten original, and may be reprinted only with permission.[1]

My Midnight with Anton

"LaVey Speaks"

JACK FRITSCHER: Aleister Crowley claimed he could summon the Devil
   to appear bodily in a room. Christians also believe in the physical presence of Satan. The New Testament is like "Starring Satan, Live, In Person." Like Jesus, Satan is incarnated. In their famous duel, Satan tempts
   Jesus to fall down and worship his Satanic body.

ANTON LAVEY: I don't feel that raising the Devil in an anthropomorphic
   sense is quite as feasible as theologians or metaphysicians would like to
   think. I have felt his presence but only as an exteriorized extension of
   my own potential, as an alter ego or evolved concept that I have been
   able to exteriorize. With a full awareness, I can communicate with this
   semblance, this creature, this demon, this personification that I see in
   the eyes of the symbol of Satan—the Goat of Mendes—as I commune
   with him before the altar. None of these is anything more than a mirror image of that potential I perceive in myself.

FRITSCHER: Like the Beatles' "I am he and you are me and we are all
   together." Is the self Satan?

LAVEY: I have this awareness that the objectification is in accord with
   my own ego. I'm not deluding myself that I'm calling something that

is disassociated or exteriorized from myself the Godhead. This force is not a controlling factor that I have no control over. The Satanic principle is that man willfully controls his destiny.

FRITSCHER: The triumph of the will. So a person controls what's internal to control the external?

LAVEY: If he doesn't, some other man—a lot smarter than he is—will. Satan is, therefore, an extension of one's psyche or volitional essence, so that the extension can sometimes converse and give directives through the self in a way that mere thinking of the self as a single unit cannot. In this way it *does* help to depict in an externalized way the Devil *per se*. The purpose is to have something of an idolatrous, objective nature to commune with. However, man has connection, contact, control. This notion of an exteriorized God-Satan is not new.

FRITSCHER: Idolatry. God and Satan projected out of our own psyches . . .

LAVEY: Our sexual psyches. For instance, my opinion of the succubus and incubus is that these are dream manifestations of man's coping with guilt, as in the case of nocturnal emissions with a succubus visiting a man or of erotic dreams with an incubus visiting a woman. This whole idea of casting the blame off one's own sexual feelings onto convenient demons to satisfy the Church has certainly proved useful in millions of cases.

FRITSCHER: Bless me, Father, for I have sinned, but "The Devil made me do it."

LAVEY: That's exactly the scene when the priest is confronted one morning by a parishioner holding a stiffened nightshirt, a semen-encrusted nightgown. The priest can tell him about this "terrible" succubus who visited him in the night. They proceed to exorcise the demon, getting the parishioner off the sexual hook and giving the priest a little prurient fun as he plays with the details of its predication on some pretty girl in the village. This, on top of it all, leaves the girl suspect of being a witch.

FRITSCHER: When all else fails, blame the girl.

LAVEY: Naturally the priest can keep his eyes open. He has the power to decide who fits the succubus descriptions that he's heard in the confessional. Of course, the concept of incubi and succubi has also been used by people who have engaged in what they would consider illicit sexual relations. More than one lady's window has been left open purposely for the incubus to enter—in the form of some desirable male. They can both then chalk up the next day to demonic possession. All these very convenient dodges have kept Christianity and its foibles alive for many hundreds of years.

FRITSCHER: You mean, I think, that sex has kept Christianity in business. When I look at Satanism, I see Christianity reversed. What Christianity does with the right hand, Satanism does with the left. Like Christ and Antichrist.

LAVEY: The birth of a Satanic child is another manifestation of the need to extend the Christ myth of the virgin birth to an antithetical concept of a demonic birth, a Devil-child. *Rosemary's Baby* wasn't the first to use this age-old plot. The Devil's own dear son or daughter is a rather popular literary excursion. Certainly the Devil walks in the sinews and marrow of a man because the Devil is the representation of fleshly deity. Any animal heritage, any natural predilections, any real human attributes would be seen as the personification of the Devil.

FRITSCHER: Precisely the philosophy of Protestant Puritanism and Catholic Jansenism. Humans are essentially depraved, evil animals.

LAVEY: And the Devil is proud of them. Just as the Devil would have offspring and be proud of them, antithetic as they are to Christianity. Christians are ashamed that the child was conceived in sin and baptized out of sin. The Devil revels in the lust-conception of his child. This child would be involved much more magically than one who was the by-product of an environment that sought to negate at first opportunity the very motivating force—the carnal desire—that produced him.

FRITSCHER: So when baptism washes away original sin, it also washes away magic and sex.

LAVEY: Not just Christianity. Religion itself demeans our carnal nature. Religious artists' desexualizing of the birth process—Christ coming out of the bowels of Mary—has caused women to suffer childbirth pains much more than they need to because of the age-old collective unconsciousness that women must suffer this and the periodic suffering that comes every twenty-eight days. Both these are attempts to stamp out or discredit what are in the animal world the most passionate female feelings when the animal comes into heat at that time of the month. The "curse" of the menstrual cycle is a manufactured thing, manufactured by society that recognizes this period as one of great desire. Automatically, we have overemphasized its pains, tensions, turmoil, cramps. This taboo is not just Christian. Women have been placed in huts outside many villages. Every culture has thought women would cause more jealousy and turmoil at this time because of this increase in her passions.

Male animals fight more when the female is in heat. Having been a lion tamer, I know even the females are more combative at this time.

Christianity has subjected modern women to even more self-recrimination. This is the big difference between tribal customs and Christian. In the tribe, the woman is considered bleeding poison. In Christianity the woman is not only considered taboo, but she has to endure her pain as a "moral" reminder of her mortality and guilt. The primitive woman can give birth relatively painlessly and return to the fields. She goes through the physical act, but not through the moral agonies of the Christian woman. Such is the compounding of guilt. This kind of hypocrisy is my "Enemy Number One."

FRITSCHER: That's why the establishment fears you. Your voice adds to the counterculture revolution.

LAVEY: Out there in the streets, I don't think young people can be blamed too much for their actions and antics. Although they coat their protests in ideological issues, I think what they resent most is not the actions of older adults, but the gross hypocrisy under which adults act. What is far worse than making war is making war and calling it *peace* and *love* and saying it's "waged under the auspices of God" or that "it's the Christian thing to do." Onward, Christian soldiers and all that! I think that the worst thing about Christianity is its gross hypocrisy, which is the most repugnant thing in the world to me. Most Christians practice a basic Satanic—

FRITSCHER: Satanic?

LAVEY: —Satanic way of life every hour of their waking day and yet they sneer at somebody who has built a religion that is no different from what they're practicing, but is simply calling it by its right name. I call it by the name that is antithetical to that which they hypocritically pay lip service when they're in church.

FRITSCHER: They burn people like you at the stake.

LAVEY: Precisely. Take, for example, the roster of people executed for witchcraft in the Middle Ages. They were unjustly maligned because they were freethinkers, beautiful girls, heretics, Jews . . .

FRITSCHER: Homosexuals . . .

LAVEY: And lesbians, or people who happened to be of a different faith than was ordained. They were mercilessly tortured and exterminated without any thought of Christian charity. The basic lies and propaganda of the Christian Fathers added to the torment of the people. Yet the crime in today's streets and the mollycoddling of heinous criminals is a by-product of latter-day Christian charity. Christian "understanding" has made our city streets unsafe. Yet helpless millions of people, simply because they were unbelievers or disbelievers, were not "understood." They were killed. It's not right that a mad dog who is really dangerous should be "understood" and those who merely dissent from Christianity should have been killed. At the Church of Satan we receive lots of damning letters from people condemning us in the most atrocious language. They attest they are good Christians, but they are full of hate. They don't know if I'm a good guy or a bad guy. They only know me by the label they've been taught: that Satanism is evil. Therefore they judge me on the same basis those people did in the thirteenth through sixteenth centuries.

FRITSCHER: The Inquisition has never stopped.

LAVEY: These very same people hardly ever get worked up over a murderer.

FRITSCHER: They fear that your Satan debunks their Jesus.

LAVEY: They fear. I think. Christ has failed in all his engagements as both savior and deity. If his doctrines were that easily misinterpreted, if his logic was that specious, let's throw it out. It has no place. It is worthless to a civilized society if it is subject to gross misinterpretation. I'm not just protesting the "human element" in Christianity the way Christians do when something goes wrong with their system. I void the whole of the system that lends itself to such misinterpretation.

FRITSCHER: Protestantism made Catholicism worse. Rome dictated exactly what the Bible meant. Protestants reacted and opened the Bible up to private interpretation.

LAVEY: Why the hell didn't the writers mean what they said or say what they meant when they wrote that stupid book of fables, the Bible? This is the way I feel about it.

FRITSCHER: How do you feel, then, about Wicca, or white magic? Pagans I've talked with feel robbed because early Christianity sucked up their beliefs and rites the way the Church turned the Roman Empire into the Holy Roman Empire, which turned into the Vatican that rules more people than Caesar ever conquered.

LAVEY: Anybody who takes up the sanctimonious "cult of white light" is just playing footsy with the Christian Fathers. This is why the bane of my existence are these white witches, white magicians, people who'd like to keep their foot in the safety zone of righteousness. They refuse to see the demonic in themselves, the motivations Satan's majesty and nature has placed inside them for their terrestrial goal. Materialism is part of Satanism, but a right kind of materialism. Everyone wants to acquire. The only thing wrong with money is it falls into the wrong hands. This makes it a curse, a disadvantage rather than an advantage. The marketplace is full of thieves. Easy wealth may be something would-be Faustian Satanists would like to get hold of.

FRITSCHER: You can "make things happen"? Certain things that people want? Practical magic?

LAVEY: In my experience, people have come to me after I had opened doors for them. They got what they wanted. Very quickly, they come back wanting to know how to turn "it" off as they have more troubles than they had before. Once I offer to people what they think they want, given a week to think it over, they get cold feet.

FRITSCHER: Ah. You are saying, like Saint Theresa and Truman Capote, that there's more tears shed over answered prayers.

LAVEY: Success is a threat. Threatened by success, most people show their true colors. They show they need a god or an astrological forecast to really lay the blame on for their own inadequacy in the threatening face of imminent success.

FRITSCHER: Your basic tenet: Everything is personal, rooted in the person.

LAVEY: Man needs religion, dogma, and ritual that keeps him exteriorized outside of himself to waylay his guilt and inadequacy. Men will always, therefore, search for a God. We should, however, be men in search of man.

FRITSCHER: Satanism is the ultimate humanism.

LAVEY: That at least makes sense I can see, hear, and touch. The man in search of God is the masochist. He is the world's masochist. There are more than we imagine.

FRITSCHER: Religion attracts masochistic exhibitionists who like to suffer public penances and denial of the flesh. It's common.

LAVEY: In the beginning. I may not have intended Satanism to evolve into an elitist movement. But experience has taught me that Satanism can be a mass movement only insofar as its basic pleasure-seeking premise is concerned.

FRITSCHER: Attached to sexual freedom.

LAVEY: You build a better mousetrap, and people are going to flock to it. A pleasure principle is going to be more popular than denying plea-sure. I can't help attracting the masses. As for the people who practice a truly Satanic way of life, you can't expect the masses to transcend mere lip service to the pleasure-seeking principle and get into the magical state of the Absolute Satanist.

FRITSCHER: Is the Absolute Satanist transcendent? Self-reliant? Self-creating?

LAVEY: The Absolute Satanist is totally aware of his own abilities and limitations. On this self-knowledge he builds his character. The Absolute Satanist is far removed from the masses who look for Satanic pleasure in the psychedelics of the head shops. We Satanists are magically a part of all this surface culture. I realize what my magical lessons have done, the things I've stumbled upon. We necessarily spawn our neo-Christian masses seeking their sense of soma through pills and drugs. Certainly I don't oppose this for other people who get stoned out of their minds. When they do this, the more material things there will be for me and my followers since all those people who freaked themselves out on drugs will be satisfied with their pills and will move off to colonies based on drugs. The rest of us, the materialists, will inherit the world.

FRITSCHER: So Absolute Satanism is humanism and materialism. But is Satanism narcissism? Drugs, which you have always denounced, are very narcissistic.

LAVEY: Actually, I'm very much opposed to drugs from a magical point of view, from a *control* point of view. I feel drugs are antithetical to magic. The pseudo-Satanist or pseudo-witch or self-styled mystic who predicates his success on a drug revelation is only going to succeed within his drugged peer group. His miracles go no farther than his credibility. This type of witchery is limited. This, I say, despite the fact that the druggies are no longer just a marginal group, but are a very large subculture which threatens to be the "New Spirituality" or the "New Mysticism" or the "New Non-Materialism."

FRITSCHER: So the drug culture, despite its visions on peyote and acid, is narcissistic in that it turns in on itself and accomplishes nothing. Witchcraft, on the other hand, is a means to an end.

LAVEY: The whole concept of witchery is manipulation of other human beings, as means to the end you want.

FRITSCHER: You give an essential definition, and clear motivation.

LAVEY: Druggies don't realize that. Druggies are not manipulative witches. To manipulate someone you've got to be able to relate to that someone. Their idea of witchery is not witchcraft so much—in the sense of witchery being manipulative magic—as witchery equaling revelation of a spiritual nature.

FRITSCHER: Two different goals. Power and mysticism.

LAVEY: Their superego gets developed through the use of drugs. This superego can be the earmark of a new world of drones who, through soma, would attain superegos which allow them while so controlled to think they have superiority over those really enjoying the fruits of the earth. This is why as the leader of the Satanic movement I have to examine these popular movements in the culture from a very pragmatic point of view.

FRITSCHER: Which is why I thank you for us sitting together tonight. You and the Church of Satan are perfectly relevant to the study of popular culture.

LAVEY: The point is there will always be, among the masses, substitutes for the real thing. A planned way of life—not drugs—gets the materialist what he wants. There's nothing wrong with color TV and cars in the garage as long as the system which provides them respects "law and order"—a terribly overworked term.

But as long as people don't bother other people, then I think this is an ideal society.

I'm in favor of a policeman on every corner—as long as he doesn't arrest people for thinking their own way, or for doing within the privacy of their own four walls what they like to do.

FRITSCHER: You are speaking, are you not, of your operating your Church of Satan? Which is, of course, the freedom to practice your religion. You are wise to have chosen San Francisco, which has always been an open city.

LAVEY: We haven't been hassled too much by the law because we have so many policemen in our organization. I'm an ex-cop myself. I worked in the crime lab in San Francisco and I've maintained my contacts. They've provided for me a kind of security force. But all in all we have a very clean slate. [*He laughs.*] We are very evil outlaws in theological circles, but not in civil.

How could we murder? We—unlike Christians—have a real regard for human bodies.

The Satanist is the ultimate humanist.

The Satanist realizes that man can be his own worst enemy and must often be protected against himself. The average man sets up situations for himself so he can be a loser. We Satanists have ancient rituals which exorcise those needs for self-abasement before they happen. We wreck Christians' tidy little dreams.

When you have a born-again Christian rolling orgasmically on the floor at a revival meeting claiming an ecstasy, you tell them they're

having a "forbidden" orgasm and they hate you for enlightening them.
You've robbed them of their "succubus"—

FRITSCHER: You're so evil, you're good.

LAVEY: —Of their freedom from guilt. They push their evilness on to us.
In this sense, then, we are *very* evil.

FRITSCHER: How does the public person you are impact your private life?
Americans know you baptized your daughter into the Church of Satan.
Does she go to school with Rosemary's baby?

LAVEY: I needn't send my child to a private school. Why should I, when children are, in fact, all natural Satanists, perfect at manipulating everyone.

FRITSCHER: Undoubtedly, she will be a perfect heir.

LAVEY: My daughter has no trouble at school. The majority of our members are from the middle class. At least fifty percent of our members have
children. But our members do not proselytize at their children's schools.
Our members rarely discuss sex, religion, and politics with outsiders.

FRITSCHER: What about your own politics? What about law and order
and civil rights?

LAVEY: I was very liberal in my younger years. I would have been thrown
into prison during the [Senator Joseph] McCarthy purge [1951–52] had
I been of any prominence.

FRITSCHER: You would not have cooperated with the government.

LAVEY: I was ultraliberal, attending meetings of the Veterans of the Spanish Civil War, the Abraham Lincoln Brigade, the revisionist movements
of Israel's founding. This was all very liberal at the time. I was always
for civil rights. I had Negro friends when Negro friends weren't fashionable. A man should be judged on his accomplishments, his kindness
and consideration for others. A certain planned form of bigotry may be
a little healthy. I mean, if a person is the worst that his race has produced, he should be prevented from using his race as a means to make
his way unless he is a credit to his race, religion, whatever it is.

FRITSCHER: You mean revolutionaries like Huey Newton? Eldridge Cleaver?
The Black Panthers?

LAVEY: Martin Luther King was killed because he was an articulate gentleman, concerned about his wife and family. He tried to do things in
a mannerly way. A man like that belongs on a pedestal. But these loud
baboons—and I choose the term—are nothing but rabble-rousers, spew-
ing venom. The more a person has at stake the more he watches his p's
and q's. This is my test of a person's sincerity. The public is no judge.
The public is not too particular in its choosing of heroes.

FRITSCHER: Yours is a powerful voice saying things that scare people who fear what they don't understand.

LAVEY: I voted for George Wallace to act out a magical ritual.[2] I performed the political ritual—knowing Wallace would not win, but wishing simply to cast my runes. Wallace's advantage was he would have been helpful in the inert area between *action* and *reaction*. The pendulum is swinging. I've been misinterpreted when I've said people like [Ronald] Reagan and [Richard] Nixon are doing a lot to help Satanism because they are causing tremendous popular reaction—whereby we're getting off the hook in Vietnam.

FRITSCHER: Racial anarchy, war, social chaos, women's lib. Your opinions are interesting in these first years of your Church of Satan, insofar as right now you *are* the Church of Satan. You have many opinions. Are they subject to change?

LAVEY: Even the Church of Satan will change as time goes by.

FRITSCHER: What do you make of these changing times? Of popular culture versus the government?

LAVEY: Popular opinion is simply a reaction against the leaders who have made their stand so heinous that the protestors don't realize they're doing exactly what the masters want them to do: they're getting the masters off the hook. The masters are using the old magical technique of manipulating the people to think it's their idea to end the war.

FRITSCHER: So the government is using magic, or is it just reverse psychology?

LAVEY: Same manipulation. This explains the government's permissive attitude toward protest. The idealists of the early fifties during the McCarthy era were certainly just as against war; but the government then wanted a posture of cold war. So they had to be shut up fast. Currently the show of rebellion is a very magical ritual approved by the government which is trying to direct the inevitability of change.

FRITSCHER: Some say this is a magic time, because revolution—change— is upon us. Change is the essence of magic, of changing one thing into another, of tricksters shifting shapes. American parents think their hippie children are changeling babies. The hippies thing they are spawn of aliens.

LAVEY: In the change that is coming the new emphasis will be placed on staging. Life is a game and we'll realize it's a game. Life is not "God's Will."

FRITSCHER: Is it "Satan's Will"?

LAVEY: Whose will is Satan's Will? We have to go to the point of no return before we can return. We will get to the point where anybody who is establishment-oriented is suspect as being the worst kind of individual. This will happen before we return to a rather safe normality, to a sane discrimination as to who are really the contributing members of society and who are the cancerous tissue.

Satanically speaking, anarchy and chaos must ensue for awhile before a new Satanic morality can prevail. The new Satanic morality won't be very different from the old law of the jungle, wherein right and wrong were judged in the truest natural sense of biting and being bitten back. Satanic morality will cause a return to intrigue, to glamour, to seductiveness, to a modicum of sexual lasciviousness. Taboos will be invoked, but mostly it will be realized these things are fun.

FRITSCHER: Fun already is the heart of movements like the hippies and gay lib, and maybe women's lib.

LAVEY: The various liberation fronts are all part of the omelet from which the New Satanic Morality will emerge. Women's Liberation is really quite humorous. Supposedly women were liberated after the Industrial Revolution when they got out of the sweatshops. Women are going to defeat themselves, because they're not using the ammunition of their femininity to win as women. They're trying to reject their femininity, which is their greatest magical weapon.

FRITSCHER: This I know. *The Satanic Bible* tells me so.

LAVEY: Women are parodying themselves.

FRITSCHER: Some people will not want to hear that.

LAVEY: Speaking of parody, Christians will not want to hear this. The historical Black Mass is a parody of a parody.

FRITSCHER: You mean the Black Mass where the woman is the altar, and sex and sacrilege are committed on her body to defy Christ . . . the way the French revolutionaries did on the altar of Notre Dame.

LAVEY: Making fun of the Catholic Mass, yes. The Black Mass parodies the Christian service, which parodies a pagan. Every time a man and woman go to church on Sunday they are practicing a Black Mass by parodying "ancient earth rituals" which were practiced by their ancestors before they were *inverted* by the Christian Fathers.

FRITSCHER: Not *converted*?

LAVEY: *Inverted.* Our Satanic Mass is not a parody of the Catholic Mass. Our Satanic Mass celebrates the power of the self, the beauty of the self. We ritualize that. Our Mass is catharsis. The women's lib-ists, for the same kind of catharis, should simply use their femininity by taking the Devil's name and playing the Devil's game. They should take the stigma that cultural guilt has thrown at women and invert the values. Just as words have power, the semantic reversal of those words is also powerful.

FRITSCHER: So if someone calls a woman a witch, or worse, she should co-opt the epithet and turn it into a compliment; change a bad word into good?

LAVEY: This is the essence of what we have done in Satanism. What theologians have supplied in stigma we change to virtue. We therefore have the attraction of the forbidden. This has greatly aided our success.

FRITSCHER: On the subject of women, how exactly was Jayne Mansfield connected to the Church of Satan?

LAVEY: I know I have been rumored to have cursed Jayne Mansfield and caused her death in that car crash.[3] Jayne Mansfield was a member of the Church of Satan. I have enough material to blow sky-high all those sanctimonious Hollywood journalists who claim she wasn't. She was a priestess in the Church of Satan. I have documentation of this fact from her. There are many things I'll not say for obvious reasons.

FRITSCHER: Say what you can.

LAVEY: Her lover [lawyer Sam Brody, also killed in the front seat of the car], who was a decidedly unsavory character, was the one who brought the curse upon himself. There was decidedly a curse, marked in the presence of other people. Jayne was warned constantly and periodically in no uncertain terms that she must avoid his company because great harm would befall him. It was a very sad sequence of events in which she was the victim of her own—as we mentioned earlier—inability to cope with her own success. Also the *demonic self* in her was crying out to be one thing, and her *apparent self* demanded that she be something else. She was beaten back and forth in this inner conflict between the apparent self and the demonic self. Sam Brody was blackmailing her.

FRITSCHER: About what?

LAVEY: He was blackmailing her. I have definite proof of this. She couldn't get out of his clutches. She was a bit of a masochist herself. She brought about her own demise. But it wasn't through what I had done to curse *her*. The curse, that she asked me to cast, was directed at *him*. And it was a very magnificent curse.

FRITSCHER: Your *Satanic Bible* is dedicated to a pop culture pantheon from Rasputin and Ragnar Redbeard to a bevy of Hollywood blondes.

LAVEY: The dedication of my *Satanic Bible* to Jayne Mansfield, Marilyn

Monroe, and Tuesday Weld [the blonde movie star of *Pretty Poison* and the black comedy *Lord Love a Duck* in which she sold her soul to Satan] was, in Marilyn's case, homage to a woman who was literally victimized by her own inherent witchery potential, which was there in her looks. I think a great deal of the female mystique of beauty, which was personified in Marilyn's image. In the case of Tuesday Weld, it's part of the magical ritual. She is my candidate of a living approximation of these other two women. Unlike them, Tuesday has the intelligence and emotional stability to withstand that which Marilyn Monroe could not. For this reason Tuesday is not in the public eye as much. Her own better judgment has cautioned her not to bite off more than she can chew.

FRITSCHER: The way you reference history, you are very successful at reminding America how deeply ingrained Satanism is in society from colonial times to the present.

LAVEY: History is character. Modern Puritans need to know that the popular American hero, Ben Franklin, was a rake without question. He was a sensual dilettante. He joined up with the British Hellfire Club. Their rituals came to them from the [Knights] Templars and other secret societies. We practice some of these same rituals secretly in the Church of Satan. Not only did Ben Franklin influence the activities of the Hellfire Club, his very association sheds some light on the *quality* of members of what would appear to be a blasphemous group of individuals. This proves the Devil is not only a gentleman, but a cultured gentleman.

FRITSCHER: Pop culture brags that we live in an age of "beautiful people." You like blonde women. What about physical beauty, or the lack of it? Thomas Aquinas says grace builds on nature. What does Satanic grace build on?

LAVEY: Beauty, yes. And the eye of the beholder. Throughout history, the witch most feared is the witch most antithetical to the physical standards of beauty. In Mediterranean cultures, anyone with blue eyes would have been the first to be named as a witch. The black woman Tituba in Salem was antithetical to New England physical standards of race. Anyone who is dark has an edge because of all the connotations of black arts, black magic, the dark and sinister side of human nature. Tituba probably was not only more feared but also more sought after. She was set apart physically from the rest of the people. She was the magical outsider.

FRITSCHER: Homosexuals are outsiders. Does a queer stand a chance in hell?

LAVEY: In terms of homosexuality, the Church of Satan does not invite males as altars simply because the male is not considered to be the receptacle or passive carrier of human life. He possesses the other half of what is necessary to produce life. Woman is focal as receiver of the seed in her recumbent role as absorbing altar. A male would defeat the purpose of receptor unless he were fitted out with an artificial vagina and were physically and biologically capable of symbolizing the Earth Mother.

FRITSCHER: So you conjure on the basic heterosexual act. Yet, alternatively, Aleister Crowley used male sodomy to conjure Satan, and the white magician Alex Sanders used mutual male masturbation to create a spirit guide.

LAVEY: They're British, aren't they. [*He laughs.*] We do, however, accept homosexuals. We have many in the Church of Satan. They have to be well-adjusted homosexuals—and there *are* many well-adjusted homosexuals who are not on the daily defensive about their sexual persuasion. Many have a great amount of self-realization. Of course, we get the cream of the crop. Because, however, homosexuals cannot relate to the basic heterosexuality of the Church of Satan, whatever they do must be modified. Care would have to be taken, because if the homophile were involved in defining the dogma of our Church, it could become very imbalanced for the masses of people with whom we deal. The homosexual would very easily like to substitute a male for the female altar.

FRITSCHER: Many Catholic priests are homosexual, as are many Protestant ministers, as are many white witches.

LAVEY: And most heterosexual congregations don't mind, because it's a fact that a heterosexual can accept homosexuality more readily than a homosexual can accept heterosexuality. Relating to the existence of the opposite sex is something that *must* be in evidence. Women cannot be denied their function in our Satanic Church. Needless to add, man-hating women cause us a great lack of, shall we say, sensual scintillation.

My book *The Complete Witch; or What to Do When Virtue Fails* is a guide for witches. It doesn't stress the drawing of pentacles on the floor. It smashes all the misconceptions that women have had, not only about witchery, but about their own sexuality. I think of this book like Simone de Beauvoir's *The Second Sex.* Even if a woman is a man-hater, she can use her femininity to ruin that man. This book tells her how to do it. If she wants to enjoy men, this book will open her eyes to a few things about her power.

FRITSCHER: Fetishes are important in magic, but what about sexual fetishes in the Church of Satan?

LAVEY: Sexual fetishes we find natural. Everybody has one. These should be catered to. Sexual deviations are only negative factors when they present an obstacle to one's success. They present an obstacle when they are carried out of the ritual chamber, out of the fantasy room into the world where others will see them disapprovingly.

FRITSCHER: So homosexuals and sexual fetishists can belong to a Satanic coven as long as their impulses do not impede ritual or self-realization.

LAVEY: As long as the men pursue their male power, and the women their female power, and they do not try to apply their sex power to manipulate others of the same gender. Self-realization, more than the sex act, is the main tenet of Satanism.

FRITSCHER: You mean the way Rosemary realized by the end of *Rosemary's Baby* who she was, and accepted her child?

LAVEY: I must tell you something quite amusing. *Rosemary's Baby* did for us what *Birth of a Nation* [Hollywood epic, 1915] did for the Ku Klux Klan. The first Satanic Year was 1966. *Rosemary's Baby* premiered in 1968. I never realized what that film could do. I remember reading that at the premiere of D. W. Griffith's *Birth of a Nation* there were recruiting posters for the KKK in southern cities. I chuckled because at the premiere of *Rosemary's Baby,* there were posters of the Church of Satan in the lobby. Here at the San Francisco premiere there was a great deal of consternation, but the film started an influx of very worthwhile new members. Since *Rosemary,* the quality of membership has gone up. Immeasurably.

Since that film with Roman Polanski, I am constantly confronted with scripts by thick-skulled exploitation producers who want me either to be technical advisor or play the role of the Devil or the Satanic doctor in their new films. They think to one-up *Rosemary.* What they don't realize is that *Rosemary's Baby* was popularly successful because it exploded a lot of the preconceptions of Satanism. It didn't chop up the baby at the end. Rosemary took her baby to her breast exactly like Christianity's Virgin Mary. It threw all the crap down the drain and showed the public who was expecting the sensational the real image of the Satanist. It will remain a masterpiece.

FRITSCHER: Hollywood pop culture explains Satanism.

LAVEY: *Rosemary's Baby*, of course, was the allegory of the Christ Child told in reverse. The baby represented the birth of the New Satanic Age, 1966. The year 1966 was used in *Rosemary's Baby*, as the date of the baby's birth, because 1966 was our Satanic Year One in the Church of Satan. The birth of the baby was the birth of Satanism. *Rosemary's Baby* stands foursquare against the popular image of child sacrifice. The role that I played in the picture—the Devil in the shaggy suit—was not from my point of view anything other than it should have been. I was man, animal, bestial, carnal nature coming forth in a ritualized way. The impregnation of Rosemary in that dream sequence was to me the very essence of the immodest, the bestial in man, impregnating the virginal world-mind with the reawakening of the animalism within oneself. This impregnation was very meaningful because it showed the spawning literally, in the movie, of the Church of Satan. Among all the rituals in the film, this was the big ritual in *Rosemary's Baby*.

These other moviemakers who want my opinion on their scripts are simply producing more trash of the blood-sacrifice variety. In *Rosemary's Baby*, the girl who went out the window and landed on the pavement died in the pure Satanic tradition. She had made it clear—although the people who saw the film didn't realize it—that she was a loser. Everything she said pointed to it. She'd been kicked around. She'd been on the streets. She'd been on dope. She was obviously the wrong girl to be a carrier. Satan saw her lack of maternal instinct, of winning instinct, of spunk to carry this baby out into the world. She, therefore, sort of fell "accidentally" out the window. The end of the film shows Rosemary throw away her Catholic heritage and cherish the Devil Child. The natural instinct of Satanism wins out in her woman's heart over manmade programming.

FRITSCHER: Rosemary wins.

LAVEY: Rosemary is a triumphant woman, because she reaches self-realization.

FRITSCHER: Satan wins in your parallel to Christianity. Most movies have a traditional moral ending where good triumphs. You and Polanski are announcing a new ending.

LAVEY: Even though I have done the consulting for *Mephisto Waltz* for Twentieth Century Fox, that film still has the old elements of witchery.

FRITSCHER: More old cliches rather than modern blasphemy?

LAVEY: It's going to take a lot to come up with a film that's as much a blasphemy as *Rosemary's Baby*. Polanski's other film, *The Fearless Vampire Killers*, is like nothing else that's ever been done before in the film world. That film explodes all the puerile Christian myths about vampires. The old professor, sort of a Count Dracula, is shown to be not only the doddering old fool he really is, but also the real victim at the end. There's more to real Satanism than that.

FRITSCHER: You mean Satanists now resist the Inquisition.

LAVEY: We'll never be victims again. Satanism is self-realization. Self-realization is power.

FRITSCHER: As the Black Pope, you must protect yourself, your family, your Church. How do you cope with the tragedy that befell Roman Polanski when his wife, his unborn baby, and his wife's guests were butchered by the Manson Family?

LAVEY: The fact that all those unfortunate murders took place at Polanski's home—his wife Sharon Tate and all the rest—was used by the press to highlight Polanski's interest in witchery and Satanism. The deaths had nothing to do with the films. The Polanski household was simply plagued with hippies and drug addicts. If I were to allow it, my house would be full of sycophantic loungers.

FRITSCHER: You are like a rock star.

LAVEY: I was in showbiz. I know. If I allowed hangers-on, if I neglected them, they'd be paranoid. I would have been put in the same position as those people at Polanski's house had I allowed it. Polanski attracted, as people in Hollywood do, all the creeps, kooks, and crackpots. He wasn't around to stop it, or was too nice to put his foot down. He, in a sense, put himself in much the same position as Jayne Mansfield.[4]

Those people that were killed at Polanski's house were all freaked out of their minds anyway. They were people who were only a little better than the killers. As far as their warped outlooks on life, their senses of values, it was a case of the blind destroying the blind. Sharon was probably the victim of her environment, but I can't find it in myself to whitewash these murdered people. I know firsthand how the people at Warhol's Factory and the Daisy discotheque and these other nightclubs behave. They're quite indiscriminate as to the people they take up with.

FRITSCHER: If anyone knows, you do: What *does* the Devil look like?

LAVEY: The Devil in *Rosemary's Baby* was depicted as a combination of many anthropomorphic ideals of the bestial man: the reptilian scales, the fur, claws. A combination of the animal kingdom. It was not a red union suit with a pitchfork. Nor was it Pan transmogrified by Christians into a cloven-hoofed Devil. *The Cloven Hoof* title of our newsletter was chosen precisely for its eclectic image in the popular mind as one of the Devil's more familiar and acceptable traits. Cloven-hoofed animals in pre-Christian times had often been considered sacred in their association with carnal desire. The pig, goat, ram—all of these creatures are consistently associated with the Devil. Hence our title.

The truest concept of Satan is not in any one animal, but is in man, the evolutionary epitome of all animals. That's what Satan looks like.

FRITSCHER: Catholicism teaches that hell is hot; witchcraft says that Satan's penis is cold.

LAVEY: The historical notion that Satan has an ice-cold penis is a very pragmatic thing, because when Satan had to service the witches who would assemble to draw from his power at the Sabbaths, he could actually remain erect either with those who stimulated him—that is, the magician who portrayed Satan—or until he became expended of his sexual vigor. Naturally then, under his fur cloak or garb, he had to strap on something of an artificial nature, a bull's pizzle, a dildo. In the night air, it would cool off. So the witches all swore that the Devil's penis was cold. He would have to use something like this to maintain his position as the Devil.

FRITSCHER: Then a gay man could service a female witch? Or not . . . because he'd have the artificial member, but he wouldn't have the real desire.

LAVEY: There would be no self-realization.

FRITSCHER: Witch hunters in their hysteria often see the mark of Satan.

LAVEY: It is of interest to me that hippies and Hell's Angels tattoo themselves with the markings of Satanism and other symbols of aggression. Tattooing is an ancient and obscure art. One of the few books on it is called *Pierced Hearts and True Love* by Hanns Ebensten [1953]. There's also George Burchet's *Memoirs of a Tattooist* [1958]. Certainly much needs to be said of the relation of Satanism and witchery to tattooing. We have members that were tattooed long before the Hell's Angels made it fashionable. One man has the Goat of Bathona, the Satanic goat, tattooed across his back. Beautifully done. The Devil-headed eagle is on his chest. Then on each thigh he has the figure of Seth. He's quite spectacular. He has a shaven head and the build of a professional wrestler. He is extremely formidable when he is in ceremony wearing only a black pair of trunks with a very small mask across his eyes. His tattoos are very symmetrically designed attempts at using tattoos for ritualistic purposes.

FRITSCHER: You paid your dues in burlesque, the circus, and Hollywood. What about witches in popular culture? You were a hit with your Topless Witches Sabbath in North Beach.

LAVEY: Witchcraft has a lot of show business in it. Religious ritual, after all, was the first theater. For this reason, I think, *Dark Shadows* and *Bewitched* are fine. White witches think these TV shows are terrible because they play the witch as a pretty girl who can snap her fingers and get things done. They try to impress the world that Wicca is not up to that sort of thing. They try to play that they're an intellectually justified Old Religion. The popular image of the witch is a gal who can get things done in apparently supernatural ways. Like *I Dream of Jeannie*. Why not take advantage of the glamorized witch? If this has been the very element that has brought witchcraft out of a stigmatized, persecuted stereotype, then why put it down? It is the glamorization of witchcraft that gives the erstwhile white witches the free air in which to breathe. Why knock it?

FRITSCHER: What about these white witches? They back away from the black arts.

LAVEY: This gets me to Gerald Gardner, another British type, whom I judge a silly man who was probably very intent on what he was doing. He was motivated to call himself a "hereditary witch" because he had opened a restaurant and needed a gimmick to get it filled with customers. He had taken over a not-too-successful tea shop and had turned it into a museum. He had to say he was a research scholar. He got the term *white witch* from a coinage in *Witchcraft's Power in the World Today*. Gardner used the term because witchery was illegal in England at the time. To avoid persecution he opened his museum under the guise of research. He stated he wasn't a witch until the repeal of the laws in 1953. Then he made it very clear he was a "white witch." That's like saying, "Well, I'm a good witch. The others are bad witches. So don't persecute me." Gardner did what he had to do, but I don't think he was any more of an authority on the true meaning of witchcraft than Montague Summers.[5] I think that he simply followed Summers's crappy rituals of circles and Elohim and Adonai. They used the name of Jesus and crossed themselves.

FRITSCHER: Nevertheless, what Gardner dared do in Britain in 1953 for white magic was like the giant step forward you took in the United States in 1966 for black magic.

LAVEY: True. I have broken the barrier. I have made it a little bit fashionable to be a black magician. A lot of white witches, however, are still trying to say now that their horned god is not a Devil. It is just a horned god. Well, let me tell you, until five or six years ago they wouldn't even admit to a horned god. Some of them are finally intimating that perhaps they have made pacts with the Devil. For many years the Old Religionists used the writings of Albertus Magnus, the *Sixth and Seventh Books of Moses*, the *Book of Ceremonial Magic*, crossing themselves as they turned the pages, denying theirs was a Christian-based faith.[6] Why in the hell did they use all these Christian accouterments? White witches are no more than a by-product of Christianity, or they wouldn't have to call themselves white witches in the first place. I don't think white witches have the courage of their convictions.

FRITSCHER: What about Aleister Crowley, the Great Beast, code name 666? How does your demonology doctrine handle this famous Satanist's sex, drugs, and rock-and-roll?

LAVEY: I have said that Aleister Crowley had his tongue jammed firmly in his cheek. I think Crowley was a pragmatist. He was also a drug addict [psychedelics and heroin]. The demons he conjured were the products of a benumbed mind. Basically he was a sweet, kind man who was trying to emancipate himself from the throes of a very strict upbringing. He can't be blamed for anything he did from a psychoanalytical point of view. He wasn't really that wicked of a man. He had to work overtime at being bad. All the arbitrary numbers, dogma, and so on of his magical curriculum were constructs he invented to answer the needs of his students. Crowley's greatest wisdom was in his *Book of Lies* [(1913); followed by *Magick in Theory and Practice* (1929); and *The Book of the Law* (1938)]. The particular page can be paraphrased: "My disciples came to me, and they asked, 'Oh Master, give us your secret.'" He put them off. They insisted. He said it would cost them ten thousand pounds. They paid, and he gave them his words: "A sucker is born every minute." This one line says more for Crowley than all his other work. His judgment of the popular follower was accurate. Most of the public wants gibberish and nonsense. He alluded to this in his numbering of his *Libers* which are not immense volumes but just a few bound sheets of paper. He's saying the real wisdom is about ten lines long.

FRITSCHER: Like Crowley and Gardner in Britain, in America Ray Buckland has done much to spread witchcraft.

LAVEY: Ray Buckland. Like Crowley, Gerald Gardner probably knew a good thing when he saw it and got something going that turned out to be more sanctimonious than it should be. Ray Buckland began the same way. Now he admits to being part of the "more mundane" [Wiccan] rather than the "complete esoteric" [black magician] he was once made out to be. Ray Buckland certainly knows a great deal about the occult.

He has a good synthesis of the arts. But sanctimony still comes through.
His famous chapter on black magic threatens that if a curse is not performed properly it will return to the sender. He defines things like *good*
and *bad, white* and *black* magic for those who—as I say in my *Satanic
Bible*—are frightened by shadows. I maintain that good like evil is only
in the eyes of the beholder. Ray Buckland has guts, though, to sit in his
Long Island home conducting his rituals and not caring what the neighbors think.

FRITSCHER: What about Sybil Leek? Another British white witch and
astrologer. It's like the British invasion in pop music.

LAVEY: I don't know whether Sybil Leek is as big a fool as she sometimes
seems, or whether she's laughing up her sleeve. Sybil is a good businesswoman. She helped start the health food craze and wrote some books
[*The Diary of a Witch* (1969) and *The Complete Art of Witchcraft* (1972)].
I don't want to judge her. When it comes to white and black magic, she
is a good businesswoman. She knows on which side her bread is buttered! My only complaint with Sybil—and I do know her personally—
is she has done nothing to dispel all the crap about black and white
witches. If she's after the little old ladies in tennis shoes, fine. But she
is a dispenser of misinformation.

FRITSCHER: What about that other Englishman, Alex Sanders, who inherited his white magic tradition from Gerald Gardner?

LAVEY: Alex Sanders has become more public in proclaiming himself the
"King of the Witches." He is a dispenser of misinformation too. He's not
too bad. Actually, in the stifling climate of England he's a forward man
among a backward people. He's got a big load. For this I admire him.
He's great enough to claim himself king. I don't put as much credence
in astrology as he does, because astrology is a case of the tail wagging
the dog.

FRITSCHER: Satan doesn't need the stars?

LAVEY: A competent sorcerer, however, should know his astrology because
it is a motivating factor for many people. Sydney Omarr, the popular
syndicated astrologer, is basically a level-headed guy who sees through
a lot of the fraud.

FRITSCHER: Against the white noise of all these white witches, there you
stand: the Black Pope of black magic.

LAVEY: I'll be the first to give Sybil Leek and Louise Huebner [the official witch of Los Angeles County] and all these people their due. They
don't say, "We witches don't want publicity." That takes moxie in a

sanctimonious society. They're not like these damn cocktail party witches who can't defend their self-styled reputations when called to do it. These people give me a pain. It's part of being a witch, the ego-gratification of being a witch, to want to talk about it in detail in public.

AFTERWORD

Anton LaVey remains as controversial dead as alive. Although he died on October 29, 1997, his death certificate in the San Francisco coroner's record initially stated that he died October 31, Samhain, Halloween, a few days after he completed his last book, *Satan Speaks*.

Anton LaVey founded the Church of Satan on Walpurgisnacht, April 30, 1966. Thirty-five years later, on Walpurgisnacht, 2001, the eve before May Day, the feast of Beltane, the Church of Satan moved from San Francisco to New York. On October 17, 2001, the owners of 6114 California Street tore down the famous Black House where Anton LaVey founded the Church of Satan. Word got around. On October 31, driving to the annual gay Halloween party that mobs Castro Street, I stopped and set a bell, a book, and a candle on the curb to mark where once stood the door to the house of a man who, like my pal Robert Mapplethorpe,[7] was a cosmic gent.

If in the best books the reader can hear the author's voice, then *The Satanic Bible* is essential LaVey. His work, philosophy, and personality continue with the worldwide Church of Satan under the direction of Magus Peter H. Gilmore with High Priestess Magistra Peggy Nadramia and can be visited at www.ChurchofSatan.com. Anton LaVey's surviving companion, Magistra Blanche Barton, who is rumored to be an ex-nun, is the actual mother of his only son, Satan Xerxes LaVey, and the author of the intimate memoir, *The Secret Life of a Satanist: The Authorized Biography of Anton LaVey*. Barton's official title is "Magistra Templi Rex." She is also the author of the book *The Church of Satan: A History of the World's Most Notorious Religion* (1990), and is the editor of *The Cloven Hoof*, the official newsletter and journal of the Church of Satan.[8]

You can take Salem out of the country,
but you can't take the country out of Salem
—RADIO AND TV COMMERCIAL JINGLE,
SALEM CIGARETTES

CHAPTER 1

The Medium as Medium

WITCHCRAFT, WOMEN, AND LAW

How Witchcraft Measures Law, Human Rights, Sex, and Drugs
and Makes for Great Cocktail Party Conversation

*L*AW, *COVEN, CULT, AND CONSCIOUSNESS; the*
Inquisition, the holocaust of witches; The Witch Manifesto;
The Hammer of Witches; Celtic fairies; Halloween; hags;
werewolves; virgin sacrifice; Hitler and Jewish magic; astrology;
shape-shifting; and W.I.T.C.H. (Women's International
Terrorist Conspiracy from Hell)

Popular witchcraft is a strange country. Bounded on the left by science
and on the right by religion, this "Mesopotamia of the Mind" lies somewhere between the flowing together of two great rivers: one a natural
stream, the other a human-designed canal. According to Egyptologist
Margaret Murray's theory, Wicca, or the Old Religion—the religion of
nature and human nature—predates Judeo-Christianity. The other witchcraft, a latter-day media phenomenon, has long since been channeled by
the alternately commercial and hysterical tides of Western culture.

Left to itself, witchcraft could have maintained a quiet flow as sup-
portive to the Christian mainstream as Merlin was to Camelot. Can society educate away its fears? Damned by laws, however, witchery has always
risen boiling to civilization's floodgates. Can society legislate away its fears?
The establishment, controlling nature with technology and suppressing

dissent with politics, uses the legal system to repress witchcraft, which it sees as too powerful and threatening. "Rebellion is as the sin of witchcraft" (I Sam. 15:23). Witchery, more often than not, has led the charge of human rights and social revolution: without witches there would be no feminism, no gay liberation, no civil rights for racial equality.

Both the Old Testament and the New Testament are full of demonology. The archetypal biblical story of rebellion features the Archangel Lucifer, whose name means "Light-Bearer." Fighting God, Lucifer fell from heaven to hell to wander the earth as the wild one—the new Satan—in search of souls. The brightest becomes the darkest. The conservative state ethic of Western culture—rarely separated from muddled-class churches—has long seen the need to write laws protecting the status quo from the threatening freedoms of the progressive human rights movements, including the various occult liberation fronts.

Babylonian King Hammurabi in 1900 BC legislated against witchcraft and image worship because too many of his tribes had too many exorcists telling people too many things that contradicted Hammurabi's political control. The outlaw status of seers and witches can be seen by connecting the dots from the ancient Bible to the most modern state laws, all of them influenced by the canon law of the Roman Catholic Church, which, as reported in a 2003 update by *Newsweek*, is the oldest functioning legal system in the world. Mosaic Law, written for a Middle Eastern ethic that originally had no Devil, said, "Thou shalt not suffer a witch to live" (Exod. 22:18). In Christianity, magic and mysticism are called Gnosticism, and in Judaism, Kabbalah. Islam, Hinduism, and Buddhism each handle the mystical esoterica behind their standard creeds with, respectively, Sufism, Tantrism, and Dark Zen.

The Bible is a written collection of oral folktales from a popular culture of four thousand to two thousand years ago that had an opinion on absolutely everything. It is the traditional weapon of choice used by literalists to support their review-proof opinions. Always quoted as the ultimate argument from authority, the Bible is a gun. Often it is aimed at thinkers, scientists, occultists, women, homosexuals, and dark-skinned races. The Bible is a catch-22 that, in its circular argument, fails Logic 101: "Believe the Bible because the Bible says you must believe the Bible." The Old Testament is the folklore of primitives wandering the flat earth of the ancient desert. The New Testament contains the monotheistic stories and letters popular in the polytheistic Roman Empire, yet it has power. It threatens contemporary people who cannot shake the superstition that the Bible is some kind of magic book. Waving a Bible at a Christian is like holding up a crucifix to a vampire: both crumble before the symbol.

History tells how this conditioning became the superstition that "the Bible will get you if you don't watch out." Scriptural quotations have been invoked for centuries to control people, to judge people, to convict people, and to kill people. Thus the Bible, like a loaded handgun, scares people. And why not? For centuries, for instance, in cases of occultism, Bible quotes have been offered in evidence at more than one witch trial, and have bent lawmakers' attitudes toward the occult from ancient law to contemporary law.

The Bible is based on the fundamental belief in God and angels, as well as in Satan and devils, and in all of these spirits must Jews, Catholics, and Protestants believe.

Once upon a time, in the Bible stories of sex and violence, a (no doubt, priapic) Satan dressed in black leather boldly bragged that all the kingdoms of the world were his to give when he tempted Jesus Christ to kneel in Satanic worship. "Again, the Devil took Him to a very high mountain, and showed Him all the kingdoms of the world, and the glory of them, and the Devil said to Him, 'All these will I give You, if You will fall down and worship me.' Then Jesus said to him, 'Begone Satan! For it is written, You shall worship the Lord your God and Him only shall you serve.' Then the Devil left Him, and, behold, angels came and ministered to Him" (Matt. 4:8–11).

In the polar battle between good and evil, "Witch, be warned and beware!" In the antiwitch hysteria between the years 1500 and 1900 more than 250,000 people were tried, tortured, and killed. This is the "Withering of the Witch," according to an assortment of biblical laws that are so unnerving, it may be helpful to remember that in the classic American opera *Porgy and Bess* (1934), lyricist DuBose Heyward has a black preacher sing the warning that what one reads in the Bible: "It Ain't Necessarily So."

Lev. 19:26: "[N]either shall ye use enchantment nor observe dreams."

Lev. 19:31: "Regard not them that have familiar spirits, neither seek after wizards, to be defiled by them. I am the Lord your God."

Lev. 20:6: "And the soul that turneth after such as have familiar spirits, and after wizards, to go a-whoring after them, I will even set my face against that soul and will cut him off from among his people."

Lev. 20:27: "A man also or woman that hath a familiar spirit, or that is a wizard, shall surely be put to death: they shall stone them with stones; their blood shall be upon them."

Deut. 18:10–12: "There shall not be found among you any one that maketh his son or his daughter to pass through the fire, or that useth divination, or an observer of times, or an enchanter, or a witch, or a charmer, or a consulter with familiar spirits or a wizard, or a necromancer. For all that do these things are an abomination unto the Lord: and because of these abominations the Lord thy God doth drive them out from before thee."

2 Kings 9:22: "What peace, so long as the whoredoms of thy mother Jezebel and her witchcrafts are so many?"

2 Kings 23:24: "Moreover the workers with familiar spirits, and the wizards, and the images, and the idols, and all the abominations . . . did Josiah put away."

Isa. 8:19: "When they say unto you, Seek unto them that have familiar spirits, and unto wizards, that peep and that mutter, should not a people seek unto their God?"

Gal. 5:19–20: "Now the works of the flesh are manifest, which are these: adultery, fornication, uncleanness, lasciviousness, idolatry, witchcraft."

When worlds collide, change happens.

Constantine the Great (274–337) was a pagan warrior who in 324 became emperor of the entire Holy Roman Empire. He grafted witchcraft and Christianity together, until he didn't. He was, as Roman emperor, a God as well as the Pontifex Maximus (the high priest) of paganism. In combining church and state, he refused to choose between the Old Religion of paganism and the new religion of Christianity. He put the *byzantine* into Byzantine Roman emperor as he ruled the western and eastern Roman empires from the city of Byzantium, which he renamed Constantinople in 324. That city carried his name until 1930, when it was named Istanbul.

As Constantine united the empire politically, he united religion theologically—after he had a little, well, séance. He mixed together the Sun God with Christ on the cross after seeing—just before a battle—a vision of a cross appear in the sky. He heard the words "In hoc signo, vinces," which means "In this sign, you will conquer." This led inevitably to the cross that the Crusaders soon emblazoned on their shields as they first marched against Islam. That Latin phrase of those onward-marching Christian soldiers entered modern popular culture as the motto on every pack of Pall Mall cigarettes. Because Constantine won the battle as the vision predicted, he legalized Christianity with the Edict of Milan in 313. In a way, he introduced a brief period of religious tolerance into the Roman Empire, because he also allowed the ancient practices of paganism to continue.

In fact, in an act of cultural genius, Constantine invented the official fusion of paganism and Christianity.

As emperor, he interpreted the antiwitch laws in the Bible to be against workers of evil charms only. As legally as Christian priests, pagan priests attended to the public altars and observed traditional pagan worship. In the middle of his reign, Constantine began to co-opt paganism by baptizing it. His mixmaster legislation made the birthday of the Sun God into Christmas, and Sunday into a day of rest. His laws turned the pagan rites of spring into Lent and Easter. He minted pagan Gods on coins even while he dug out the site in Jerusalem of the crucified, buried, and risen Christ, where he built the Church of the Holy Sepulcher and prohibited any residency by Jews. His mother, Saint Helena, unearthed the "true cross of Jesus," which can be found in splinters in Catholic churches around the world, most accessibly in Sainte-Chapelle, Paris.

Emperor Constantine, straddling the fusion of the Old Religion and the new, lived a holy Roman life, leaning with politics more toward the Christian, though he refused to be baptized until he was on his death bed. In his old age, he had tried for a time to stamp out paganism, but shortly before he died, still straddling the Old Religion and the new, he confirmed the privileges of the pagan priests serving ancient Gods. His waffling did not please the Catholic Church, but the second of his sons, Constantius, his favorite, militantly persecuted pagans, heretics, and particularly women and homosexuals for whom in 342 he legislated "exquisite punishment." He closed the temples and wrote, "Let superstition cease. Let the folly of sacrifices be abolished." Constantius was a Christian triumphalist. He and his successors wrote extremely stringent Holy Roman laws against witchcraft and paganism in their crusade to control sexual behavior. Those laws, ironically written by these reformed pagans, set up the fall of civilization into the Dark Ages and the Middle Ages that eventually led to the Inquisition, which was the Holocaust of Witchcraft.

Constantine also mixed some of the pagan redes into the sayings of Christ, who said, "Do what you will, but do unto others as you would have them do unto you." Centuries later, the thumbnail aphorisms of the rede tradition summed up the creeds of Saint Augustine, the "Great Beast" Aleister Crowley, and the founding high priest of the Church of Satan, Anton LaVey.

POPULAR REDES

Jesus Christ said, "Love is the greatest commandment. Do unto others as you would have them do unto you."

Saint Augustine wrote, "Love God and do what you will."

Aleister Crowley wrote, "Do what you will is the whole of the law. Love is the law. Love under will."

The Wiccan rede—or pagan rule of white magic—is, "And it harm none, do what thou wilt."

The devilish rede for Anton LaVey's modern Church of Satan is, "If it harms no *undeserving* person, do what you will."

The gay rede is, "If it harms only yourself, do what you will."

Aleister Crowley (1875–1947) was a lawyer, legislator, and inventor of the Western tradition of black magic. He was born into a strict Puritan family from whom he rebelled after his mother told him he was the Devil himself. Taking her seriously, he joined the Order of the Golden Dawn, founded in 1887 out of the secret societies of the soldier mystics of the Knights Templar, the Masons, and the Rosicrucians with emphases on yoga, guardian angels, and the laws of the mystical occult. Later, as head of the Golden Dawn, which counted mystical Irish poet W. B. Yeats (who hated Crowley) in its secret membership, Crowley taught the practice of magic, the tarot, and the Kabbalah. These were his ways to cause social change and to raise self-consciousness, according to his Greek code word *thelema*, meaning the "free will to create one's real self." He wrote nearly one hundred books, including *Magic in Theory and Practice* (1929), *The Book of the Law* (1938), and *Magic without Tears* (posthumous, 1954).

Born in England, traveling worldwide, and living in Scotland, where he enjoyed flashing his kilt, he was known to cynics and churchmen as the "other Loch Ness Monster." Long a famous attraction through books, stage lectures, and radio, Crowley achieved popular canonization four years after his death when his literary executor, John Symond, published his controversial biography, *The Great Beast* (1951). Had he lived until the 1960s and 1970s, Magister Crowley would have been everything pop culture expects of the essential hippie guru: the larger-than-life personality who is charismatic author, teacher, naturist, sexual satyr, and drug conjurer advocating free love, self-help, and the repeal of repressive laws.

Crowley would not have done well under the draconic Justinian Code written in 534 at the order of the Roman Emperor Justinian who hated paganism and its witchcraft and sexuality. Paganism meant tribalism.

Tribalism meant trouble to imperial Rome. In the Migration of Nations, wandering tribes of Vandals, Visigoths, and Huns were terrorists attacking the sprawling Roman Empire. Justinian needed to pull Rome's huge self together. The spinning centrifuge of empire was flying apart, trying to control millions of people in thousands of cultures across hundreds of thousands of square miles. Justinian knew that a common language (Latin), a common religion (Christianity), and law applied universally could tame the outsiders. The Justinian Code, also known as *Corpus Juris Civilis*, was based on the logic of Greek legal principles. Justinian's ten judges reviewed thousands of ancient laws scattered through previous civilizations. They codified the dissonance into four thousand laws that in a Christian context became the code of one comprehensible Roman law. This was not an abstract doctoral dissertation, nor a Gallup Poll. Justinian *acted*; he made the code into actual law. His modernization of law still serves as the base of contemporary civil law, which, with English common law, governs the modern societies of Western civilization.

The Justinian Code came down to a rede of natural law: "To live an honest life, to harm no one, to give each person what he actually deserves, and to attribute to each what is his own."

The problem for witchcraft is that the term *natural* is so open to private interpretation. The Nazis painted the third line, "To give each person what he actually deserves," on a sign over the entrance to the Bergen-Belsen concentration camp. Justinian, trying everything to avert the coming fall of the Roman Empire, feared tribal paganism, heathen homosexuality, and female sorcery as practiced, for instance, by the wild Goth women he fought. So he pronounced the lot of them "unnatural" and persecuted them all in bloody shows at the local Hippodrome where the cross once seen by Constantine was multiplied in thousands of fiery crucifixions. Justinian and his actress wife Theodora were made legendary in the tell-all book written by Procopius, *Secret History* (*Historia Arcana*, 1623). Justinian's "phobic authority" influenced medieval judges to embrace a relative moral law that was not necessarily an absolute natural law. In this way, a fearful church and state, owning religion and law, yanked the focus of history. Witches, healers, pagans, and homosexuals didn't need astrologers with crystal balls to know their rising sign was in *merde*, and they'd best go way underground. As Justinian appropriated ancient laws he liked, the Church continued Constantine's appropriations of ancient folk traditions.

Christianity, particularly as preached from city to city by both Jesus Christ and Saint Paul, was characteristically always an urban religion that had a certain attitude about the simple folk who lived in the country or on the heath. *Pagan* in Latin means simply "someone who lives in a rural area." *Heathen* means "someone who lives out on the heath or the moors." *Witch* may derive from the old Anglo-Saxon word *Wicca*, meaning "wise," in the way *werewolf* (*weirwolf*) and *weird* come from the word *weir*, meaning "country."

Constantine had begun the fusion. Popular culture followed his lead. The pagan feast of the Winter Solstice was eagerly accepted as the Christ Child's Christmas. The pagan celebration of spring, Beltane, with its maypole, became the May Day procession to crown the Blessed Virgin Mary with flowers. The pagan autumn feast of Samhain (pronounced sow-en), which celebrates the crossing between the world of the living and the world of the dead, became Halloween, the Eve of All Saints, the night before the Christian feast of All Souls Day. The Catholic Church took to its popular heart the functions of white magic because, to be accepted beyond politics, the new religion had to comfort old human needs with religious rituals previously addressed by the Old Religion. As quickly as pagan white magic became Christian ritual, heathen sorcery that could not—and would not—be absorbed was written up into church law as sin, heresy, and witchcraft. The good women of white-magic covens went to convents. The rebel women of black-magic circles remained outside the pale. Thus, early on, squelching the competition, primitive Christianity, by the time it turned positively medieval, gave the Catholic Church a monopoly on bell, book, and candle. Contemporary blessings, exorcisms, and most of Catholic ritual are remnants of this baptism of the old white magic.

Centuries before John Van Druten (1901–57) wrote the 1950 Broadway hit comedy *Bell, Book, and Candle* (filmed in 1958, with Kim Novak as a white witch whose brother writes a book on black magic), the Catholic Church had co-opted these three conjure symbols. For instance, the "minor orders" leading up to the major ordination to the Catholic priesthood are, in fact, historical vestiges of white sorcery. These are four.

The order of *porter*, bestowed as the sound of one *bell* is rung once, entrusts the keeping of the church door to the cleric who admits only the initiated to the heart of the consecratory rites.

The order of *lector*, with its giving of the sacred *book* to the ordained, symbolizes more intense study of the tenets of the sect.

The third order of *exorcist*, bestowed amid much *incense*, remains the militant equivalent of the white magician's use of his power to break curses and cast out evil forces.

The last minor order, that of *acolyte*, gives the cleric not only the duty of tending the *candles* but also the privilege of blessing objects like bread, salt, houses, and automobiles.

Grimoires, which are books of spells (handled by the lector of the coven), talk of witches' ability to blow into locks to open doors, and to blow on candles that light themselves. Again and again, Christendom helped itself to what it preferred in pagan religions and named what was left over the work of Satan.

Pope Innocent VIII (1432–92) ruled popular culture because the medieval Catholic Church was the sole medium of its time, reaching the people through pulpit, epistle, and pronouncement in papal bulls. For the first fourteen centuries of Catholicism, witch hunting was sporadic and unorganized, though often intense. On December 5, 1484, Pope Innocent issued his papal bull, *Summis Desiderantes.* His intent was to ratify the "antiheretic" campaign of Jacob Sprenger and Heinrich Kramer. What he did was fan the smouldering fires against witchcraft to full flame. The Bible taught that witchcraft was real. The Church taught that witchcraft was a sin because it was a lapse back into paganism. *Summis Desiderantes* codified the Catholic laws against witchcraft in much the same way that the *Justinian Code* (534) modernized the ancient laws into new laws.

Pope Innocent's *Summis Desiderantes* made witchcraft more than a sin. It made it a heresy, and turned witch hunting into a blood sport. Its ratification of Sprenger and Kramer led the two Dominican priests and sadists to write their witch-hating book, *Malleus Maleficarum*, also known as *The Hammer of Witches* (1486). Never underestimate the murderous power of *Malleus Maleficarum*: it was the seminal document that systematized Christian doctrine defining witchcraft as heresy, and women's sexuality as Satanic. *Malleus Maleficarum* invented and prescribed "everything anyone had ever wanted to know" about witchcraft and its erotic practices, including the form of trial by torturers who were "not afraid to ask anything" in their sadomasochistic interrogations of any person accused of witchcraft.

Malleus Maleficarum was the perfect book for the Gutenberg printing press, invented thirty years earlier. Johannes Gutenberg had been motivated to publish the Bible in a mass-market way so that everyone could have a copy. *Malleus Maleficarum* was a kind of lurid cautionary tale of witchcraft, sex, and womanhood, and the ways to strip, torture, and kill witches and women. *Malleus Maleficarum* was a best seller, second only to the Bible for the next two hundred years until John Bunyan's *Pilgrim's*

Progress was published in 1684. *Malleus Maleficarum*'s first twenty-nine editions averaged a new printing every six years until four years after the Salem, Massachusetts, witch trials in 1692. Printed in German, French, Italian, and English, the sadomasochistic erotica of the document "turned on" the whole of the European continent, and particularly Spain, where Hispanic panic over witches rose to the formal level of the Inquisition (1478–1808). The Spanish Inquisition, codified by *Malleus Maleficarum* and authorized by Pope Sixtus, was administered by King Ferdinand and Queen Isabella. They funded the voyage of Christopher Columbus who landed in a whole new world of heathens, magic, and gold.

In his twenties, the gay British dramatist Christopher Marlowe (1564–93) focused on humankind's pact with Satan in his *Tragical History of Doctor Faustus* (1592, published 1604), which director Peter Brook staged in London in the 1940s with Aleister Crowley as technical advisor. In 1584 in England, Reginald Scot wrote the popular *Discourse of Witchcraft* to refute the fantasies of the hundred-year-old *Malleus Maleficarum*. Scot aimed to defend the simple, the poor, the aged, and particularly women, who, when they were melancholy and old, were accused of sorcery as defined by the hate-filled *Malleus Maleficarum*. In *The Tempest* (1610), William Shakespeare, who often used white magic (*Midsummer Night's Dream*, ca. 1594) and horror (three witches open *Macbeth*, c. 1606) in his works, reflected the European mind-set characterizing the new American world and its native inhabitants. His antagonist, the dark Caliban—the deformed offspring of Sycorax the witch, clashes with the white-magic powers of his protagonist, Prospero, who controls the genial spirit, Ariel.

Queen Elizabeth I caused the first real persecution of witches with the first English Witchcraft Act, 1563. Her advisors were first-generation Protestants. They were so fearfully antipapist, and so terribly British, that they confused folk magic with Catholicism, because Rome, so far away in Italy, had incorporated so much of the Old Religion in its rituals. As goes witch hunting, so goes art. In 1642, Puritan censors closed Shakespeare's Globe Theatre because in England as in New England, playhouses, music, dance, and laughter were things of the Devil. But of course! Furthering the anarchy, mystic British poet and painter William Blake (1757–1827), in *The Marriage of Heaven and Hell* (1790), defined the Devil as "the imagination." A powerful elite of British aristocrats in the eighteenth century celebrated Satan, attended the Hellfire Club founded in London by Sir Francis Dashwood, and desecrated an altar or two. The Greek goddess Hecate, who ruled the underworld, became their goddess of witchcraft.

Salaciously detailed, the *Malleus Maleficarum* merchandised itself as theology, but its subtext was its sadomasochistic obsession with naked women, deviant sex, and blood-lust torture.

Not to believe in witches was as much heresy as the practice of witchcraft.

No one in that absolutely theological time could, really, dismiss the *Malleus Maleficarum* as a mad Dominican porno book, for that would be heresy, too.

In 250,000 words, *Malleus Maleficarum* builds many specious arguments. Arthurian scholar Rossell Hope Robbins (1912–90), in the *Encyclopedia of Witchcraft and Demonology* (1959), reveals how the book's premise depends on the fantastic sacrifice of logic to fit a preconceived theological line. In the worst case of linguistics ever, the Dominican authors say that *femina* (woman) is derived, quite erroneously, from *fe* (faith) and *minus* (less); and *diabolus* (devil) from *dia* (two) and *bolus* (death), which kills body and soul. In all three parts of *Malleus Maleficarum*, rational arguments are ignored. The first two parts deal all the witchcraft cards from the Bible to prove witchcraft is a reality all people must confront. The third part details the procedure for the ecclesiastical court's trial of the witch, whom the civil court would then order to execution. Such casuistry meant that from a legal standpoint the church courts themselves never ordered an execution. The *Malleus Maleficarum*, with its fine legal persuasiveness, transcended sectarian lines and became conveniently ecumenical. Robbins connects the dots of the Christian conspiracy against witchcraft: "The Protestants, who otherwise so strongly opposed the Catholic aspects of the Inquisition, accepted the *Malleus Maleficarum* as their authority and code against witches."[1]

When the Catholic priest Martin Luther basically announced Protestantism on Halloween 1517 by nailing his theses to the Wittenburg church door, he remained for all his humanist reformation a firm believer in the punishment of witchcraft because he believed that each Christian was personally living a life constantly in battle with the real presence of Satan. The Protestant Reformation was a pious and fundamentalist movement based on an absolutely literal interpretation of the Bible that leads directly to today's American fundamentalism, which thinks popular culture itself is Satanic. Terrorized by the biblical image of Satan, all of Western civilization—Catholic and Protestant alike—pivoted around the *Malleus Maleficarum* and its fundamentalist medieval cartoons (as simplistic as stained-glass windows) of the Devil and his witches copulating at midnight sabbaths where easily seduced women oiled Satan's privates with the juice of unbaptized babies. The H. Adrian Smith Collection at Brown University includes thousands of books, texts, and graphics from the sixteenth century onward that depict both truths and popular fantasies about witchcraft and magic.

Almost as suspect in Western civilization was the concept of "Christian mysticism." Male mystics were often self-punishing monks who meditated in pederastic union with the infant child Jesus and the adolescent Jesus teaching in the temple, or in homosexual union with the naked, athletic, crucified Jesus. Female mystics, also often sexually self-abusive, sought mystical union in erotic terms with the nursing infant Jesus and the powerful adult Jesus. While women like Hildegard of Bingen, Julian of Norwich, Saint Catharine of Siena, and Saint Teresa of Avila may well have achieved pure mystical marriage with Christ, popular culture—with its fantasies of women behind bars—has long considered convents to be covens.

Aldous Huxley, most famous for *Brave New World* (1931), portrayed this sexual-religious hysteria in his historical novel *The Devils of Loudun: A Biography* (1951), based on an event in a French town in 1632 when the local priest was accused of bewitching a convent of nuns. The book became the 1965 Broadway play *The Devils*, by John Whiting. In 1971, British director Ken Russell used the book and the play to create his outrageous and much-censored film *The Devils*, a brilliant excess of sex, violence, and camp urged on by the set design of the gay British painter and filmmaker Derek Jarman.

In the marriage of these two prejudices of "witchcraft" and "Christian mysticism," the cross-dressing Joan of Arc was burned at the stake at Rouen on May 30, 1431. When Joan after her death was deemed to have worked certifiable miracles, the Catholic Church, by then long expert in co-opting the alternative world, ruled that her magic was not the work of a witch but of a saint and canonized her, whom they had burnt, as Saint Joan of Arc in 1920. Joan was always popular. Her execution drew ten thousand people, largely because the "English authorities in France . . . in many ways were less interested in Joan the heretic than in Joan the witch" whose trial fell "at a period when witch-persecution was quite rapidly on the increase. . . . She insisted too much on the visions she said that she had" and "she died, too, for her defiance of the established theological orthodoxy of her time" which, of course, made her an outsider, a sorceress, a witch.[2]

The *Malleus Maleficarum* is typical of hysterical laws that gain so much popular momentum that they become enforced for their own sake to maintain the establishment status quo rather than for the protection of individuals in a just society. For instance, the Catholic charge of "witchcraft," ironically—like the earlier imperial Roman charge of "Christianity" by Nero, and like the contemporary American charge of "marijuana"— was a convenient crime to trump up in order to persecute people who had been guilty of no more than perhaps radical views. Each charge in its day led to conviction.

Christianity has done more for witchcraft than the Old Religion left to its own devices could ever have popularized for itself. Most of the popular image of witchcraft comes from confessions of people being murdered by Christians who tortured them until the victims said what they were forced to say. People under torture have very few original ideas. George Burr, in *Johnson's Encyclopedia* indicated how Christianity forced witchcraft into a polar opposite: "Born into an atmosphere of belief in magic, the early Church seems never to have questioned its reality, while she greatly broadened its scope by systemizing as magic all the marvels of rival faiths. Her monotheism and her identification of religion with ethics led her to look on the gods of the heathen as devils and on their worship as witchcraft. Her conversion of the Germanic people brought in a host of fresh demons; and it is the name of the seers of this northern faith, *witega*, *Wicca*, which gives us the word *witch*."[3]

Until the Age of Reason (1650–1800), intellectual skepticism toward anything was the exception, because everyone believed on faith in magic, witchery, and shape-shifting. Until Francis Bacon, René Descartes, Immanuel Kant, and John Locke in the seventeenth and eighteenth centuries, the Church, the state, and art reinforced the ancient popular notions. In the Old Testament, David's harp had exorcised Saul's bad spirits, because music, wrote William Congreve, has "*charms* to soothe the savage breast." This axiom is often misquoted as "charms to soothe the savage beast" to cover lycanthropy, the ability to turn oneself into an animal—specifically, a werewolf. In the *Book of Daniel*, Nebuchadnezzar, the king of Babylon, was changed lycanthropically into a wolf, in the way that Dracula changes into a vampire bat, or that in a movie a man implanted with an animal heart by a mad doctor becomes the animal. Such shape-shifting is part of both white and black magic. Merlin changed Arthur into many different animals. Satan is always a trickster changing shapes. As the pagan horned God he appears as a goat, and in the Old Testament as a serpent, and in the New Testament as a pig.

In modern popular culture, Dr. Frankenstein, who began studying

alchemy, which is essentially about changing essences, is able to alchemize a man-beast in Mary Shelley's novel *Frankenstein* (1818). The book—
when all popular genres, horror to comedy, are considered—seems largely
the Greek legend of Pygmalion, which has also been updated by George
Bernard Shaw in *Pygmalion* (1916), and reconceived by Alan Jay Lerner
and Frederick Lowe as the musical-comedy *My Fair Lady*. More than seventy movies have "Frankenstein" in their title. Thomas Edison was the first
to film *Frankenstein*, in 1908. Gay Hollywood director James Whale contributed the first great addition to Mary Shelley's original myth when he
created the "sympathetic" monster in his movie *Frankenstein* (1931). Director Herbert L. Strock added the "changeling angst of teens" in the 1957
drive-in movie *I Was a Teenage Frankenstein*. Director Paul Morrisey made
the arty addition of soft-core erotica in the film *Andy Warhol's Frankenstein* (1974). Mel Brooks added "comedy and camp" in *Young Frankenstein*
(1974). Off-Broadway, the Frankenstein myth secured the franchise on
camp, homoerotica, cosmetics and masks, as well as narcissism in the
"shape-shifting drag" character of Doctor Frank N. Furter in *The Rocky
Horror Show* (1973, London; 1975, Broadway). Shape-shifting is an infinite
and essential "magic" ritual constantly repeated in the makeover of the
"plain" girl so often featured on television talk shows, and in film comedies such as *Auntie Mame* (1958). The purpose of the makeover is universally to create the girl into a sorceress with power over men.

In the New Testament, Christ met with Satan repeatedly, casting out
evil spirits as, at one showdown, he drove the Devil—who had taken the
shape of swine—off the sea cliff. The Greek and Roman literary classics
reinforced the popular biblical imagination. Plato, Pliny, and Zeus Lycaeus
all write of metamorphoses of man to animal. In fact, Ovid's most famous
book is titled *Metamorphoses*, and is the mythic history of shape-shifting
from the beginning of the world to Greco-Roman times. Ancient storytelling has an enduring fascination with man-beasts such as centaurs
and satyrs. Inevitably, according to format, Satan is the bright archangel
changed to the Dark Beast. The erotic satire *Satyricon*, written in 61 A.D.
by Petronius, featured a folktale episode in which a vengeful wizard keeps
setting perpetual fire to the thighs of a young witch, who burns all
the way into 1970, when Federico Fellini was nominated for an Academy
Award as best director for his 1969 film *Fellini Satyricon*. In Merrie Olde
England, where the continental legislation of *Malleus Maleficarum* carried
no weight because sheer distance from Rome made papal decrees ineffec-
tual, witchcraft was considered, before the Protestant Reformation, as rarely

more than a minor felony. Minor felonies, however, often received major punishment.

Mary Stuart, Henry VIII, Elizabeth I, and James I—all politicians panicked by rebellious witches—legislated most vociferously against witchcraft, which, ironically, seems so much a part of English culture. Parliament under George II, one reign before the American Revolution, minimized Henry VIII's "Statutes against the Egyptians," naming necromancers at worst as merely rogues and vagabonds. Such increasingly permissive attitudes toward witchery stem largely from the popular belief, as horror-film actor Vincent Price has pointed out, that the British witches brewed up the storm that sank the Spanish Armada in 1588. In the 1940s, several British covens, led by Gerald Gardner, announced that their collective powers prevented Hitler's total invasion of England. Nevertheless, witchcraft collided with law during World War II. In 1944, Helen Duncan became the last person jailed in England under the Witchcraft Act of 1735. She served nine months for trying to raise the dead spirits of war victims so their survivors could receive messages. The press was simultaneously thrilled, outraged, and finally sympathetic.

As a result, in 1951, the enlightened, perhaps grateful, repeal of English antiwitch laws sprang British practitioners Gerald Gardner and Sybil Leek from their underground activity. Gardner then taught the craft of Wicca to the young Ray Buckland (born 1934), a Brit of Gypsy descent, who, out of his lineage as a Gardnerian witch, has become one of the most popular writers on the history and rituals of the occult. Buckland often appears on television talk shows, and was advisor to Orson Welles on his film *Necromancy* (1972) and to William Friedkin, director of *The Exorcist* (1973). The influential Buckland, who came to America in 1962, is almost single-handedly responsible for the fast growth of the Old Religion in the United States. His classics *Witchcraft Ancient and Modern* (1970) and *Buckland's Complete Book of Witchcraft* (1986) serve as a perfect guides to Wicca. He has authored more than twenty-five books, including *Color Magic: Unleash Your Inner Powers* (1983), *Advanced Candle Magic: More Spells and Rituals for Every Purpose* (1996), and *Gypsy Witchcraft and Magic* (1998).

American legislation has followed the British pattern toward permissiveness. As laws against witchcraft have disappeared, so have laws outlawing sex. The first colonial legislation against witches appeared in 1655 in the Puritan laws of New England. William Bradford, writing his diary *Of Plymouth Plantation* (1642–50), legally detailed the crime and punishment of a list of sins common among the colonists: bacchanalian drunkenness, witchcraft, homosexual sodomy, and buggery, as in the case of the young Thomas Granger who for "buggering a mare, a cow, two goats, diverse sheep, two calves, and a turkey" was hanged on September 8, 1642, but only after the mare, the cow, the goats, the sheep, the calves, and the turkey were killed before his eyes.[4] In 1691 and 1692 at the Salem trials, the 1655 definition was invoked: "Witchcraft is fellowship by covenant with a familiar spirit, to be punished with death." The score at the Salem witch trials was 144 accused, 54 confessed, and 19 hanged.

American embarrassment over the Salem hysteria has caused modern legislation concerning occult practice to be rather "hands off." The constitutional right to free exercise of religion supports occult practices performed in the name of the Old Religion. The First Amendment to the U.S. Constitution reads, "Congress shall make no law respecting an establishment of religion, or prohibiting the exercise thereof. . . ." As a result, where state laws exist, they are carefully worded, and rarely enforced. Where once American legislation supported by theologian John Wesley banned witchcraft as "in effect giving up the Bible," religious righteousness against witches has given way to religious protection of witches.

In the jurisprudential history of American crime and punishment, state laws are, in fact, in a curious state and getting curiouser. In Delaware, cameras are forbidden at the whipping post and dueling is as taboo as movies that ridicule religion. California laws legislate about frog-jumping contests, train wrecking, and dumping sawdust into Humboldt Bay. Louisiana has statutes on interracial dancing, the tattooing of minors, possession of piranhas, and atheism at state universities. Indiana has outlawed glue sniffing, switchblades, and unreturned library books. In the final analysis, law more than any other social phenomenon is an index of the mind-set of the times.

Washington, D.C., has more soothsayers per capita than any other American city. One Southern congressman consults his favorite clairvoyant weekly for fecal readings, proving (like the sabbath ritual of kissing Satan's ass) that separation of church and state is more honored in the breach than the observance. San Francisco demonologist Anton LaVey, who included congressmen and senators in his Church of Satan, once claimed that Washington, D.C., has more than twice the national average of Satanists. LaVey, establishing his new grotto in Washington, found that in the bureaucratic District of Columbia, anything occult is legal as long as it is licensed.

District of Columbia. 47.2342. Mediums, clairvoyants, soothsayers, fortune tellers, palmists or phrenologists, by whatsoever name called, conducting business for profit or gain, directly or indirectly, shall pay a license tax of $250 per annum. No license shall be issued hereunder without the approval of the mayor and superintendent of police, nor shall any license be issued hereunder to any person not an actual resident of the District of Columbia for two years next preceding his date of application:

Provided, that no license shall be required of persons pretending to tell fortunes or practice palmistry, phrenology, or any of the callings herein listed, in a regular licensed theatre, or as a part of any play, exhibition, fair, or show presented or offered in aid of any benevolent, charitable, or educational purpose: And provided further, that no license shall be required of any ordained priest or minister, the fees of whose ministrations are not the private property of such ordained priest, minister, or accredited representative of such priest or minister.

The District's two-year residency requirement is simply a sophistication of the solid-citizen Maine statute against outsiders of transient status, such as Irish tinkers, gypsies, and hippies.

Maine. 17.3758. Undesirable persons generally. All rogues, vagabonds and idle persons going about in any town in the country begging; persons using any subtle craft, jugglery or unlawful games or plays, or for the sake of gain pretending to have knowledge in physiognomy, palmistry, to tell destinies or fortunes, or to discover lost or stolen goods . . . be committed to jail or to the house of correction in the town where the person belongs or is found, for a term of not more than 90 days.

New England laws typify American occult legislation: every statute builds on the premise that the occult is essentially a fraudulent business. The emphasis is caveat emptor.

Connecticut. 53.270. No person shall advertise, by display sign, circular or handbill or in any newspaper, periodical, magazine or other publication or by any other means, to tell fortunes or to reveal the future, to find or restore lost or stolen property, to locate oil wells, gold or silver or other ore or metal or natural product, to restore lost love, friendship or affection, to reunite or procure lovers, husbands, wives or lost relatives or friends or to give advice in business affairs or advice of any kind to others for or without pay, by means of occult or psychic powers, faculties or forces, clairvoyance, psychometry, psychology, spirits, mediumship, seership, prophecy, astrology, palmistry, necromancy or like crafty science, cards, talismans, charms, potions, magnetism or magnetized articles or substances, oriental mysteries or magic of any kind. No person shall obtain money or property from another by fraudulent devices and practices in the name of palmistry, card reading, astrology, seership or like crafty science or fortune telling of any kind where fraud and deceit is practiced. No person shall hold or give any public or private meetings or seance of any kind in the name of any religious body, society, cult or denomination and therein practice or permit to be practiced fraud or deception of any kind with intent to obtain from another anything of value. Any person who violates any provision of this section shall be fined not less than twenty-five nor more than one hundred dollars for each offense or imprisoned not more than six months or both. The provisions of this section shall not be construed to prevent advertising or holding any bona fide meeting of spiritualists for purposes of worship according to their faith.

In Michigan and Colorado, seers Jeane Dixon and Peter Hurkos are legally Bonnie and Clyde. Jeane Dixon is the syndicated newspaper astrologer who, much in demand in Washington, D.C., political circles, in 1956 predicted in general terms the death of President John F. Kennedy. Dixon was the official astrologer whom Nancy Reagan called upon to advise Ronald Reagan when elected governor of California in 1966 and again in 1970. Later, in the White House, Joan Quigley was Nancy Reagan's astrologer. Hurkos, whose "God-given gifts" Pope Pius XII praised, was the psychic detective who tracked the Boston Strangler, and worked on the Manson Family's Tate murders.

Michigan. 150.270. If any person shall publish by card, circular, sign, newspaper or any other means whatsoever, that he or she shall or will predict future events, the said publication may be given in evidence to sustain an indictment under this chapter. Any person whose fortune may have been told as aforesaid, shall be a competent witness against all persons charged with any violation of this chapter. Nothing contained in . . . this act shall be deemed to apply to services conducted by a duly ordained minister of any spiritualist church incorporated under the laws of the State of Michigan.

Colorado. 40.24.1. Practice of clairvoyancy—unlawful. No person shall practice or exercise the vocations or calling of clairvoyancy, palmistry, mesmerism, fortune telling, astrology, seership, or like crafty science, readings, sittings or exhibitions of a like character within the state of Colorado, and for which a fee or charge is made or accepted.

Colorado. 40.24.2. Advertisements barred. No person shall advertise that he carries on or conducts such a vocation or calling within the state of Colorado.

Colorado. 40.24.3. Penalty. Any persons violating any of the provisions of this article shall be guilty of a misdemeanor punishable by a fine not to exceed five hundred dollars or imprisonment for a term not to exceed six months, or by both such fine and imprisonment.

Massachusetts, in the most telling about-face of American jurisprudence, legislates not so much against witchcraft as it does against the actual motivation of its own Salem trials. In seventeenth-century Massachusetts the plaintiff's motivation was frequently—exactly as in the Inquisition—simple lust for the property of the accused. In modern Massachusetts the approach is reversed, but the destination is the same: the occult can be allowed until it interferes with the rights of property owners. Like British psychic Sybil Leek in her famous fight with the landlord who evicted her because she was a witch, witches in Massachusetts must be careful not to devalue property—even through infamy, which is a kind of theft.

Massachusetts. 266.75. Whoever, by a game, device, sleight of hand, pretended fortune telling, or by any trick or other means by the use of cards or other implements or instruments, fraudulently obtains from another person property of any description shall be punished as in the case of larceny of property of like value.

Supplemented by laws against cursing God the Father, denying God the Son, and reproaching God the Holy Ghost, Trinitarian Massachusetts shies understandably away from overt proscription of anything possibly supernatural.

Pennsylvania, similar to many states in statute revision, has amalgamated all its old legislation against occult practice into neat statements allied more to Better Business Bureau legalese than to theological disputation. The Pennsylvania statutes, in fact, read as if the famous Dutch hex belt no longer exists in the very real way that Arthur Lewis chronicled it through tape-recorded interviews in his book, *Hex: A Spell-Binding Account of Murder in Pennsylvania* (1969).

Pennsylvania. 4870. Fortune telling. Whoever pretends for gain or lucre, to tell fortunes or predict future events, by cards, tokens, the inspection of the head or hands of any person, or by any one's age, or by consulting the movements of the heavenly bodies, or in any other manner, or for gain or lucre,

pretends to effect any purpose by spells, charms, necromancy, or incantation, or advises the taking and administering of what are commonly called
love powders or potions, or prepares the same to be taken or administered,
or publishes by card, circular, sign, newspaper or other means that he can
predict future events, or for gain or lucre, pretends to enable anyone to get
or to give good luck, or to put bad luck on a person or animal, or to stop
or injure the business or health of a person or shorten his life, or to give
success in business, enterprise, speculation, and games of chance, or to win
the affections of a person, or to make one person marry another, or to induce
a person to make or alter a will, or to tell where money or other property
is hidden, or to tell where to dig for treasure, or to make a person dispose
of property in favor of another, is guilty of a misdemeanor, and upon conviction thereof, shall be sentenced to a term of imprisonment not exceeding
one (1) year, or a fine not exceeding five hundred dollars ($500) or both.

New York typifies the American feeling that even black witches are
straight out of Halloween and Hallmark cards, and are not to be taken
seriously except when they attempt to peddle fraud to the public. In the
states that bother with legal notice of occultists, the accused can be guilty
of no more than a class B misdemeanor as a disorderly person.

New York. 165.35. Fortune telling. A person is guilty of fortune telling when,
for a fee or compensation which he directly or indirectly solicits or receives,
he claims or pretends to tell fortunes, or holds himself out as being able, by
claimed or pretended use of occult powers, to answer questions or give
advice on personal matters or to exorcise, influence or affect evil spirits or
curse, except . . . for the purpose of entertainment. . . . Fortune telling is a
class B misdemeanor.

Louisiana exports artifacts of voodoo and black sorcery to the world.
Yet, despite its Catholic culture, Louisiana has no state laws restricting the
incoming revenues from the multimillion-dollar sales. On the other hand,
Hawaii was influenced by a Puritan Christianity of the kind dramatized by
James Michener in his 1959 novel *Hawaii*, which became the 1966 movie
starring Julie Andrews as a prim New England missionary. Again, those
always onward-marching Christian soldiers have legally stamped out many
practices native to the Polynesian culture. Hollywood has twice filmed
Bird of Paradise (1932 and 1951) because of the pagan exotica of totem and
taboo. Popular culture cannot resist curses cast on stolen locks of hair and
a Polynesian chief selecting his beautiful daughter as a virgin sacrifice to

the volcano god. Once upon a time immersed in spirits, Hawaii has made it legally—but not really—impossible to get back to *mana*, or supernatural powers.

Hawaii. 772.6. Sorcery, etc.; penalty. Any person who attempts the cure of another by practice of sorcery, witchcraft, anaana, hoopiopio, hoounauna, hoomanamana, or other superstitious or deceitful methods, shall be fined not less than $100 nor more than $200 or imprisoned not more than six months.

Hawaii. 772.7. Fortune tellers; penalty. Any person who pretends to tell fortunes for money or other valuable consideration shall be fined not more than $1000 or imprisoned not more than one year, or both.

Illinois, one of the more legally enlightened states, repealed its statutes against occult practices on July 28, 1961. In 1962, Illinois was the first of the states to modernize its sexual code, making homosexual acts legal. The repeal of both laws shows how closely witchcraft and sexual behavior are connected. Historically, in both instances, the laws have tended to be attempts by a few to legislate the morality of the many.

In Ohio, individual rights of morality and religious practice become even more complicated when combined with education. Some American educational institutions, such as Bowling Green State University; Brandeis, New York, and Northwestern Universities; and the Universities of Alabama and South Carolina have pioneered courses in witchcraft history and practice. However, establishing a school specifically for occult education is legally difficult in mid-America.

Ohio. 5141. The secretary of state is not authorized to accept for filing articles of incorporation for a corporation not for profit whose purpose it is to establish and conduct schools for the study of astrology and allied subjects.

Ohio, so often retrograde in progressive social thinking, has also ruled on statute 2911.16, finding that "it does not violate Art. I.7 of the Constitution of Ohio which guarantees religious freedom."

Ohio. 2911.16. Practicing astrology, fortune telling, clairvoyancy, or palmistry. No person, not legally licensed to do so, shall represent himself to be an astrologer, fortune teller, clairvoyant, or palmister.

Whoever violates this section shall be fined not less than twenty-five nor more than one hundred dollars or imprisoned not less than thirty days nor more than three months, or both.

Beyond all the statutes lies the barrister's admission of occulta to the courtroom. Robert Heinselman of the California Bar has written "The Effect of Superstitious Beliefs and Insane Delusions upon Competency," an article applicable to cases like that of Charles Manson.

The Manson Family, guided by its insane guru, Charles Manson, killed the pregnant movie-star wife and the unborn child of Roman Polanski, director of the 1968 film *Rosemary's Baby*. Besides stabbing Polanski's wife Sharon Tate, who had made her 1965 Hollywood debut in *Eye of the Devil*, the Manson Family slaughtered five others in the Polanski home on the night of August 9, 1969: Abigail Folger, heiress to the San Francisco coffee fortune; her lover, Voyteck Frykowski, Polish playboy and photographer; teenager Steven Parent; and famous hairstylist Jay Sebring (Thomas J. Kummer) who, the press alleged, as if the victim were somehow responsible, had leather clothes, whips, and chains stored in the trunk of his car.

Overnight—literally, as Friday night turned to that infamous Saturday, August 9—the Tate murders in Hollywood changed the way American popular culture regarded the occult. The hoopla of Halloween turned to a terror of cult and commune. In all media, suddenly, American popular culture seriously began to believe in witches, sex cults, and devil worship. By coincidence, later on that same Saturday, August 9, Disneyland—the epitome of children's popular culture—cut the opening ribbon on its scary "Haunted Mansion" ride. Critics on Friday, August 8, had grumbled that, because the mansion's white gothic architecture resembled the White House, it seemed poor taste to have a death-ride so soon after the assassination of John F. Kennedy. Before the end of opening day, August 9, a man had smuggled a gun onto the Haunted House ride and fired off a shot, just as the news media were revealing the bloody massacre up at the Polanski mansion.

Ghosts rarely show up in courtrooms, as one does in William Makepeace Thackeray's *Irish Sketchbook* (1842) to say, "Here am I that was murdered by the prisoner at the bar." Ghosts do cause occasional legal decisions. The Supreme Court of Indiana, in a family-property suit (*Craven v. Craven*, Ind. 103 N.E. 333), ruled that "a ghost which fails, for a period of 45 years, to appear and make known a will disposing of real estate in a certain manner, is guilty of laches, so that one claiming under the will cannot set up the record title against a title acquired by adverse possession."

Consequently the Craven nephew did not inherit his uncle's estate. The court ruled that the forty-five-year statute of limitations for ghosts "must be the law, else no title would be secure, however long it may have been occupied under a 'claim of right.'"

Similarly, charges that a person is a witch have been deemed too ridiculous to take the time of busy American courts. However, "While a charge of witchcraft is no longer libelous *per se*, the jury may find it libelous when published in a community whose members believe in witchcraft to some extent, concerning a woman whose livelihood depends upon the respect and goodwill of members of the community." This decision was handed down in the case of *Oles v. the Pittsburgh Times* (2 PA. Superior Court 130). The case concerned a newspaper article stating that a young boy was obsessed by devils through contact with an elderly woman whom the child's parents believed to be a witch.

In November 1969, in Newall, West Virginia, Frank Daminger asked damages of $150,000 from ten neighbors who, he contended, called him "a male witch, warlock, and Devil's consort, burned a cross on his lawn, and tried to hire thugs to beat him up." One of the defendants, Thelma Franszek, countered to the jury that Daminger took her and two other women to moonlit Nessly Chapel cemetery and performed what he called a "black mass." She said he scattered salt, muttered incantations, and promised on a weathered tombstone he would "communicate with the dead." Daminger's lawyer said his client was trying to debunk the occult, but the women ran away before he could make his point. Whether horse-trainer Daminger was a "warlock" or not, the contemporary legal system obviously allowed witches at long last a courtroom role other than that of defendant.

In general, occult legislation where it exists aims more to protect society from adventurers into the occult than to repress the occult itself. Throughout history the witch has been not only persona non grata but psychological measure of the "zeitgeist fright-geist" of his or her times. Since legislation is one of the surest touchstones of popular feeling, the changing legal posture regarding witchcraft indicates the changing attitudes of Western culture as it widens its concepts of psychology and religion to embrace paranatural phenomena and practices. The decline of the witch laws indicates the generally decreasing attempts to legislate choice in moral, religious, and political beliefs.

No longer does the United States outlaw the *use* of witchcraft; only the *abuse* is proscribed. Washington, D.C., may be full of soothsayers, but those witches have their license to practice so long as they do not defraud. Since the 1914 case of the *United States v. Fay* (83 Fed 839), American witches are permitted to use the U.S. Mail for their own purposes. The U.S. Postal Service has long been a national tool of occult and erotic censorship efforts. For instance, the ban against mailing images of full frontal nudity effectively censored the content of heterosexual and homosexual publications until the U.S. Supreme Court ruled in 1969 that images of full frontal nudity were legal, thus launching the adult entertainment industry, changing the centerfolds in *Playboy*, and allowing the start-up of the modern gay press. Similarly, in 1914, the Supreme Court liberated the literature of witches, whose brochures may now be as outrageous as they like in their claims, so long as these claims are patently absurd and do not exploit desperate hope.

To be guilty of fraud through the federal mail, witches' circulars "must involve something more than absurd claims which could not appeal to a rational being." Permissible, therefore, ruled the 1914 Court, was a witch's "manifest hoax and humbug, like a proposition to take a person on a flying trip to the moon, to fit out a traveler for a submarine voyage . . . (or any such thing that) belies the . . . laws of nature (and) cannot, in the nature of things, deceive any rational being." What else have witches promised that came true? Not permissible would be a claim to cure disease. Healing places with healing waters, such as the shrine at Lourdes where the Blessed Virgin appeared to visionary Bernadette Soubirous, are very careful of claiming cures and miracles that, as they actually occur, are thoroughly researched and documented.

The state of witchery, like most popular culture, is always aggressive to the status quo, and has always been more sophisticated than the laws of its times. Essential witchcraft is about the liberation of the individual from the traditional morality and self-restraint that impede self-realization. Occultists, more individuated and isolated than politicians and popes, are easy targets for crusading lawmakers seeking dragons to slay for political, religious, or business agendas. Fighting such prejudice is the work of the very serious legislative lobby called the American Federation of Astrologers (AFA), in Washington, D.C.

SNAPSHOT: Headquarters American Federation of Astrologers, Washington, D. C., May 11, 1970, two tumultuous days after 150,000 demonstrators, mostly students, marched on Washington protesting the deaths of four students shot by the National Guard at Kent State University, May 4, 1970.

Located in Library Court, a tiny mews of garages three blocks east of the U.S. Capitol building, the AFA resides in a two-story whitewashed brick office guarded by its astrologically chosen incorporation date, 4 May 1938, 11:38 A.M. E.S.T. Heaps of books, as well as a friendly German Shepherd sleeping near the door of the hectograph room, make the office seem a cozy enterprise. Actually, the AFA is the world's largest astrological membership and accreditation association. It is also a small publishing house whose brochures and books are neatly displayed. Titles of pamphlets include "Aims and Objectives," "Codes of Ethics," and "Applications for Membership," the cost of which is $15.00.

The AFA spokesperson, a tad dismayed at the hippie popularization of astrology, is weary of the uninitiated adventurers who call out of "like, you know, *curiosity.*" He wishes that the Broadway musical *Hair* (1967, off-Broadway; 1969, Broadway) had never announced "The Dawning of the Age of Aquarius." He recommends *Astrology* (1964) by Louis MacNeice as the best history of the subject, and *A to Z Horoscope Maker and Delineator: The #1 Astrology Text in the World* (1910) by Llewellyn George (1876–1954) as the astrological bible. He explains that in 1901 Llewellyn George established his Llewellyn Publications Company as well as the Portland School of Astrology in Oregon, where he separated the science of astrology from magic and witchcraft, setting the tone for the AFA. As a publisher, the AFA has a long tradition of producing historical books, such as *The Five Books of Manilius* (London, 1697; transcribed and published by the AFA in 1953), as well as contemporary books such as *The Astrologer's Guide* by Guido Bonatus and Jerome Cardan, and *The Textbook of Astrology* by Alfred John Pearce (both 1970). Once callers have studied some basic books, the AFA's Astrology Liberation Front can recruit them into its purpose-driven lobbying with both legislative groups and mass media.

Then, as now, the AFA aims to unite astrologers and local astrological organizations into a standard system of study and practice for their own protection, to encourage students of astrology, and to clarify astrology as a science. The AFA proposes to accomplish its objectives by:

a. Establishing a definite Code of Ethics to be subscribed to and practiced, particularly by professional astrologers and teachers, and to use every means at its disposal to eliminate the charlatan and faker.
b. Establishing standards of practice in accordance with the Code of Ethics and by securing the enactment of legislation which will require these

standards, thus protecting both the public and the ethical astrologer, and bringing legal recognition to astrology as a science.

c. Carrying on a public educational program as to the value of astrology as a means to a fuller and richer life.

d. Conducting scientific research into astrological problems, encouraging and assisting scientists in other fields of knowledge to honestly and conscientiously investigate the claims of astrology and publicize their findings. This work has already started and a central depository has been established for former and contemporary astrological writings at the nation's capital, Washington, D.C.

Such militancy is not confined to the AFA. The revolutionary 1960s, particularly the founding of the Jewish Defense League by Meir Kahane in 1968, inspired many liberation movements to stand up for themselves. The Occult Liberation Front has linked itself to various popular movements, a phenomenon that prior-generation witches like seer Sybil Leek never predicted. Witchcraft and the new liberal, in fact, hardly seem strange bedfellows. Revolution grows from the oppressed minority, from the subculture caught outside the established power structure. At Salem, it was the Caribbean outsider Tituba—the black woman in a white community—who was blamed for the colony's woes. The Devil, himself defined biblically as an outsider, has always provided Christians with a convenient scapegoat to blame for their own sins. Witches, their image cast in the Devil's image by *Malleus Maleficarum*, have always found—like Jews and homosexuals—their ostracism to be constant. Their persecution rests on a premise of establishment fear: coming from outside the pale, the witch has knowledge (and consequently power) that those conditioned within the establishment can never have to wield against that very establishment.

SNAPSHOT: Gay Witch Leo Louis Martello (1931–2000), New York, 1972.

Professional Manhattan mystic Dr. Leo Louis Martello, who calls himself "The Gay Witch," has surfaced in the mainstream media through his popular books: *How to Prevent Psychic Blackmail* (1966); *It's Written in the Cards* (1968); *The Weird Ways of Witchcraft* (1969); *Black Magic, Satanism, and Voodoo* (1971); and *Witchcraft: The Old Religion* (1973). Martello is familiar to television audiences from his frequent appearances on popular [1970s] talk shows hosted by Allan Burke, Mike Douglas, Gene Rayburn, and David Susskind. Born a Catholic in 1931, he exited the Catholic Church and founded the American Hypnotism Academy in New York in

1950, when he was only nineteen. Bearded and hip, Dr. Martello is both a "witch lib" and a "gay lib" activist who was one of the founders of the Gay Activists Alliance of New York (GAA) in 1970.[5] Martello uses witchcraft to introduce and interpret his sexual preferences to a mainstream culture that frowns equally on witchcraft and homosexuality.

Although he speaks respectfully of Anton LaVey's Church of Satan, Dr. Martello claims to be neither a white-magic nor a black-magic sorcerer. He follows the hereditary line of his grandmother, who was a Sicilian witch, or *strega*. Like her, he is an Old Religionist. In his book *Witchcraft: The Old Religion* (1973), he defines witchcraft as the underground religion of outsiders whose rituals of sex are sacred.

As pioneer and militant occultist, in 1968 Martello wrote his famous *Witch Manifesto*, demanding $500 million in damages from the Catholic Church and $100 million in reparations from the city of Salem, Massachusetts. Further demands were for the repeal of the remaining laws against witchcraft, and for a National Witches Day Parade similar to Saint Patrick's Day parades. On Halloween, 1970, with the support of the American Civil Liberties Union, he created and hosted a "Witch-In" in New York's Central Park, forming one of the first public magical "faery circles," which drew more than a thousand people. The Witch-In was filmed as a documentary by the production group then known as Global Village. He also founded the Witches Anti-Defamation League, one of the first pagan civil rights organizations.

"The 1964 Civil Rights Act," Martello claims, "can be the basis for the establishment of Witchcraft Temples. If convents can have tax free status, so can covens, from which the former derived their name. Witchcraft seminaries are not constitutionally obliged to follow the same pattern as Christian theology schools. Witches, recognized by their own covens, their work, their beliefs, are entitled to the same privileges as other priests and ministers."[6]

Martello's New York activist coven, balancing the gender power of male and female, intends to use witchcraft as a form of guerrilla theater and psychic warfare in order to liberate witches as human beings. "A witch," Martello maintains, "is a human being subject to the same trials and tribulations as anyone else. The one difference is the witch's capacity to adjust, to use mind power, and to right wrongs. *Witch* comes from the Anglo-Saxon *Wicca* meaning *wise*. All witches were innate psychologists long before the word ever existed. It's the ability to penetrate the surface to detect subtleties."[7]

Martello's will to power, self-consciousness, and self-help is optimistically American. He follows Ralph Waldo Emerson, the transcendentalist guru, who taught self-reliance and personal divinity. Martello makes the Old Religion seem akin to Yankee ingenuity. "In the Old Religion of witchcraft which identifies with nature and with reason," he notes, "power comes from self-mastery. A witch controls his own Wheel of Fortune. He is not a creature of fate or luck or destiny. He directs his Destiny. He uses the Fates. He makes his own Fortune."[8] Witches stand next to Norman Vincent Peale, author of *The Power of Positive Thinking* (1952), and Mary Baker Eddy, the founder of the Christian Science movement and its philosophy of self-help.

The new exorcism is not against witches; the new exorcism comes from witches who themselves cast out pessimism and infirmities from the human condition.

Louise Huebner, the "official witch of Los Angeles County," reigning from 1968 on through the millennium, promises health and wealth in her *Power through Witchcraft* (1969). Three titles of Alfred Canton spell their own ritual exorcism: *Unitrol: The Healing Magic of the Mind* (1963), *How to Heal Yourself* (1964), and *Ridding Yourself of Psychosomatic Health Wreckers* (1965). To negotiate through the dangers in the underworld of magic, Dion Fortune (real name: Violet Firth) authored *Psychic Self-Defense* (1965). A militant gender separatist on the offensive, Ms. Fortune wrote *Winged Bull* (1971) to portray her nemesis, Aleister Crowley, as a bisexual villain ambivalent about gender. Fortune was a Sapphic witch in search of a utopian matriarchy featuring a dominant Goddess correcting, of course, the misfortunes of Ms. Fortune herself. She preferred the Wicca of Gerald Gardner because Gardner emphasized the role of the Goddess, which made a High Priestess essential. The library of occult books grows larger daily as people seek self-help solutions to problems unanswered by religious institutions.

Witch Power, because it develops natural abilities, has always helped humans evolve toward social improvement. Leo Louis Martello views history with a cool that accounts for his enormous popularity in the hip underground, as well as in the ranks of gay liberationists who have followed radical activist Harry Hay (1912–2002). In his writing, Martello referenced the Mattachine Society, a virtually "secret network of homosexuals" founded by Hay in Los Angeles in 1951. The biography of Harry Hay, the "Father of the Radical Faeries," is *The Trouble with Harry Hay* (1990), written by Stuart Timmons, who popped his title off Alfred Hitchcock's classic film *The Trouble With Harry* (1955). Former Catholic Martello was part of the 1960s surge in gay spirituality that, born in witchcraft and issues of masculinity, emerged as the pagan Gay Faerie movement founded by former Catholic Harry Hay with Don Kilhefner in 1979. In the way that Harry Hay invented a totally new identity for gays as "a distinct minority of outsiders" exactly like African Americans and women, Martello defined radical "gay witchcraft" as a distinct entity with an essence equal to heterosexual wicca and witchcraft. Their playing the "gay card" of gay identity changed everything in American culture's march toward equal civil rights, including gay marriage.

Actually, Richard Feiherr von Krafft-Ebing invented the word *homosexual* in 1893 so that he could analyze sexual "outsiders" for what he was the first to claim was not simply behavior, but an indelible part of personality. U.S. military policy, invoking Krafft-Ebing, confirmed this outsider personality: in 1940 the military stopped punishing soldiers for homosexual *acts* and began discharging them for *being* homosexual. Such personalizing of discrimination—by definition against a person's true self—was actually an upgrade in the social and legal evolution of gay identity, "grateful" at that time for even backhanded recognition.

While Martello had trouble with the New York Police Department, the radical Harry Hay, as double outsider (both gay and communist), in 1951 was called before the U.S. Senate's House Un-America Activities Committee (HUAC) because he demanded the repeal of antigay laws. Editor Marvin Cutler published some of Hay's writing as well as information about the founding of the Mattachine Society in his book *Homosexuals Today* (1956), which followed hot on the heels of Gerald Gardner's *Witchcraft Today* (1954). The secret society of homosexuality is important because it mirrors the secret societies of both mainstream religion and the pagan occult, and is often the unspoken soul of both insofar as so many priests, ministers, and practitioners are, at heart, homosexual, which means they are born open to psychic and religious impulses.

The Mattachine Society's name comes from the Italian word *mattachino*: a court jester who dares to tell the truth to the king. When in the 1950s Harry Hay tried to tell the truth, the gay truth, and nothing but the gay truth to the HUAC, the senators dismissed him as irrelevant because he came off more pink (homosexual) than red (communist). According to Martello, it was Harry Hay, among others during the 1960s counterculture rise of hippie consciousness, who began expressing a new idea about the visionary value of the separate consciousness of "radical faeries." This was a compliment generally to the consciousness-raising of the GAA, and specifically to activist Martello who had already by 1968 advanced the idea of radical gay Wicca in two of his books, *Witchcraft: The Old Religion* and *The Witch Manifesto*. Typically, radicals in the 1960s and 1970s have taken terms of aspersion thrown at them and turned those negative words positive, as in the case of the epithet *fairy*. In gay culture, the mattachine jester with powdered face and outrageous clothes came out beyond "radical faery" into the comic, drag, and benevolent burlesque of the Sisters of Perpetual Indulgence, founded in San Francisco and perpetually threatened with lawsuits by the Catholic Church, which claims some kind of trademark on "nuns."

Folklore fairies easily came to be pop-culture gays and drags. With the exodus from Ireland during the famed Potato Famine of the 1840s, Irish immigrants brought to the United States from their pagan-basted Christian culture their celebration of Halloween, the Celtic New Year. The introduction of this Celtic feast of Samhain has as a holiday become one of the best loved (by gay men and lesbians) and most feared (by born-again fundamentalists) in the American calendar of pop culture feasts.

All gussied up with fairy dust, Halloween has never been revealed more romantically or fearfully than through the eyes of the Irish-American actress Margaret O'Brien in *Meet Me in St. Louis* (1944). This classic MGM musical comedy is one of nostalgic perfection infused with the gay sensibility of director Vincente Minnelli and the star, his wife, the gay icon Judy Garland. Minnelli anchored his notion of Halloween on seven-year-old O'Brien, who had "the map of Ireland on her face." Cross-dressed as a hobo boy, O'Brien charged out bravely into a Halloween of tricks and treats, scary neighbors, haunted houses, and bonfires. The enormity of the night soon sent her running home crying. Minnelli said he intended his Halloween mise en scène to invade the repressed unconscious of the audience. Minnelli's young actress hit a pop-culture nerve. She was innocence in search of mischief. She was every girlchild growing up pagan on the Irish heath. She channeled so much primal power, such wizened pathos, into her performance that she was awarded a special Academy Award as an outstanding child actress. This gay, Irish notion coming out of Samhain is not everything about all fairies, but it is a distinct thread through the Celtic fairy realm that leads to the changeling underground of American pop culture, where gay fairies continue to evolve from traditional to radical.

In Celtic lore, where time is cyclical, the two major fairy feasts are May Day (Beltane) and Halloween (Samhain), when fairies come from their underground mounds, called *Sidhe*, to celebrate the natural world of spirit, of unbridled eros, and of imagination. On ancient pagan Halloween—a trickster feast—men dressed as women, and women as men; some dressed as animals, and others wore masks and swept the paths clear with brooms. They went knocking door-to-door in order to confuse the fairy spirits on the night when the border between the shadow world separating the dead and the living was so at its thinnest that the fairies could escort the dead, who had come back to look into their old haunts. In 1518, Johannes de Tabia identified as witches the Mascarae, who blackened their faces to become the blind man of conjure rituals, which for the Mascarae consisted of dancing to ecstasy and drinking henbane to cause visions. The Mascarae enter popular culture in the words *mask, mascara,* and *masquerade.*

In Irish lore, fairies were originally the Tuatha de Danaan, the supernatural warrior people of the goddess Dana, who first conquered the Firbolgs, the original people of Eire. In turn, the fairy Tuatha were conquered and driven underground from where they emerged as the wee folk, leprechauns, and banshees to live mischievously alongside humans who ambivalently loved and feared the "fair folk." Fairies had "glamour" or "enchantment," which is the ability to turn one thing into another, and the inability to leave well enough alone, always going too far. To protect themselves from fairy mischief, people nailed horseshoes over doors, carved faces in pumpkins, hung wreathes of dried pansies in the closets, and sprinkled rooms with urine to scare off fairies too fastidious for human soil. To attract fairies and their angelic favor, women, as a sign of their trust in "healing fairies," hung hollyhock in their closets to prevent miscarriage, put shepherd's purse under their beds to avoid hemorrhage, and tucked yarrow in their pillows to tighten the uterus and cause contractions to bring down the afterbirth. Like witches and magicians, homosexuals get most of their power granted from the straight world, which fears their fairy evil eye.

The "fair folk" were so powerful, and so respected for both good deeds and mischief, that humans thought it was bad luck to call the Tuatha de Danaan or the Sidhe by their actual names, so they shortened "fair folk" to *fairy.* (Ancient Jews likewise would not say the name of Yahweh.) In modern times, the invented words *homosexual* and *gay* actually follow in time the traditional and legitimate term *fairy.* Then as now people thought they had to be careful of their attraction to fairies, because too much time spent with the "fair folk" meant a person could get a "fairy stroke" and become too all-knowing to speak straight, or act straight—that is, simply, without "glamour."

Irish hags, the women who most interacted with fairies, were women who interpreted that the "wise blood" of menstruation meant the spirit of the Goddess was in them. These hags joined the Danaan Sidhe in their pursuits of hunting and fighting, as well as in the dancing, music, and cruising about in finery beloved by all fairies. In modern culture, as the word *fairy* has evolved from simple Celtic identity to slur to badge of pride, so has the rhyming term *fag hag* inched toward acceptability.

Chasing Danny Boy: Powerful Stories of Celtic Eros (2000), the first international anthology of gay Irish fiction, has its title story set on the Summer Solstice and Midsummer's Eve. The story is a homosexual retelling of the traditional Irish myth of Dermid (Dearmid) and Grania, as once collected by Lady Augusta Gregory in her *Complete Irish Mythology* (1902), with a preface by W. B. Yeats (of the Order of the Golden Dawn). Dermid and Grania are the Celtic Romeo and Juliet who must overcome, and then positively use, the tidal pull of seductive fairies and benevolent fag hags who help them become a heterosexual couple united under the white magic veil of the seven Bridal Sisters. Dermid's adolescent rock group dare go by the ancient name Tuatha de Danaan, and their fairy energies, conjured by eros, involve music, fighting, priapism, changing sexual identity, and shapeshifting with drugs that take them to the underworld of the "Other World."[9]

Radical witches and radical faeries operate off the word *radical*, which comes from the Latin, *radix*, which means "root." Radicals of whatever type are actually people trying to live at the root of things. Radical witches and radical faeries, who are an evolving identity step beyond standard gay fairies, come in as many denominations as Protestants. They may be druids, or they may be followers of the Old Religion of Wicca, and they might practice either white or black magic.

Gay witch Martello, acknowledging the radical visionary value of straight and gay women, has written,

> In the Middle Ages the *witch* was the only truly liberated woman. All others were forced into roles as wife, mother, mistress, nun, etc. The witch was usually single and she had sex with whom she pleased. She was respected, envied, feared, and somewhat held in awe. But because she was anti-establishment, she represented a threat to male chauvinists. Her independent free spirit prevented them from having any real hold on her.
>
> The female witch was the first suffragette, the forerunner of today's Women's Liberation Front, and the Women's International Terrorist Corps from Hell (W.I.T.C.H.). The latter are *political witches* using street and guerrilla theater, as have the Hippies, the Yippies, the Crazies, and many

other radical groups. Combining the profound, the profane and the put-on, modern political witches are using the same techniques [as] the Medieval Mattachines (who were court jesters who cleverly told the truth in disguised, play-acting form. . .). This technique is effective because it uses other people's ammunition against them. For centuries the church and society have ruled by guilt and fear. One of their chief weapons was sex. Today modern witches are using liberated sex as a hex to "blow the minds" of the Establishment. Revolutionary witches can properly be called WITCHES (Wit plus Che, from Che Guevara).[10]

At the First Washington Peace March in October 1967, Abbie Hoffman's yippie legions made a match: "Pentagram versus Pentagon." They formed a magic circle around the Pentagon in order to levitate the Pentagon building and exorcise its demons. Their famous attempt, however much a put-on, affirmed the enormous popularity of the occult in the guerilla theater of the new politics. The second American revolution calls together different minorities, and includes their excluded bodies, hearts, and minds through meditation, astrology, ritual gatherings, drum circles, drug mysticism, and music-induced trances. For centuries, witches have been the artificial niggers, the artificial Jews, the artificial radicals because the Christian power structure has cast them as the ultimate outsiders.

A premise explaining popular bigotry is that the lowest class of the "overculture" hates the outsider (for example, immigrants) because it feels the outsider threatens to enter the overculture and surpass the lowest class, proving that the lowest class is indeed the bottom it always feared it was. Consequently, blue-collar whites voted for George Wallace for president in 1968 to keep African Americans out of industrial management. New York construction workers beat up student intellectuals who pointed out that the hard-hat workers were dupes of the military-industrial complex. The lowest classes of the overculture are always uneasy riders in every rising subculture.

James Baldwin knew a thing or two about subcultures. His message, in his book of essays The Fire Next Time (1963), can be summed up as, "To affirm you're not the bottom, you've got to point out by pecking order who the bottom is." A black American homosexual who escaped from the United States to France, Baldwin wrote about outsiders in his book of essays Nobody Knows My Name (1961), in his drama Blues for Mister Charlie (1964), and in his shockingly frank homosexual novel Giovanni's Room, which was published in 1956, shortly before Tennessee Williams's Suddenly

Last Summer (1958) dared dramatize one homosexual, two female witches, and cannibalism of the queer outsider eaten alive by the underclass.

Racism and witchcraft have been of a piece since Christianity, in epistles by Saint Paul and in diatribes by Martin Luther, named the Jew as a demonic outsider who in medieval times was accused of causing the plague of the Black Death by poisoning the wells of Europe. In his 1965 book *The Devil and the Jews: The Medieval Conception of the Jew and Its Relation to Modern Anti-Semitism*, Joshua Trachtenberg prepared a composite portrait that "though lacking a single allusion to the Jews . . . is as descriptive of the medieval conception of the Jew as of the heretic and sorcerer and witch it actually delineates. . . . The 'demonic' Jew was the product of a transference *in toto* of a prevailing corpus of belief concerning one hated and hunted class in European society to another whose conspicuous independence placed it in a similar category."[11] Rabbi Trachtenberg meant that when reading about *witches, heretics, homosexuals,* or *Jews,* all four words become synonyms, because all outsiders were treated the same by the established culture of church and state.

History has taught Jews, witches, women, and homosexuals that exclusion leads to elimination, which leads to extermination. While Adolf Hitler, who was no stranger to the occult, was creating the Third Reich in the 1930s, Rabbi Trachtenberg was writing the seminal book *Jewish Magic and Superstition: A Study in Folk Magic* (1939). More details than overview have come to light regarding Hitler's use of occult symbolism and philosophy: for instance, Aryan superiority based on an ancient society of elite warriors as expressed by the Thule Society. Hitler the artist turned the legs of the ancient swastika to the *left,* which, in magic, is a sign of turning *sinister, to evil,* so the swastika becomes, with its axis in Berlin, a moving circular scythe with four blades mowing down territory in a wide magic circle being cut *widdershins*—counterclockwise.

Although Hitler, whose Nazi propaganda accused the Jews of practicing witchcraft, later publicly turned against anything occult, early on he was trained as a public speaker and greatly influenced by his tutor, Dietrich Eckart, who was an anti-Semitic publisher and leader of the occult Thule Society. For all that, it is odd—in the precise way that the hidden core of magic is always odd—that in an American popular culture always looking for a new documentary or dramatic angle on history, no one has, on page, stage, or screen, ever delved into the story and particulars of the actual 1930s struggle of overt "Nazi Magic" *versus* overt "Jewish Magic."

In 1966, Bernard Malamud won the National Book Award and the

Pulitzer Prize for his novel, *The Fixer*. The book became the 1968 film scripted by the famous Dalton Trumbo, who as a member of the Hollywood Ten (who were mostly all Jews) had suffered during the inquisition of the communist witch hunts of Senator Joseph McCarthy in 1951. *The Fixer*, based on a real incident, depicts a Jewish handyman—a fixer— accused of the ritual murder of a young Christian boy whose blood is drained for some imagined Passover celebration. Jews, according to malignant legend, murder Christian children as a way of continuing to kill Christ. This never-ending blood libel against Jews, resurrected by Mel Gibson's film *The Passion of the Christ* (2004), is typical of modern prejudice against all cult and all outsiders who must continually try to prove their innocence, and therefore their right to exist, against the most bizarre accusations. It has not been historically helpful that the first mention of witches' sabbaths in the eleventh century used the words *sabbath* and *synogogue* interchangeably as synonyms.[12]

In 1897, for instance, the controversial *Protocols of the Elders* first surfaced. The *Protocols* claimed that Jews were working a Satanic pan-national master plan to take over the Christian world. Repeatedly discounted as a slanderous forgery written by anti-Semitic authors, *Protocols* keeps resurfacing among right-wing groups eager to profile whoever is their outsider. To calculate *Protocols'* universally applicable absurdity, for the word *Jew*, again substitute the words *witch, Satanist, homosexual,* or *woman*.

The increasingly vociferous independence of women, African Americans, Native Americans, homosexuals, druggies, students, and witches—all in league with the American Civil Liberties Union—has shocked the American middle class. Attacked for the first time in its history, middle America, having rooted out Jews who were Communists in the 1940s and 1950s, seeks to continue to eliminate anyone who seems to need reporting to some kind of House Un-American Activities Committee. The black woman Tituba, the Jewish fixer, and the popular witch are all pagans, heathens, fairies, and weird folk who all live "outside the pale" of Saint Augustine's urbane City of God. The forest (the *weir*) is the place of the suspicious outsider, of the *weird folk* and the *werewolf*. "Country hill folk," "city ghetto folk," "witch folk," and "queer folk," because their ways are not mainstream, are all outsiders come to ruin the law and order of the white Anglo-Saxon Protestant God's established city as biblically defined in the Colonial-American literature of fire-and-brimstone sermons. So when "Sinners" as famously threatened by Jonathan Edwards in 1741, are caught "in the Hands of an Angry God," they need the Devil as a scapegoat to blame for their sin.

Why else would American southern-gothic novelist Flannery O'Connor state so dramatically the fears of her own Catholic religion in *The Violent Bear It Away* (1960)? In that novella, the hitchhiking protagonist Tarwater is drugged and raped by a traveling salesman who wears a lavender neckerchief. Tarwater, a religious boy, should have known the color code that *lavender* indicates *homosexual*, and *salesman* denotes a traveling *outsider*. His should have been no surprise when he regained consciousness. After all, in O'Connor's southern gothic world, a queer pusher from the outside can be none other than the Devil himself. In precisely this way, Middle America is afraid that it will be drugged by hippies putting LSD in the water supply, or raped by Satanists on motorcycles, or murdered by cultists like Charles Manson. When one knows that a woman who has the spirit of the Goddess in her has "wise blood," then O'Connor's novel, menstruationally titled *Wise Blood* (1952), takes on a new level of meaning. She echoes Emily Dickinson, who wrote that a person didn't have to be a house to be haunted.

Like the chicken and the egg, witchery's connection with drugs is legendary from the brewing of potions to the rubbing of ointments that give the sensation of flying.

British poet Thom Gunn (1929–2004), interviewed in 1970 while on a national reading tour, said, "The traditional witch's trip by broomstick was probably a mere phallic high on something like LSD. All their potions were simply primitive gestures at medicine. Witches quite obviously were the first pharmacists."[13]

Having taught previously at Princeton University, Stanford University, and the University of California at Berkeley, Thom Gunn may provide an insight into the occult, drug, and sex scene in San Francisco as much as into the traditional craft where secret *nostrum* vendors of potions—that is, drugs—have long been the norm. Thom Gunn's poetry is known in the mainstream of world literature as well as in the "gaystream" of masculine literature for his shaman's insight into the leather psyche, ranging from *The Sense of Movement* (1959) to *Touch* (1968) to *Moly, and My Sad Captains* (1971).

As the 1950s Beat scene of San Francisco grew into the 1960s hippie scene and then into 1970s gay liberation, art and sex and magic and drugs combined as never before in American popular culture. These real facts are more than right-wing fundamentalist fears. As sure as Benjamin Franklin was a member of the Hellfire Club, American politicians are constantly rumored to be members of secret societies and practitioners of Satanic rituals—for instance, in the all-male Bohemian Club, founded in San Francisco in 1872. Every Midsummer's Eve in the redwoods north of the Golden Gate Bridge, the rich and powerful meet at the Bohemian Grove to take over the world—which, ironically, is already their oyster. The Bohemian Grove is located in Monte Rio, California, which is part of Guerneville, the gayest resort west of Provincetown, Massachusetts. The rumor in San Francisco, leaked by the gay waiters serving at the Bohemian Club and the Bohemian Grove, is that after his election as governor of California, Ronald Reagan, on the advice of Nancy Reagan's astrologer, sacrificed a goat at the Bohemian Grove so that he would not be assassinated while in office.

American artists also stand accused of secret agendas. After years underground, occult-inspired art has dared rear its head. Religion has long inspired art; so has the occult. Since the 1960s, artists in music, film, and theater have openly injected into mass media the civil disobedience of the first rebel, Satan; the magic rituals of witchcraft; the drugs and wisdom of Wicca; the sexual liberation of cult; and the erotic imagery of the occult.

Some artists, rock stars, and filmmakers are deadly serious. Some are merely toying with a fad. But it's no wonder that religionists are frightened by what they see boiling to the surface of America's popular youth culture. Fright is the point of this new age of the witch, where, as in act 1, scene 1 of Shakespeare's *Macbeth*, the three witches chant revenge: "Fair is foul, and foul is fair." As religionists use the Bible as a gun to frighten nonconformists, so do those same outsiders sometimes use witchcraft as a weapon of revenge to terrify Bible-thumpers.

It is, of course, only a "born-again urban legend" that the queer eye can be an evil eye. For instance, is there really any gay cause and effect when the Bible Belt, where homosexuality is most proscribed by law and religion, is repeatedly hit by hurricanes, tidal waves, floods, drought, and killer bees? Concordantly, fundamentalism mongers who believe in a provident God dipping his hand into human affairs go on television and specifically blame homosexuals, ACLU Jews, and free-choice women as the cause of evil such as the September 11, 2001, terrorist attacks. Within seventy-two hours, on September 14, 2001, Protestant preachers Jerry Falwell and Pat Robertson, sounding like Little Sir Echoes of *Malleus Maleficarum* authors Jacob Sprenger and Heinrich Kramer, appeared on Robertson's *700 Club* TV show to discuss the attacks on the Twin Towers of the City of God—the City, actually, of their "Angry God" straight out of Jonathan Edwards. Stereotype became archetype as Falwell pointed his finger the way society has always pointed at the witch.

"Throwing God out . . . of the federal court system . . . . The abortionists have got to bear some burden for this [attack] because God will not be mocked. And when we destroy 40 million little innocent babies, *we make God mad.* [Emphasis added]

The pagans and the abortionists and the feminists and the gays and the lesbians who are actively trying to make that an alternative lifestyle, the ACLU, People for the American Way—all of them who have tried to secularize America," Falwell continued, "I point the finger in their face and say 'you helped this [terrorist attack] happen.'"

"Well, I totally concur," responded Robertson.[14]

In the history of witchcraft, this is a modern replay of medieval villagers accusing women of killing babies, Jews of causing plagues, and Gypsies of poisoning wells. Knaves—very like Falwell and Robertson—with their torches and pitchforks have always been the ignorant hotheads leading the mob up the hill to storm Frankenstein's castle.

Churches cast out demons; covens summon demons. What gullible person, required by religious dogma to believe that evil spirits actually exist, wouldn't run when someone cocks a left eyebrow, raises a hand in a wizard-like gesture, and intones,

Evil Spirits from all around,
walk upon this human ground.
Because they utter words of hate,
let them suffer a terrible fate.

Legendary filmmaker Kenneth Anger, in San Francisco, Los Angeles, and London, mixed sex with the drugs and magic of Aleister Crowley in his classic underground films of the "Magick Lantern Cycle" titled *Scorpio Rising* (1964), *Invocation of My Demon Brother* (1969), and *Lucifer Rising* (1969). Shot at the turbulent end of the 1960s, *Lucifer Rising* starred Anton LaVey, high priest of the Church of Satan, and Bobby Beausoleil, reportedly Anger's lover, and definitely a member of the Manson Family, who was sentenced to life in prison for murder. A disciple of Aleister Crowley, guru Anger said his idea of filmmaking was casting a spell using *chaos* and *eros*.[15]

Aleister Crowley, besides his draft synopses for six articles on drugs, told all in his alchohol-and-heroin confessional, *Diary of a Drug Fiend* (1922). Aldous Huxley, turned on by his research for *The Devils of Loudun,* swallowed hallucinogenics in the 1950s and wrote about it in *The Doors of*

Perception and Heaven and Hell (1954). Because of this Huxley title, pouty rock star Jim Morrison named his group the Doors. The Beatles paid both Crowley and Huxley homage by including images of them on the cover of *Sergeant Pepper's Lonely Hearts Club Band* (1967). Was it coincidence that *Sergeant Pepper,* released exactly twenty years after the death of Aleister Crowley, opened its lyrics by referencing the "twenty years ago today" when Sergeant Pepper—a stunt double for Crowley?—"taught the band to play"?

Also in 1967, immediately before Anger included footage of them in *Invocations of My Demon Brother,* the Rolling Stones released the album *Their Satanic Majesties Request.* Mick Jagger composed the synthesizer score for Anger's *Demon Brother,* as well as taped sounds for *Lucifer Rising.* Upon the arrest of Mick Jagger and Keith Richard on drug charges, sixty British pop-culture personalities, including the Beatles, took out a full-page ad in the London *Times,* July 24, 1967, protesting the marijuana laws. The advertisement was "officially" signed by an organization called the Society of Mental Awareness, or, SOMA, from Aldous Huxley's euphoric drug in *Brave New World.* Stanley Kubrick used Huxley's drugged "vision quest" in the spacey last act of *2001: A Space Odyssey* (1968). Huxley, of course, never saw the movie; he had died five years earlier, on November 22, 1963—the same day John F. Kennedy was assassinated. Huxley, writing about Shakespeare and religion, noted that Shakespeare, tempering himself with common sense, believed sorcery between humans and devils existed, and that magic did indeed work—albeit unreliably—because magicians, witches, and sorcerers are as fallible and foolish as all other humans. In Huxley's genius notion, people who fear witches can find some solace. No witch has any more power over a person than that person allows.

While such a bibliography of witchcraft, sex, and drugs will forever be a growing library, America's leading Satanist, Anton LaVey, has noted that drugs are escapist and contrary to the realistic values of the Church of Satan because they cloud the ability to exercise choice.

Even on the comic side of family entertainment, witchcraft and drugs have entered pop culture. Jerry Herman's twenty-five-minute film, *The Winter of the Witch,* is a contemporary child's fable about a witch (Hermione Gingold) who haunts a house owned by a boy and his mother. The witch confides to the boy that witches don't get the respect they used to. To prove her own powers, the witch whips up some "Alice B. Toklas" hashish pancakes. So turned-on are the boy and his mother that they open a restaurant, and with typical "head" fervor try to convert the rest of their straight neighborhood to a constant high. *Parents* magazine commissioned and distributed this 1969 film. This theme repeats in other films such as *Babette's Feast* (1987) and *Chocolat* (2000). Stéphane Audrun as Babette, the heroine of Isak Dinesen's adapted short story (1949), cooks with ingredients so epicurean and esoteric her Puritan guests fear she's preparing a witch's Sabbath. In *Chocolat*, Juliet Binoche, costumed as a mysterious high-fashion outsider dressed in scarlet, comes to town, opens up a shop, and whips up secret recipes that magically and sensually transform the locals' cold hearts. The witch as "cook" always alters states of consciousness.

Marijuana, acid, and mescaline do not a warlock make—except perhaps in Los Angeles, where the appearance passes for the reality. When East Coast newspapers termed Charles Manson an occultist, it was not a true witch they were meaning. *Occult* was used as an innuendo code word for *drugs.* An opium den frequented by drug users is not the same as a coven of witches.

A Hollywood starlet interviewed by Tom Burke in *Esquire* magazine's pop-sational occult issue (March 1970) admitted the "witches" she knew were acid-freak poseurs in the occult. Bonafide witches, she said, "loathe publicity. And they're about as sinister as Donald Duck. They've always been here. They're nice, harmless people who got disillusioned with churches and started reading the *Book of the Dead* at home. And *none* of them are heads! They get their kicks from *prescribed* ritual—spreading rings of salt. . . . Acid freaks *make up their own rituals* as they go along. That's their danger."

Historically, however, witches have been purveyors as well as users of drugs. Long before a big-bucks corporation invented priapic Viagra, the aphrodisiac Spanish Fly was the sole knowledge of the witch, as were aconite (wolfbane), belladonna, poppy, and castor oil. "Tannis root," popularized by *Rosemary's Baby*, was sold at the 1969 Detroit County Fair; but "tannis root" seems, with literary convenience, to have been *Rosemary's* author Ira Levin's purely phonetic invention from the word *Satanas.* Dorothy Jacob, author of *A Witch's Guide to Gardening*, wrote in *Popular Gardening Magazine* (December 1965) that "what the physician prescribed to cure, the witch administered to kill. The difference lay in the strength of the dose and the occasion." Obviously all witches worthy of the name had their own herbarium. The witch in *Romeo and Juliet*, disguised as the priestly Friar Tuck, works his white magic through concoctions from his own garden apothecary that has nothing to do with Catholicism. Parsley was sowed on Good Friday for use in abortions; knotweed was the polygonum used to stunt a child's growth to make him into a dwarf; and hemp, needless to say, was marijuana.

Contemporary witches, according to the *Washington Post*, anger Columbia University anthropologist Michael Harner when they overanxiously disavow any use of drugs. "Their witchcraft," he said, "is no more than a ritualistic survival, without the subjective experience that comes from the hallucinogenic trance state." In short, he maintains, witchcraft requires drugs.

As interest in witchcraft spread across America in the wake of the Manson Family's Tate murders, the *Washington Post/Potomac*, May 10, 1970, reported: "Early witches were familiar with drugs and, from time to time, scholars claim to have discovered the original recipe. Erich Will Peuckert, a philologist at the University of Goettingen, revealed in a 1960 interview that he had created an ointment from ingredients recorded in a 16th-century work, *Matica Naturis*. The recipe included thorn apple, belladonna, parsley, and fat of an unbaptized infant. Peuckert explained that he successfully substituted supermarket lard for the last ingredient. The professor and a friend rubbed their bodies with the salve, fell into a 20-hour trance and described visions of a witches' sabbath that, 400 years ago, would have led them speedily to the stake."

When witches were not causing health, illness, or hallucination, they were receiving the blame for everything from missing children to plague to insanity. Often in the Middle Ages (which lasted from the fall of Rome, in 476, to Columbus arriving in America), entire villages were frequently gripped by hallucinatory behavior that seemed to be "the Devil's work." Of course, witches were blamed for what modern science has determined was ergot poisoning. In his book *The Day of Saint Anthony's Fire* (1968), John G. Fuller goes deep into a modern news story that exonerates witchcraft. In 1951, in the tiny French village of Pont Saint Esprit, 150 people tripped out into hallucinatory behavior when LSD was spontaneously formed in the village bakery where rye flour had been contaminated with an ergot fungus. A hippie acid trip taken voluntarily for mystic reasons is a different experience than that of a town of men, women, and children going erotic and psychotic and seeing God, who has the—omigod—tongue of Mick Jagger. The lesson is that as science—increasing knowledge—shrinks medieval theology, it also shrinks medieval witchcraft by clarifying cause and effect that is not based on superstition.

Will science eventually explain away both God and the Devil, both priest and witch?

Ask Galileo.

If the black witch has become a devotee of mind-altering drugs, then the white witch has been refined into a gourmet.

More saucy than the books of Zen macrobiotic cooking are Carroll Righter's *Your Astrological Guide to Health and Diet* (1967), Sybil Leek's *Astrological Cookbook* (1968), Dr. Leo Louis Martello's guide to gay meals of destiny, *Foods of Fate* (1969), Marcello Truzzi's *Cauldron Cookery: An Authentic Guide for Coven Connoisseurs* (1969), and *Cooking with Astrology* (1970), which brings together syndicated newspaper astrologer Sidney Omarr and gourmet Mike Roy "to guide you along the Stars' path to master chefdom."

The canon of metaphysical books is enormous. Early in the low-tech 1970s, publisher Samuel Weiser—fronted since 1926 at his venerable shop "Samuel Weiser Esoteric and Antiquarian Books" on 4th Avenue in New York—listed more than five thousand diverse occult titles. By the millennium, when Weiser moved to the web, the number of occult books had exploded exponentially. So, buyer, beware. Nowhere in the occult world have so many coughed up so much for so little as in the sideshow of astrology. Although essentially respectable as the science the American Federation of Astrology claims it is, astrology—even more than its sibling palmistry—has a fatal attraction for everyone from the Time Pattern Research Institute to San Francisco's Zodiac Killer, a serial murderer who wrote, "I am collecting souls to serve me as slaves in the afterlife."

The *New York Times* reported that Time Pattern Research was mass-marketing computer horoscopes (thirty-page one-year projections) in 350 department stores and on 2,000 college campuses. In 1970, Atlanta's "Aquarescope" mixed, for $10.50, "IBM Technology" with "the Wisdom of the Ages" for a six-month forecast. At that same time, for three dollars, "Kodiatronics" programmed its clients into its computer and allowed four free phone calls "day or night, to hear an expert reading of your next 24 hours." Subsequently, a dollar a month (billed quarterly) entitled the client to four calls a month. Each call, after four a month, cost twenty-five cents additional. "Maric Enterprises" offered "Dial-Your-Stars" in major cities with free telephone forecasts interrupted midway by a recorded commercial for deodorant or headache relief. Another horoscope-computer sold a zodiac-compatible dating service.

In a send-up of telephone psychics, the actress Judy Holliday, working as a switchboard operator for "Suzanswerphone" ("Sue's Answer Phone") in the Betty Comden and Adolph Green musical *Bells Are Ringing* (1956), spun a pop-culture plan for American business to cash in on star-crossed lovers:

"Hello Veronaphone. Yes Mr. Romeo, Juliet Capulet [the trickster] called. The message is: 'To avoid getting married to other fellow am playing dead [shape-shifting]. This Friar Lawrence [the white witch] gave me a great big sleeping pill [the drug, the potion], but when I wake up [from the spell] we'll head for the border [we'll go beyond the pale].' Oh, don't thank me. But if I'd got that message [actual education] through on time, those two kids would be alive today!"[16]

In occult culture as in pop culture, there is nothing new under the sun. At the crucial moment when the 1960s sine-waved into the 1970s setting the tone for the rest of the century, occult offers updating the past were everywhere. For those who preferred to cast their own horoscope, the Universe Book Club offered Grant Levi's *Heaven Knows What,* which was a chart maker costing only ten cents when four occult book selections were purchased during the first year's membership. For those who desired more than Jeane Dixon's or Sydney Omarr's newspaper daily scopes, the *Chicago Sun-Times* entered the 1970s with "Astrodata," a column based on a mammoth computer installation logging twenty-seven million bits of zodiac information. The *Sun-Times* readers, perhaps never wondering about the mystic title of the newspaper itself, could check out their natal signs, their rising signs, and their moon signs. Parker Brothers jump-marketed a new astrology game to complement its fast-selling ouija board. Both were copyrighted almost perversely in—where else?—Salem, Massachusetts.

Perhaps the successful Parker Brothers consulted Donald Bradley who opened an entirely new field of financial astrology in his groundbreaking book *Stock Market Prediction: The Historical and Future Siderograph Charts and Software* (1948). Building on Bradley, David Williams cited his own trustworthy credentials as former president of the Astrologers Guild of America and as a retired naval lieutenant commander (who knew how to guide a ship by sextant) when he wrote his book *Astro-Economics: A Study of Astrology and the Business Cycle* (1959). In fact, Williams anticipated every major bear and bull market of the 1960s by previously charting the time and place of a business's incorporation as well as zodiac data on investors and speculators. In 1968, Thomas Reider entered the expanding field with *Sun Spots, Stars, and the Stock Market.*

On the other hand, white witches like Alex Sanders claim they can make only others than themselves rich. Most witches concur that when they use their powers for selfish gain, their powers immediately diminish. Books in the Alexandrian tradition of Sanders include *King of the Witches*, by June Johns (1969) and *What Witches Do*, by Stuart Farrar (1971).

For simpler taste and lower finance, pop culture once offered the Sydney Omarr set of twelve recorded albums as promotional items for several national supermarket chains. Omarr spoke enthusiastically about "love, money, health, character, and future potential." In San Francisco, public relations man James Bolen launched *Psychic*, a slick magazine of the occult, in early 1969. By the beginning of the 1970s, *Psychic* reported that in the United States there were 10,000 full-time and 175,000 part-time astrologers, each earning up to six figures; and that more than forty million Americans read horoscopes printed in over 70 percent of their daily newspapers.

The zodiac, in short, was a universal gimmick, long before the standard 1970s pick-up line, "What's your sign?" It's easy to popularize and profit from something everyone has—and has an interest in: themselves. *Self* is the main commodity merchandised by popular witchcraft, and it is at the heart of the booming "self-help" industry. Any publisher or manufacturer, appealing to at least twelve kinds of "individuality" and "self-expression," can easily market mass-produced books, zodiac dishes, zodiac dresses, zodiac jewelry, zodiac incense, and zodiac rugs ad infinitum. But after all the mania, the professional charting done by a legitimate astrologer can cost a bundle, especially if the psychic is, like the jovial, famous, and late clairvoyant Maurice Woodruff, a celebrity consultant to wealthy pop people like Pearl Bailey, Zsa Zsa Gabor, Ginger Rogers, Edward G. Robinson, and Peter Sellers. The cost for an astrologer, as a rule of thumb, should approximately equal the cost of a three-course dinner including wine, tip, and tax.

Human technology has reached the moon. Human metaphysics *interprets* the moon.

"Armstrong, Aldrin, and Collins," people muse. "The initials of those first men on the moon are the same as those of the first men on the earth. Adam, Abel, and Cain."

Someone somewhere will explain what that means.

For a dollar, a yen, a buck, or a pound.

A Brief Occult Guide to Herbs and Roots

Acacia (aids psychic development)
Angelica Root (tends to prolong life)
Ash Tree Leaves (for good luck)
Balm of Gilead Buds (mend a broken heart)
Basil (protects every part of the body)
Betony (for relief of toothache)
Black Snake Root (softens a lover's heart)
Buckeye (brings good luck and wards off rheumatism)
Clover Tops (a charm against witches and snakes)
Cloves (comfort for the sad)
Cumin Seeds (keep lovers faithful)
Damiana Leaves (aphrodisiac)
Dill (counteracts sorcerer's spells)
Elder Bark (quiets nerves and protects the home)
Flax Seed (promotes peace in the home)
Hyssop (witches wash their hands in a hyssop brew before and after casting spells)
John the Conqueror Root (for victory in battle and bed)
Kola Nut (soothes the nerves)
John the Conqueror (grows money when wrapped in a bill and carried)
Marjoram (a charm against witchcraft; anyone in league with the Devil cannot abide the odor)
Mistletoe (ensures love and devotion)
Mustard Seed (ensures fidelity)
Indian Nutmeg (for gambling luck)
Orange Flowers (beneath a pillow these ensure early and happy marriage)
Passion Flower (explains itself)
Patchouly (graveyard dust, to be mixed with evil things and buried far away from home)
Periwinkle (causes love between two people when sprinkled on the clothes of both)
Peony (for good luck in everything)
Poppy (assuages grief, aids sleep)
Rosemary (strengthens memory and the heart)
Sandalwood (carried for good luck)
St. John's Wort (causes dreams of future mate when hung over bed)
Skunk Cabbage (repels evil)

Tonka Beans (to ensure friendship forever, keep one and give the other to
    a friend)
Valerian (induces harmony between husband and wife)
Waahoo Bark (used in uncrossing spells by rubbing a brew of this on the
    head and shouting "Waahoo" seven times)
Wormwood (for female troubles)
Yarrow (worn to weddings for seven-years' happiness)

If "less is more" were true,
the world would not need witchcraft.
—JACK FRITSCHER

CHAPTER 2

The Selling of the
Age of Aquarius

𝓮𝓵

The true philosopher's stone is found within yourself.
—SABAEAN PONTIFEX MAXIMUS FREDERIC DE ARECHAGA

S*ATAN GOES HOLLYWOOD; pop music; Wiccabilly rock;*
Broadway; television; the evil eye; Camelot; The Music Man;
Mick Jagger; Roman Polanski; Kenneth Anger; Jim Morrison;
Frank Sinatra; Haxan: Witchcraft through the Ages; The Devil
Is a Woman; Freaks; *how to look like a witch; the magic capital*
of the world; nuns from hell; Hispanic botanica; and Satan with
a zip code

Mein Camp: FROM UNIVERSITY TO DIVERSITY TO PERVERSITY

Kitsch and *camp* and *pop culture*: synonyms or not? For years *kitsch* was
anything sentimental, precious, and dreadful, particularly in the art world
and its collectors' environs. *Kitsch* was Betty Boop figurines, Elvis on black
velvet, and crystal balls with shakeable swirling snow resting on dragon
claws. With Susan Sontag, *camp* emerged in the mid-1960s from the homosexual subculture into the "overculture's" straight word-hoard. What had
once meant to act *queer, gay, effeminate* in public came to mean *nostalgic,*
or something that was "so bad it was good," such as professional Las Vegas
temptress and gay icon Ann-Margret singing "Thirteen Men (and Me the
Only Gal in Town)" without any irony.

75

In the 1950s, popular culture was scorned by most intellectuals as vulgar. At that time, the University of Michigan reportedly turned down an offer from a major Hollywood studio that had offered the university library thousands of scripts of produced movies. In the late 1960s, when cinema courses bloomed in university curricula and film scholarship became serious, the library claimed it had turned down the written scripts because they weren't suitably bound. Always, some sniffy followers of the high culture of, say, academic art and literature, mock anything *popular* as *vulgar*.

Professor Ray B. Browne, literary critic and folklorist at Bowling Green State University in Ohio, founded the *Journal of Popular Culture* in 1967. With the journal's success, Browne, Russell Nye, and Marshall Fishwick, reacting against their connection with the tightly traditional American Studies Association, founded the American Popular Culture Association headquartered at Bowling Green in 1969. Their controversial purpose established the principle that pop culture itself was intellectually defensible, and that it was important to study culture as it was happening and not leave analysis of culture to historians fifty years later.

Their pioneering theory, spinning out of the work of Marshall McLuhan, said that students can be taught the essence of liberal arts and critical thinking through the serious study of film and television, as well as through William Shakespeare and John Milton. When Browne founded the Department for the Study of Popular Culture at Bowling Green, he and the American Popular Culture Association basically opened up the landscape of American "universities" to the "diversities" of what came to be termed "alternative curricula." Historically, in 1969, Browne was the first to include witchcraft and homosexuality in pop culture studies when he, as publisher of the Popular Culture Association, signed the contract for the first edition of the present volume.

Actually, *popular* means "belonging to the people," as in *people's culture*. The very democratic Latin word *vulgaris* means "belonging to common people." Pop culture, in short, is something—usually in mass media—that is known to many people: the Beatles, the Hell's Angels, the television soap opera *Dark Shadows*. Popular culture can also be measured by what people buy in large numbers: best-selling books, records, and toys. Pop culture is also a synonym for folk culture: what people make and do for themselves—for instance, family snapshots and home movies. The word *pop* by itself has also come to mean a style, particularly of art, that depicts everyday life using commercial techniques.

In Western culture, people believe there's a price to pay to gain magical powers. They think the price is one's soul. Actually, the price of witchcraft is the cost of "entertainment," coven supplies, and dry cleaning.

CUT TO

The Record Industry

Long before the French composer Charles Gounod met Faust, music was essential to witchcraft and Wicca: from druid drums to the mystical chants composed by Hildegaard von Bingen; from Kenyan ritual music to the hillbilly and rockabilly of Wiccabilly; from ancient chants written down as Gregorian plain chant to country songs sung as Christmas carols. Because folklore considers the partridge a randy bird, the gift of "a partridge in a pear tree" promises sex and fertility. Gounod adapted Johann Wolfgang von Goethe's *Faust*, the cautionary tale of a man who sells his soul to the Devil, into a five-act opera in 1859. In *Fantasia* (1938), pop-culture king Walt Disney cast his own alter ego, Mickey Mouse, as the "Sorcerer's Apprentice," from the poem by Goethe and the concert piece by Paul Dukas of the same name. Disney conjured magic and demonology, and anticipated the acid culture of LSD, by sampling the work of classical composers who were not unfamiliar with the occult: Modest Mussorgsky's *Night on Bald Mountain*, Igor Stravinsky's *Rite of Spring*, and Johann Sebastian Bach's *Toccata and Fugue in D Minor*, which was part of the "fantastic genre" of organ music from northern Germany.

Mass-media producers of movies and television try to cross-pollinate their screen titles with hit songs. Gounod's "Funeral March of a Marionette" was popularized into the theme for the suspense-driven *Alfred Hitchcock Presents* TV show (1955–62). In 1964, Jack Keller and Howard Greenfield wrote the million-selling "Theme from *Bewitched*," which helped launch the initial success of that TV series starring Elizabeth Montgomery. Robert Cobert hit the Top 10 list with his 1966 "Quentin's Theme," composed for the afternoon gothic-horror soap opera *Dark Shadows*. Wildly popular with every school kid in America, *Dark Shadows* featured the reluctant vampire, Barnabas Collins; the living head of Judah Zachery; and the man-wolf, Chris Jennings. The series was equally successful as a set of paperback Gothic novels.

Popular music frequently references magic. Tin Pan Alley, Motown, and Nashville are in love with witchcraft. Thousands of songs invoke, like Debussy's "Claire de Lune," the powers of the moon: "Shine on Harvest Moon," "By the Light of the Silvery Moon," "Moon Glow," and "Blue

Moon." These songs are more than pop tunes of love with nature rhymes. They are limned out of folk hymns of the lunar cult of the horned god and of the Roman goddess Diana, who rode the crescent moon, as Ben Jonson wrote, like "a silvery chair." The cult of the flying Diana is the archetype of witches flying. From ancient theater to Broadway and to television, the Dianic cult awes audiences every time an actress/singer/chorine sits in a silver-moon crescent and is lowered down over the stage. Since the dawn of humans, the moon in all its phases has been mystical, as when the upturned crescent moon seems to be two horns in the sky. Before there were druids and Celts, the Old Religion existed as a lunar cult. Saint Paul, preaching the solar cult of Christianity, tried to end the moon worship of Diana. "This Paul hath persuaded and turned away many people . . . so that the temple of Diana should be despised, and her magnificence destroyed, whom all Asia and the world worships" (Acts 19:26–27). Centuries later, another Paul—Anka—tapped alongside this ancient worship with his 1957 hit song, "Diana," sung by a modern young man in love with an explicitly older, perhaps ancient, woman. Whether or not Anka at age fifteen knew what he was writing, worshipers of Diana have adopted his anthem as a hymn.

In fifteenth-century Spain, the religious battle for the moon became political in art and in the Inquisition. The Catholic monarchs Ferdinand and Isabella defeated the Moors, whose symbol was the crescent moon, because Islam was infiltrating Spanish culture. Arabized Jews and Christian scholars joined the fight. Even more than before, the moon and Diana were translated into Catholic statues and art portraying the Virgin Mary, the Catholic version of Diana standing like a Ziegfeld Follies star with her feet on a crescent moon. In Christian iconography, historically, this posture signifies that Mary as the Mother of Christ—with her foot on the neck of the Islamic crescent—is stamping out the Moors to help the Christian Crusaders to victory over the infidel. Charles Gounod, having turned Faust into opera, also composed the Marian anthem "Ave Maria." Catholics, whom Protestants accuse of idolatry, explain that they do not worship the Virgin; they venerate her. The cult of the Virgin, whether pagan Goddess or Christian mother, is everywhere.

In the last three months of 1949, the hit song of the "Top 10 in the Nation" was "Our Lady of Fatima." That time around, the Virgin was iconized as an anticommunist symbol popularized by the Catholic Church after she promised world peace when she appeared to three shepherds at Fatima, Portugal, in 1917. In 1949, the Cold War had American culture shivering with fear at the "Red Menace" drummed up by Senator Joseph McCarthy and the House Un-American Activities Committee (HUAC). Pope Pius XII, an ardent anticommunist, declared 1950 to be an official "Marian Year" to coincide with his new infallible dogma, "The Assumption of Mary," which stated that the Virgin Mary upon the moment of her death rose bodily up into heaven. The song "Our Lady of Fatima" implored Mary to "show the bright and shining way"—which, of course, is a yellow brick road similar to the shining path of Wicca. In that "Red Scare" climate, "Our Lady of Fatima," sung by Kitty Kallen and Richard Hayes, was ecumenical enough to receive huge popular radio play, even with its final line, "We pledge our love and offer you a rosary each day."

The movie *The Miracle of Our Lady of Fatima* was released in the midst of a political storm in 1952. Producer Jack Warner, a well-known anti-communist, who had been tricked through byzantine communist intrigue to make the pro-Stalinist movie *Mission to Moscow* (1943), was trying to correct his left-appearing image in fear of Senator McCarthy's right-wing HUAC witch hunt, which was attacking Hollywood. What better way than a Jewish-produced Virgin Mary picture? Venerable composer Max Steiner wrote the music for the well-scripted movie, and it was popular enough to be nominated for an Academy Award for best musical score. Screen-writer Crane Wilbur typed his way from *Our Lady of Fatima* in 1952 to scripting the first 3-D horror movie, *The House of Wax* (1953), starring Vincent Price. Ten years earlier the first Virgin Mary cult movie, *The Song of Bernadette* (1943), won Jennifer Jones the Academy Award for best actress for playing the visionary peasant girl who saw the Virgin at the healing waters of Lourdes. The Beatles, known for their pursuit of Eastern mysticism, invoked the Virgin as "Mother Mary" in "Let It Be," as well as in "Lady Madonna."

Pop lyrics, more than other media, portray conquering women seductively and positively, because it's a good thing for everyone that "Whatever Lola Wants, Lola Gets" (1955). Popular songs like the Eagles' "Witchy Woman" celebrate the helpless seduction of willing men by attractive witches, vamps, and sirens. Sex appeal is one of the more delicious works of the Devil. While Bing Crosby sang the rather Wiccan "White Christmas," Frank Sinatra crooned that he was "wild" because he was "beguiled" in "Bewitched, Bothered, and Bewildered." In her first movie, *Romance on the High Seas* (1948), Doris Day sang the Sammy Cahn and Jule Styne song "It's Magic." In the cross-dressing Western *Calamity Jane* (1953), tomboy Doris Day introduced what was instantly a coded classic of gay desire,

"Secret Love," with its rebellious "outing" refrain of shouting "from the highest hills."

In the six degrees of separation, the house in which the Manson Family's Tate murders occurred was rented by Roman Polanski from its owner, Rudi Altobelli, who had bought the house from Terry Melcher, the son of Doris Day, who herself was born German-Catholic and turned to Christian Science. Melcher was a record producer from whom Charles Manson had sought a recording contract for his songs, "Sick City," "Run for Fun," and "Clang Bang Clang." When Melcher met Manson, Melcher lived at what was to become the scene of the Satanic Manson cult murder at 10050 Cielo Drive.

What did Frank Sinatra know and when did he know it? Curiously, he served his much younger wife, Mia Farrow, divorce papers, between takes, during her last days of filming *Rosemary's Baby* in 1968. Sinatra already had several hits about occult passion: "That Old Black Magic" that had him "in its spell," and "Witchcraft," with lyrics of "crazy witchcraft," meaning "cool witchcraft," sung to a woman than whom there was "no nicer witch." Known as "Old Blue Eyes," the Italian American Sinatra was so powerful that no one—female or male—wanted a disapproving glance from him, because he seemed he could back up any "evil eye" he cast. During his charmed life, American popular culture thrilled to the eroticizing rumor that the romantic Sinatra was connected to the Mafia. When Mario Puzo wrote *The Godfather* and Francis Ford Coppola turned the novel to a film, their audiences figured the subplot about the Mafia creating their own Italian-American crooner reflected this rumor of the Sinatra mystique. Who can say who sells their soul for lifelong talent, fame, and fortune? Only after Sinatra's death did the show-biz bible *Variety* dare to publish a cartoon drawing of the singer crooning in a spotlight that revealed his shadow as Satan.[1] As over the crucified Jesus the sign "INRI" was hung, proclaiming "Jesus of Nazareth, King of the Jews," is it a satirical parlor game played on a ouija board to decode the anagram of the "marquee name up in lights" of "SINATRA" into "SATAN, Rex Imperialis," meaning "Satan, King of the World"?

Why has no packager yet put out *Frankly Magic: Sinatra's Greatest Occult Hits*? Time and again he returned to composers who used popular witchcraft to tap into romantic metaphor. Without exaggeration, some of his hits sound like a sorcerer's hymn book: "Witchcraft," "That Old Black Magic," "Bewitched, Bothered, and Bewildered," "Luck Be a Lady Tonight," "Devil May Care," "Come Fly with Me," "Fly Me to the Moon," "Baubles, Bangles, and Beads," "Three Coins in the Fountain," "Dancing in the Dark," "Old Devil Moon," "I've Got You under My Skin," "I Don't Stand a Ghost of a Chance with You," "Some Enchanted Evening," "On a Clear Day You Can See Forever," "I Did It My Way," and the "glances" and "chances" of "Strangers in the Night." Add one more track to the list: in 1948, Sinatra, Nat "King" Cole, and Sarah Vaughan each made a recording of one of the most popular songs of the year, the now standard "Nature Boy." Los Angeles mystic-composer Eden Ahbez gave America a song hero who was a "strange, enchanted boy." Arriving on a "magic day," the boy evoked the coming-out archetype of the homosexual outsider with psychic-fairy ability. Ahbez hung out with the Beach Boys, one of whom—Brian Wilson— once allowed Charles Manson to live at his home. Ahbez was a New Age practitioner whose white-magic lyrics promised lovely esoterica.

Eden Ahbez's pagan saying, his *rede*, was: "The greatest thing . . . is . . . to love and be loved in return."[2] Director Baz Luhrmann revived "Nature Boy," sung by David Bowie, as the opening and closing song of his film *Moulin Rouge* (2001) in order to identify his romantic hero.

Other popular songs featured magic in the rock recipe, "Love Potion No. 9" (1959), or the novelty song "Witch Doctor (Ooo Eee Ooo Ah Ah)" (1958). The singer Cher, born Cherilyn Sarkisian, played up her Babylonian-Egyptian looks when she and her Italian-American partner, Sonny Bono, first took to the stage as Caesar and Cleo. Cher sang many hit songs about magical outsiders, such as "Gypsies, Tramps, and Thieves" (1971), "Half Breed" (1973), and the fortune lady of New Orleans in "Dark Lady" (1974). In addition, her film roles, in *Mask* (1985), *Moonstruck* (1987), and *The Witches of Eastwick* (1987), elevated her to icon status in the outsider culture of gays.

The postwar influence of Italian sorcery on white Anglo-Saxon Protestant American pop culture brought more than Dean Martin singing the 1953 song "That's *Amore* (When the Moon Hits Your Eye)." In the 1950s, Rome was the romantic destination of choice because of movies shot on location, like *Roman Holiday* (1953). Even while Audrey Hepburn and Gregory Peck played comic-horror by sticking their hands into the mouth of the great stone face of the Sun God, the Vatican guarded morality and was the center of anticommunism. Within this polarity, auteur Federico Fellini directed his *La Dolce Vita* (1960), filmed just outside the pope's windows on Rome's famous Via Veneto. The Vatican condemned Fellini and his movie, which won an Academy Award for best foreign film. The Legion of Decency warned that any Catholic who viewed *La Dolce Vita* would commit a mortal sin that would condemn the viewer to hell with the Devil for all eternity. The Inquisition never dies.

Censorship of this *dolce* morality tale was ironic, anti-art, and anti-intellectual. Fellini dramatized the Seven Deadly Sins as happening over seven days and seven nights on the seven hills of Rome. *La Dolce Vita* is rich, with magic from its opening shot of a statue of Christ flying (a true deus-ex-machina) over Rome, to its hysterical "miracle" of the Blessed Virgin, and its last shot of a dying fish (a symbol of Christianity) on the beach where the hero can no longer reach out to touch innocence. *La Dolce Vita* introduced the pop-culture term *paparazzi*, and presented Swedish actress Anita Ekberg as a glamour goddess sprung from Hecate, Artemis, and Diana. For Americans escaping Puritanism, Italy, with its sensual culture, was a destination of sex, magic, ritual, and cuisine. Italian neorealism films played in the new American "art theaters," and Italian themes entered Hollywood romantic comedies with Sophia Loren and Gina Lollobrigida, and dramas with Anna Magnani, who embodied the Italian *strega* (witch) in *The Rose Tattoo* (1955) and *The Fugitive Kind* (1960), the screen version of Tennessee Williams's pagan legend, *Orpheus Descending.*[3]

In 1954, full-page ads in the movie sections of newspapers read, "The story behind the love song that's sweeping the country! *Three Coins in the Fountain.*" Rome was so beguiling that this was the first Cinemascope movie shot on location. The hit song promised magic love in return for tossing coins in the Trevi fountain. Throwing coins in a well is an ancient folkway to make a wish as well as appease demons. In *Three Coins*, the proper American women stood on the fountain's edge. In *La Dolce Vita*, Fellini deepened the magic. At midnight, wild woman Ekberg waded into the waters of the Trevi, causing so many tourists to follow suit that fences, laws, and fines had to be created. The soundtrack of *La Dolce Vita* featured international music including the blues standard "Stormy Weather," the Cuban mambo "Patricia," and an occult version of "Jingle Bells" worked into the soundtrack by Nino Rota, who composed music for sixteen Fellini films, including the ghostly *Juliet of the Spirits* (1965), in which the spirit realm is a woman's subconscious.

Nino Rota also wrote the score for *The Ghosts of Rome* (1961) as well as for the star-crossed and potion-based *Romeo and Juliet* (1968) directed by Franco Zeffirelli. Rota won an Academy award for his controversial score for Part Two of Coppola's *The Godfather*, a trilogy about the secret society of the Black Hand—the Mafia—whose oaths and blood rituals fascinate popular culture.[4]

In these ways Italian magic continued to seep into American popular culture of the 1950s and 1960s with the discovery of the cinema of Fellini, the fast-driving Lamborghini Diablo, and the Italian liqueur Strega, which infers a specific kind of Italian female magic.

When in Paris, Gary Cooper, in *Love in the Afternoon* (1957), hired strolling violinists to follow Audrey Hepburn playing F. D. Marchetti's love theme, "Fascination." That tune became a pop-culture standard with magic lyrics of the eye and the moon: "just a passing glance" and "seeing you alone in the moonlight." *Fascination* always means *bewitchment* or *enchantment,* and in a context less romantic than director Billy Wilder's Hepburn-Cooper comedy, fascination is caused by the hypnotic "evil eye" no one can resist. In the Bible, the Book of Proverbs warns, "Eat not the bread of him who has an evil eye" (Prov. 23:6). In the thirteenth century, Saint Thomas Aquinas acknowledged the existence of the evil eye (*malocchio*) in his official theological texts written for the Catholic Church. A balanced face in all cultures equals approachability and beauty. As grace builds on nature, so do psychic powers. A green-eyed stranger looking around a brown-eyed town is always suspect. When an eye is out of alignment, as in being cockeyed like the actor Marty Feldman (especially notable in Mel Brooks's film *Young Frankenstein,* 1974), the person looks to have the evil eye. Audrey Hepburn, who made dark glasses famous in *Breakfast at Tiffany's* (1961), warded off the existential evil eye of the "mean reds" when she sang the white-magic hymn "Moon River," which won the best-song Academy Award for Italian American composer Henry Mancini.

Also on location in Paris in 1957, Hepburn filmed—back-to-back with *Love in the Afternoon*—the musical *Funny Face.* Paired with Fred Astaire, who was always in search of the Greek goddess Terpsichore, Hepburn herself plays both sprite and goddess. As a bohemian, she dances solo and does what she likes in this retelling of Cinderella. In thirty seconds of film, Hepburn forever turns from mere mortal into everyone's ideal sorceress when she descends the marble staircase in the Louvre, swathed in a red Givenchy gown with her red scarf flying up around the pagan statue of "Winged Victory," which in film magic, shape-shifts her into the goddess Nike herself. As Hepburn descends into the world of mortals, she says, "Take the picture. Take the picture." True witch she must be, because in many of her movies, Hepburn (born 1929) plies her stock in trade conjuring potency in men old enough to be her father or grandfather: *Funny Face* with Fred Astaire (born 1899), *Sabrina* with Humphrey Bogart (born 1899), *Love in the Afternoon* with Gary Cooper (born 1901), *Charade* with Cary

Grant (born 1904), *My Fair Lady* with Rex Harrison (born 1908), *Roman Holiday* with Gregory Peck (born 1916), and *Paris When It Sizzles* with William Holden (born 1918). By the time she played Maid Marian to the Robin Hood of Sean Connery (born 1930) in *Robin and Marian* (1976), both stars were middle-aged, which lent a certain nostalgic sweetness to the lore that Robin was an imp of Satan and Marian was the altar for Robin's coven of merry men who had needed her powers.

In 1968, Fellini tripled with two French directors, Roger Vadim and Louis Malle, to shoot the occult *Spirits of the Dead: Three Tales of the Macabre*, adapted from three stories by Edgar Allan Poe, featuring Vincent Price. Fellini's third of the movie, from Poe's "Toby Dammit," and titled "Never Bet the Devil Your Head," starred the always supernal Terence Stamp, coming to grief on a film shoot in Rome. Roger Vadim directed his wife and brother-in-law, Jane Fonda and Peter Fonda, as fiery incestuous cousins in "Metzengerstein." Louis Malle, in "William Wilson," cast Brigitte Bardot opposite Alain Delon as the sadomasochistic Austrian officer who kills his doppelganger and comes to a bad end when the Church will not accept his final act of contrition. *Spirits of the Dead* ambitiously introduced to the new popular culture of 1960s art-house cinema the concept of horror among "the beautiful people"—which became globally true at the Polanski house. This genre's quintessence is the Jim Van Bebber film *The Manson Family* (2004).

The *Malleus Maleficarum* warns that looks could kill. Witches can bewitch their judges with a glance. "Don't you look at me cross-eyed" is a Celtic threat. At Salem, Bridget Bishop cast her "evil eye" at the Puritan girls. Historically, the counter-charm to the evil eye has been the phallus symbolized in hand gestures, such as "giving the finger," as well as in art. Ancient Romans wore gold amulets of the flying penis around their necks to ward off the evil eye. They guarded their doors, roads, and property boundaries with phallic images.

The Greek word *phallus* was synonym to the Latin word *fascinum*: "You say *phallus*, and I say *fascinum*." Each word means *penis*, and one is the root of *fascination*. The proper name Fascinus is an alternative name for the god Priapus. Posted like a "No Trespassing" sign from an electronic alarm company, the priapic warning to the evil eye is to look elsewhere, because a fully potent defense protects the perimeter surrounding the vulnerable center of secret knowledge.

The boundaries signified by phallic piles of rock, such as the herms and cairns at crossroads, defined the pale, who was in the pale, and who was beyond the pale. This defined the outsider. For instance, to live "beyond the pale" in Ireland once meant to live outside the pickets and pales of the fence around the part of Dublin ruled by the English. To "go beyond the pale" evolved to mean "to go too far, too outside the standards of society." That is what the Florida police thought in March 1969 when they arrested doomed rock star Jim Morrison, who was "hand-fasted" (married) to self-proclaimed Celtic witch Patricia Kennealy. In one magical gesture to protect himself, the charismatic Morrison exposed his penis to ward off the thousands of eyes in his audience from whom he felt he was an alienated and magical outsider. Morrison, the LSD shaman, had sung of the isolation of being the outsider in his song, "People Are Strange (When You're a Stranger)." His was the hymn of a witch.

The sacred phallus is full-frontal taboo and full-frontal totem. For both reasons, it is censored and worshiped. The phallus is the physical world's greatest shape-shifter, and as such it is of great significance to the metaphysical world. It is worshiped by those who value its morphing magic, which changes from soft to hard and shoots its seed, blinding the evil eye. Hispanic botanicas sell phallic jewelry cast in gold and carved in crystal. The gay press has a long history of magazines featuring ads selling "fascinus" jewelry mail order. A display ad in the gay porn magazine *In Touch for Men* reads, "Exclusively from Aureus. Good-luck Charm of the ancients! From our Midnight Collection of erotic art. The word *Fascinus* comes from the ancient Romans who gave this name to penis-shaped amulets they wore as good-luck charms. Our *Fascinus* amulets are sculptured in exquisite detail and cast in 14k gold and sterling silver. Erotic quality available in two sizes. Send for free brochure. Aureus, Mission Viejo, California."[5]

Nevertheless, most censorship of art and pop culture, which has accepted the nude female form, has to do with covering the full-frontal male form, because of the mysterious power of the ultimate Devil's tool, taboo, and totem: the penis. Only in the fourth century B.C., with the *Aphrodite* of Praxiteles, did the female form in sculpture began to outnumber the male, thus dating how the *totem* of phallus turned 180 degrees into the *taboo* against male frontal nudity.

In 1970s San Francisco, Faery Shaman Gwydion and his Wicca Blues Band performed pagan rock in the faery tradition, singing songs titled "Sun God" and "Harvest Dance." The album *Gwydion Sings Songs for the Old Religion* celebrated pagan days of worship, the seasons, and love songs to the Gods. Gwydion followed the gender-equal "feri" tradition of the blind Victor Anderson (1917–2001), the grand master and founder of the "faery tradition," who had a profound affect on the Radical Faerie movement on the West Coast. Anderson, the author of *Thorns of the Blood Rose* (1970), combined Gardnerian and Alexandrian traditions of the Goddess liturgy with the magic traditions of the American south. The Wicca Blues Band extracted its sound and its themes from Irish music as well as Irish lore of fairies and witches. Gwydion's second album, *The Faery Shaman*, appeared posthumously, after he died—like the magic fairy James Dean—still in his youth in a car crash.

The rock-and-roll canon regularly reflects interest, from exploitative to serious, in the occult. In 1956, Screamin' Jay Hawkins, according to legend, dropped into a trance and began singing "I Put a Spell on You," which has become a blues and rock standard sung by many including Creedence Clearwater Revival. Hawkins—who often performed holding a skull—claimed that his mother was a voodoo priestess from New Orleans. The flip side to "I Put a Spell on You" was "Little Demon." Blues and rock-and-roll were from the first denounced by censors as Satanic.

Some of "Satan's greatest hits," popular because they tap the psyche, can fill a playful play list: Kay Starr's "Wheel of Fortune" (1951); the national anthem of Halloween, sung by Bobby Pickett and the Crypt-Kicker Five, "The Monster Mash"(1962); Pat Boone's song of a jilted boyfriend who goes to a gypsy fortune teller, "I Almost Lost My Mind" (1956); Mitch Ryder and the Detroit Wheels' "Devil with a Blue Dress On" (1966); Jimi Hendryx's "Voodoo Chile" (1968); Procul Harum's perfect "A Whiter Shade of Pale" (1967); Galt MacDermot, Gerome Ragni, and James Rado's score for *Hair*, especially, "Aquarius/Let the Sun Shine In" (1969); and Carlos Santana's: "Black Magic Woman" and "Evil Ways" (1970). New Orleans' Doctor John the Night Tripper recorded voodoo-music albums like *Gris-Gris* (1969) and, with the help of Mick Jagger and Eric Clapton, *The Sun, Moon, and Herbs* (1971). At his concerts Doctor John, always in full conjure costume, conducted voodoo ceremonies popular with his hippie following.

As the Beatles' *Magical Mystery Tour* (1967) is a British trip into pop culture, drugs, and Eastern mysticism, the Chicago group called Coven are pure Devil rock. The nine songs and complete Black Mass on Coven's first album are a guide to popular sorcery. Sexy and bad, Coven's message is explicit in the songs "Black Sabbath," "Coven in Charing Cross," and "Pact with Lucifer." Forbidden sex is coded in the initials of the song "For Unlawful Carnal Knowledge."

Coven's pop liturgy for a Black Mass has adolescent interest. Anton LaVey's liturgy for his Church of Satan appeals to adults. Unlike the seriously

engaging Anton LaVey album, *The Satanic Mass,* the melodramatic production of Coven stirs listeners to laughter for its ritual pomposity and for
the too-familiar voice of former Top 10 Detroit and Chicago disc jockey
Joel Sebastian hoking it up as "I, Joel, Prince of Bats and High Priest of
the Lord Satan." Truly fearful on this Coven recording is the untrained
teenybopper voice of the young female probationer. Her quivering voice
identifies her as willing masochist participating in the masturbatory fantasy of this occult rock album. "You look into her eyes. She can see through
your disguise. . . . You will burn until you're dead / for unlawful carnal
knowledge."

The rock occult, confirmed by the Krishna chants of Broadway's Aquarian musical *Hair,* could satisfy all those medieval alchemists who wished
to turn dross to gold. New York's Fillmore East Concert Hall turned rock
to gold on April 19, 1970, in the "First Festival of the Occult Arts." The
British invasion of witches featured Sybil Leek and Raymond Buckland as
the popular headliners. Printed under the image of an ankh, the Fillmore
poster read:

FILLMORE EAST
APRIL 19, 1970
THE FIRST FESTIVAL OF THE OCCULT ARTS
Astrology * Palmistry * Tarot * Telepathy * Prediction * Clairvoyance
Witchcraft * Reincarnation * Mediation * Audience Participation
On Stage:
Psychics Marc Reymont & Chris Phelan
The English Witch Sybil Leek on screen
Holiday Vincent, "psychic" comedienne
Edgar Cayce on film
Joshua Light Show/Cosmic Music by "Light"
Raymond Buckland, High Priest of the New York Coven
In the Lobby:
Mystic Arts Book Society/Astronash
Zotique—Occult supplies and readings
One Night Only
Two Shows: 7:00 and 11:00
All Seats Reserved: $3.50/$4.50/$5.50

The "One Night Only" hook should have been a clue to the quick-buck
festival whose caliber, although graced by legitimate professionals Leek,

Cayce, and Buckland, was only slightly above those movie-theater stage shows of the late 1950s that promised "On Stage! The Ectoplasmic Return of James Dean!" The Fillmore light show lacked even the usual psychedelia, settling for slide projections of the speakers' natal signs and characteristic tarot cards.

The Fillmore Zotique came nowhere near the abundance of a botanica. Instead it was a plastic boutique of incense, candles, and charm jewelry. The festival sellers perused such items as:

- The Warner Brothers company's fast-selling record *Seduction through Witchcraft* (1969), which is part of the Astro-stereo Zodiac series "Twelve Musical Albums of the Zodiac," featuring Louise Huebner. Each one of the dozen albums is called *The Astromusical House of* (for one) *Gemini* (with Gemini-like songs, "Call Me Irresponsible" and "Cast Your Fate to the Wind"). Each album is accompanied by a "special booklet written for the sign of the Zodiac by the world-renowned astrologer Carroll Righter."
- The RCA Camden recording *Listen to Your Stars: An Astrological Guide to Your Horoscope* (1969).
- The Glass Prism, a rock group reimagining the works of Edgar Allan Poe "to hard-rock guitar and the kind of organ you remember from the cellar of the castle where Prince Prospero stalked at midnight . . . a rather startling way of learning Poe." Such is the advertising copy of their two albums: *Poe through the Glass Prism* (1969) and *On Joy and Sorrow* (1970).

To the Zotique could have been added the album of meditation-and-incense music written, composed, and performed by Laura Huxley, widow of Aldous Huxley, titled *Recipes for Living and Loving* (1969); and Louise Huebner's two albums *Seduction through Witchcraft* and *Orgies—A Tool of Witchcraft* (1969).

The grail of recorded witchcraft, without question, is Anton LaVey's 1968 Murgenstrumm album *The Satanic Mass Ceremony*. The recording was begun on Friday the 13th of September, 1967, where Satan had a zip code—at LaVey's San Francisco Church of Satan, 6114 California Street, San Francisco, 94121. The first cut is the Satanic baptism of his daughter, which segues into the Satanic Mass. Side 1 includes the entire demonic ritual in eight steps, of which three samples are:

Step Two: The Invocation to Satan

The High Priest, encircled by the black robed figures of his assistants, stands holding the Sword of Power in his extended arm and pointing towards the altar and symbol of Satan, recites the invocation to Satan, thereby calling upon the Powers of Darkness to manifest his desires.

Step Three: Drinking from the Chalice and Benediction of the House

This continues the ritual. The High Priest "consecrates and drinks from the Chalice of Ecstasy." Also at that time another priest performs the "Benediction of the House." He shakes the phallus in four directions, "towards the four corners of the earth," as a "holy water sprinkler" of the Catholic Church. As the words point out, "The Satanic Church merely returns it to its original form before Christianity devised this parody."

Step Eight: Invocation Applied towards the Conjuration of Lust

A female member of the unholy congregation has requested a ritual for the enchantment of the man of her choice, so she may obtain the fulfillment of her voluptuous desires by her chosen lover. The High Priest strengthens this working by acting as her lover, by proxy, in the reading of the first part of the invocation for lust; then the trembling voice of the enchantress for whom the ceremony is being performed is heard, as her ecstatic entreaty comes to its climax. The strains of the syrinx are heard in the background, and the pungent scent of musk mingled with sulfur permeates the dark, highly charged atmosphere.[6]

Included with LaVey's Black Mass on side 1, besides "The First Satanic Baptism," are "The Benediction" and "The Hymn to Satan." On side 2, LaVey reads from his *Satanic Bible* (1969), which "is divided into four books: the first, *The Book of Satan,* is a Hellish diatribe; the second, *The Book of Lucifer,* is the enlightenment; the third, *The Book of Belial,* is an explanation of the meaning and performance of Satanic magic; and the fourth, *The Book of Leviathan,* contains the actual invocations used in Satanic ceremonies."

The Rolling Stones, notorious for their inversions of establishment values, dragged themselves into women's clothing for an album released a year after the total inversion of *Their Satanic Majesties Request* (1967). On *Beggar's Banquet* (1968), the lyrics for the song "Sympathy for the Devil" rant Genet-like inversions, saying "every cop is a criminal, and all the

sinners saints." Jagger calls himself an unrestrained Lucifer who warns he
is out to "lay your soul to waste."

Jim Morrison's exposing himself in concert led to decency rallies in
Florida and New York. The Stones' Mick Jagger, in some ways more exhibitionistic than Morrison, wears his zodiac sign embroidered in his clothing. Jagger, noted Everett Henderson in 1969, "is the abstracted essence of
demon sensuality; he is the symbol of our most lustful appetites; when he
sings he makes you want to do every awful thing you ever felt like doing.
Jagger is a consummate actor. He has chosen to play brilliantly the role of
Devil's advocate of obsessive and restless sex."[7]

Jagger's diabolical persona matches the witchiness of the temperamental Laura Nyro, favored by female fans. Usually dressed in black and demanding an almost completely dark concert stage, Nyro, one of the hottest
composer-poets of the 1960s and 1970s, sang a number of songs with
Satanic references. In "Time and Love," she wrote the lyrics "Don't let the
Devil fool you." In "Captain Saint Lucifer," she vows that she plans to "live
and die and rise with my captain." Her "Gibson Street" smoulders with
the experienced Faustian wisdom of a woman who has sold her soul. Nyro
(original surname Nigro, meaning "black") was popularly called "the perfect witch with the perfect pitch." She is second only to the Beatles as far
as the number of her songs that were reinterpreted and covered by other
artists.

CUT TO

Broadway

Magic is everywhere. If the American record industry is into the meta-
phors of witchcraft and the zodiac, then theater, with its very source in
old religious ritual, can be no surprising stranger to the mystical. Broadway legends Alan Jay Lerner and Frederick Loewe, familiar with magic
sources, found great luck with their changeling musical, *My Fair Lady*,
which starred Julie Andrews on Broadway (1956), and Audrey Hepburn in
the film (1964). Earlier, Lerner and Loewe wrote a musical infused with
natural white magic, *Paint Your Wagon* (1951). With the rise of interest in
the occult in the 1960s, Paramount Studio filmed *Paint Your Wagon* (1969)
starring Clint Eastwood, Lee Marvin, and Jean Seberg, who rose to fame
starring in the film version of George Bernard Shaw's *Saint Joan* (1960),
directed by Otto Preminger. *Paint Your Wagon* featured two Wiccan hymns,
"I Talk to the Trees" and "They Call the Wind Maria." When Clint Eastwood

intones "I Talk to the Trees," he also talks to "the stars," seeking astrological answers. When Lee Marvin and chorus sing "They Call the Wind
Maria," the song is an invocation of what the ancient Greek Heraclites
called the four basic elements: earth, air, fire, and water. The lyrics set the
place as being so far out in the wild that even God can't find the singer
who laments he has no star to guide him, unless it is the goddess of the
wind called Maria, pronounced Mar-EYE-ah. The character played by Jean
Seberg is a witch natural enough to lure both men, and liberated enough
to take the two of them as husbands at the same time.

In the late 1950s, Lerner and Loewe opened wide the world of popular
witchcraft. They optioned the last three sword-and-sorcery books of T. H.
White's quartet *The Once and Future King*, based on the Arthurian collection of Thomas Malory, *Le Morte D'Arthur* (ca. 1470). (Malory's work
is required reading for witches.[8]) In 1939, Walt Disney bought White's first
book, *The Sword in the Stone* (1938), and turned it into an animated film
in 1963. For centuries, the magical story of King Arthur, Queen Guenevere,
Lancelot, Mordred, Merlin, and the Knights of the Round Table has been
the popular trellis around which twines the whole of Anglo-Saxon and
Celtic magic—white and black—mixed with Christian folk magic. Lerner
and Loewe musicalized the legend in *Camelot* (1960), which transcended
itself when the star-crossed young president John F. Kennedy named it as
his favorite musical.

The score opens with the benediction canticle, "Camelot," which heralds
how magical is the unspoiled Eden of Arthur's realm where nature rules.
Magician Merlin's spirit guide Nimue, the Lady of the Lake, sings the absolutely Wiccan song of seductive white magic, "Follow Me." Lost in the winter woods, Guenevere, who brings irony and lust to Camelot, invokes her
Christianized namesake "Saint Genevieve" and in spring celebrates the
pagan feast of Beltane in "The Lusty Month of May." Later, she sings the
love lament built around the formal magic word *gaze*, "Before I Gaze at
You Again." Arthur, an idealist without guile, sings a song that, if sung
with sincerity by every man in the Middle Ages, might have averted the
holocaust of the Inquisition: "How to Handle a Woman." Merlin's answer
is, "Simply love her."

In a duet specifically about magic, Guenevere, curious about "tribal
sorcery," asks Arthur, "What Do the Simple Folk Do?" Arthur teaches her
a list of "ancient native customs" practiced by the simple folk to "chase the
goblins" and make "their spirits rise," such as invoking the sun god Apollo
and the moon goddess Venus, whistling to cast "a spell," and dancing "a

fiery dance" till they "whirl" uncontrolled into a "violent trance" that makes life happy and "gay." Lancelot becomes heroic by working his white magic to bring a knight back to life. In "If Ever I Would Leave You," he invokes the powers of spring, summer, winter, and fall as he contemplates the impossibility of separating from Guenevere, who has "bewitched" him so. In the duet "I Loved You Once in Silence," Guenevere and Lancelot voice all the anxieties and dangers of every subculture's secret love when forbidden by the authority of the state. When the nights of the Round Table split, the evil knights, who are into dark sorcery, call upon Beelzebub and sing the Satanic hymn "The Seven Deadly Virtues," with its chorus "Fie on goodness." When Guenevere, like Joan of Arc and all witches, is sentenced to be burned at the stake, it is the state—that is, Arthur the King rather than Arthur the husband—executing her for political reasons, because sexual betrayal is political. Arthur's final reprise of "Camelot" is a lament for a world of white magic destroyed by the collision of black magic with sex magic.

Some people see witchcraft where it is not, and miss it where it is. That shape-shifting quality is witchcraft's big joke, because witchcraft is like the two-ton elephant in the room where people rarely mention the elephant. Meredith Willson turned the fairy tale of the Pied Piper of Hamlin into the Broadway extravaganza *The Music Man* (1956). So instantly did the surface of *The Music Man* jump into red, white, and blue Americana that no critic or director has yet scraped off its nostalgic veneer to reveal the darker characterization of a woman who out tricks a trickster and helps him trick her own town. Willson himself seduces the audience with music and words streaming so fast that the subtext of magic and sorcery bubbles just below the surface—a subtext that, of course, directors, critics, and audiences can choose to acknowledge or not. *The Music Man* is a duplicitous musical. The lyrics spin on double entendre in the same way that the slow, sentimental love song, "Goodnight, My Someone" is the same melody as the faster march, "Seventy-Six Trombones." In many ways, "Goodnight, My Someone" is a conjure song sung in order to read the future. *The Music Man* may as well have been titled *The Magic Man*.

When the traveling salesman—often the disguise of the Devil—takes the fake name of Professor Harold Hill, he rides into River City on huge clouds of steam from the coal-fired railroad car. He has sinister plans to use the town's children to swindle the know-it-all townspeople who are so "Iowa stubborn" that they are righteously fundamental about everything; they are even famous for tarring and feathering anyone who isn't

like them. The other salesmen in the opening song "Rock Island" explicitly sing that Hill is so slick that when he "dances, the piper"—that is, the
Devil—"pays him." Willson's archetype is the serpent entering Eden, but
this time the Eve he meets is more Lilith, who is his match.

The seemingly innocent Maid Marian became the librarian when an
elderly local tycoon died and left her all his books because she had, as the
townswomen sing in "Pick a Little, Talk a Little," made "brazen overtures"
to him who had no friends before Marian came to town. The orchestra-
tion under "Marian, the Librarian" is a threatening moan and vamp that
cues the darkness underlying the outsider Marian, who is so cold she
would let a lover's dead body turn to "carrion." In the library, no one dares
break Marian's strict rituals of behavior. The ladies gossip that Marian is
not like the rest of the women, and even the men of the volunteer fire
brigade are afraid of Marian for what she would do if her books were
burned. In turn, Marian expresses a low opinion of the townspeople. She
controls the secret knowledge hidden in books, particularly *Balzac*, which
sounds pornographic to the women who sing "she advocates dirty books"
like "Chaucer, Rabelais," and "Balzac." Marian sings "My White Knight" as
a prayer to the explicitly named goddess Venus, and is adamant that her
knight is quite the opposite of Lancelot or an angel.

When the devilish Professor Hill enters River City, this witchy Maid Marian recognizes him faster than he recognizes her. They are the perfect left-
handed cult couple, and the plot revolves around their realizing their match.
Hill directly cites Satan to threaten the fundamentalist River City with
the "trouble" caused by the game of pool, which he announces is, like all
pleasures, "the Devil's tool." He also triggers their fears by reminding them
"the idle brain is the Devil's playground." He plays upon Puritan heritage
to hoodwink the River City Protestants by reminding them of "Plymouth
Rock and the Golden Rule" which is, of course, the rede of Christianity.

Willson specifically calls Marian "Irish," thus identifying her as Catholic,
and mentions that she is twenty-six. Marian lives at home with her six-
year-old brother and their widowed mother, who prays to Saint Patrick and
Saint Bridget. This might add up to zero if Willson did not have Harold
Hill reference Hester Prynne, living with her six-year-old daughter, Pearl,
in Hawthorne's *The Scarlet Letter*. In the song, "The Sadder But Wiser Girl
for Me," Hill sings the punch line, that he hopes and prays "for Hester to
win just one more 'A.'" Willson thus gives away the "unspeakable truth"
that Marian is an unwed mother whose own mother claims the child is
Marian's sibling. Such a cover story was once a staple white lie told when

a family's unmarried daughter became pregnant. Marian is so troubled by her "brother's" speech impediment that when Hill teaches the boy how to speak clearly—in fact, more like Hill himself, the silver-tongued Devil—Marian falls for him.

Hill is into things more mysterious than mythology when he sings, "for no Diana do I play faun." In fact, he knows that the only way to seduce Marian is with the power of "moonlight," which he invokes in "Marian, the Librarian." With Marian's secret sexual past of books and baby, Willson codes internal evidence that reveals her true character to Hill, who pursues her because she is in fact, he figures out, "sadder but wiser." Once this Maid Marian finds out that Hill is a trickster she connives to save her Robin Hood, even to the point of offering sexual favors to another salesman who threatens to reveal Hill's plan to fleece the coldhearted town that deserves to be swindled, the way that Robin Hood only steals from the rich to give to the poor. By the finale, Professor Harold Hill and Marian are a triumphant couple; they succeed in fleecing the entire town, which is too stubborn to notice it's been beguiled. Like Mr. and Mrs. Pied Piper of Hamlin, Hill and Marian march arm in arm down the Main Street of River City, leading away all the children whom they have taught the transforming charms of music—that is, magic. In short, the interlopers from the outside world have come into the domestic small town and done the very thing witches always do: teach the children alternative values.

Because straightlaced Wall Street, always casting runes of one kind or another, is reading David Williams's *Astro-Economics: A Study of Astrology and the Stockmarket* (1959), it follows that when investors merge with artists, paranatural confrontations may not be at all unusual. Before he brought his antiwar hippie musical *Hair* to Broadway in 1968, producer Michael J. Butler found everything he touched was star-crossed. But Joseph Papp's Off-Broadway *Hair*, at the Shakespeare Public Theater (1967), taught that "when the moon is in the seventh house," astrology can "steer the stars." In one of its signature songs, *Hair* announced "the dawning of the Age of Aquarius."

The uncrossed "stars" of Butler's original *Hair* have been young actors well-steered indeed. Shelley Plimpton and Ronnie Dyson moved on to films like Robert Downey's *Putney Swope* (1969); Hiram Kellar to *Fellini Satyricon* (1970); Lynn Kellogg to the Las Vegas and TV circuit; Melba Moore to Broadway stardom and a Tony Award for the musical *Purlie* (1969); and Diane Keaton to Hollywood stardom beginning with *The Godfather* (1972). Butler, for all practical purposes, avoided the "Caesar Syndrome"; he was very aware of the Ides of March. He put his soothsayer on the pay roll. In fact, no production of *Hair*, even though *Hair* was the first certified global village hit, opened anywhere any day without the approval of Maria Crummere, *Hair*'s official astrologer.

If American witchery has a popular stage classic comparable to the screen's *Rosemary's Baby*, it is Howard Richardson's drama *Dark of the Moon*. No political allegory like Arthur Miller's *The Crucible* (1953), *Moon*'s forlorn folktale of Barbry Allen (Capulet) and Witchboy John (Montague) brings together two strains of American popular culture. Originally, in 1945, *Dark of the Moon* established in drama the Barbry Allen of oral folk tradition. In revival in 1970, at the Mercer-Shaw Arena Theater, producer William Berney crossed *Moon* with the almost obligatory nudity that *Hair* generated on the American stage in the late 1960s. Although some of the *Moon* flesh belonged to strawberry-blonde actress Claudia Jennings (*Playboy*'s Miss November 1969 and Playmate of the Year 1970), when *Dark of the Moon* stripped down, the flesh padded more than the box-office receipts. It polarized the estranged worlds of Christianity and sorcery.

If ever witches were libidinous, the nude athletics of the 1970s *Dark of the Moon* verified what audiences always suspected about "sabbaths." There on stage at the opening of the second act, director Kent Broadhurst's two witchboys gambol naked with three female witches. They celebrate their primeval sabbath in Hawthornian woods. Lightning mixes with thunder. Dead leaves hang in their hair. They quaff great quantities of blood from human skulls.

They pass Barbry's stolen shift in ritual circle. The Dark Witch dons the gingham dress and the coven works its curse. The coals of the witch fire intensify to angry red. The Fair Witchboy mounts the Dark Witch while the others chant the rhythms of the naked coital choreography. They couple in the flames with an inverted cross resting on the Fair Witchboy's bare buttocks. According to set, prescribed ritual, the witches work their curse on Barbry Allen.

Like Rosemary, Barbry gives birth to a Satanic incarnation. But Barbry's baby, with no coven to protect him, is burned newborn by the righteous Christian community. Barbry herself is then raped, compliments of the Baptist congregation. The Christians' unset, unprescribed, ad-lib ritual of exorcism is, by comparison, a more orgiastic and dangerous rite than any coven's. While randy Marvin Hudgins strips naked to penetrate and thus exorcise Barbry on the sanctuary floor, the congregation dances in a circle chanting hysterically the refrain "Blood of the Lamb."

Dark of the Moon is good coven theater. Anti-Christian, it peels back the obscenities masked under malpracticed Christian righteousness. It is the Christians who are superstitious, and the witches who are theologically knowledgeable. It is the Christians who adhere to the letter of the law; it is the witches who catch the free spirit of it. "Bein' human," the witches say, "is to be never gettin' what you want." That's the curse of having a human soul. It's what Jagger sang: ". . . can't get no satisfaction." "A witch," Witchboy John tells Barbry, "ain't got no soul. He lasts three hundred years and then he just be fog, nights, on the mountain."

With the 1970s demand for occult theater, it seemed only a matter of time before someone like producer Hilliard Elkins (*Oh, Calcutta!* 1970) brought a nude musical version of *Dark of the Moon* to the Broadway stage. Elkins also produced the Gore Vidal play *An Evening with Richard Nixon* (1972), featuring Susan Sarandon, who later starred in *The Witches of Eastwick* and was famously photographed by Robert Mapplethorpe with her toddler daughter, Eva Amurri. John Bishop, Mel Marvin, and Bob Satuloff, the Broadway musical adapters of Sinclair Lewis's novel *Elmer Gantry*, which denounces fake Bible-thumping preachers, announced shortly after their singing-dancing *Gantry* failed in the 1970 season that they were turning from religious themes to a new show on witchcraft. Broadway has beckoned musically as well to eminent British astrologer Maurice Woodruff, who was actor Peter Sellers's personal astrologer, brilliantly acted by Stephen Fry in the film *The Life and Death of Peter Sellers* (2004). Woodruff's biography of his mother, titled *Woody* (1967), details the flamboyant life of Vera Woodruff, the lionized clairvoyant of the 1920s and 1930s. From the classic occult of Shakespearean revivals through the dramatized horror of Henry James and Arthur Miller to a variety of Broadway hits, the credentials of Occult Broadway are historical enough for a Ken Burns television documentary.

A few lighter occult titles include *Blithe Spirit* (1941), a comedy by Noël Coward in which a medium contacts the dead; *One Touch of Venus* (1943), in which the goddess of love falls in love with a human, to music by Kurt Weill, lyrics by Ogden Nash, and book by S. J. Perelman; *The Lady's Not for Burning* (1948), a tale of women and witchcraft by the modern Arthurian playwright Christopher Fry; John Van Druten's *Bell, Book and Candle* (1950), in which a man falls under the spell of a witch whose cat has the traditional name of a familiar, Pyewacket; *Damn Yankees* (1955), the musical comedy by George Abbott with music and lyrics by Richard Adler and Jerry Ross, in which Faust meets baseball when a fan sells his soul to Satan to become the world's greatest player, tempted by the beautiful witch Lola (who gets what Lola wants); *Li'l Abner* (1956), in which Mammy Yokum has conjure visions while Evil Eye Fleegle casts his spell on the town of Dogpatch, where the vamp named Stupefyin' Jones stops men dead in their tracks and a mysterious potion shape-shifts scrawny hillbilly husbands into bodybuilders uninterested in sex with their wives (based on the enormously popular *Li'l Abner* comic strip, and written by Al Capp, with music by Gene de Paul and lyrics by Johnny Mercer); Alan Jay Lerner and Barton Lane's *On a Clear Day You Can See Forever* (1965), in which reincarnation is inspired by the 1950s popularity of hypnotically regressed Bridey Murphy; Stephen Sondheim's *Into the Woods* (1987), which acknowledges the magic, myth, and mystery of the heath, the weir, and the forest, replete with witches and a real curse; and Stephen Schwartz's *Wicked* (2004), a musical spinning out the back story of *The Wizard of Oz* from the novel by Gregory Maguire, *Wicked: The Life and Times of the Wicked Witch of the West* (1996). Sondheim also wrote *Assassins* (1991 and 2004) featuring as characters two women of the Charles Manson family, Lynette "Squeaky" Fromme and Sara Jane Moore, both of whom attempted at different times in 1975 to assassinate President Gerald Ford. Henry James provides a through-line of America's constant occult obsession. His 1897 ghost-story novel *The Turn of the Screw* was a Broadway hit in 1950 as *The Innocents*, as adapted by William Archibald; it subsequently became a 1954 opera by Benjamin Britten, and a 1961 movie starring Deborah Kerr.[9]

Farther Off-Broadway, *National Close-Up Magazine*, April 27, 1970, reported on the California "Orgasmic Theater of the Supernatural." Using popular folk gossip wishfully disguised as an eyewitness report, drama critic John Nevin assured his *Close-Up* readers of a theater of extreme assault and cruelty. According to the testimony of one "Esther Miles," "A bright light glared on the erection of a hooded male on stage. . . . He stroked himself right out there in public and put fluid in a vial. He raised it to the ceiling and muttered a prayer with a lot of Satans in it. . . . Then these two young girls with things hanging between their legs came running out and put their arms around him (her husband, Mort Miles). They pulled open his drawers and stroked him and led him on stage. They did the same with two other men and called to the god, Astaroth, to bless their doings. Lured on stage, the three gents sat in a triangle and let the duo bi-sex them. As the gents started to quiver, a gowned Satan stormed on stage and pranced up to the writhing bodies. With a sword, he lifted the orgasming men's heads and slit their jugulars just as they jolted their last."[10]

Supposedly fleeing to the hills where Charles Manson and his cult camped, the actors disappeared, according to policeman "Carl Wright," who told *National Close-Up*, "They left a sacrificed dog lying in the dressing rooms and a black cross on the wall. We have nothing to go on except for three slain bodies. They're occult, alright! There's a lot of it going around!"

Whether or not the "Orgasmic Theater of the Supernatural" ever made it on stage, it made it on the printed page and as such is part of the popular occult. As Judy Garland once sang from lyrics written for the MGM musical *Bandwagon* (1953), by Howard Dietz, "When a ghost and a prince meet / and everyone ends in mincemeat / That's entertainment!"

CUT TO

The Movies

Always as much De Sade as DeMille, the movies mated early with the showy horrors of the supernatural. An illusory art, film's special effects easily provide the seeing that is believing. The camera is a magic instrument that penetrates reality to reveal secrets. It is every bit as much a stealer, or a presenter, of soul and spirit, as Native Americans early on believed.

Greta Garbo, in the final scene of *Queen Christina* (1933) was directed by Rouben Mamoulian to stare into space and think of nothing. Yet the magical camera peels her mask and reveals more female and human secrets than entertainment probably should. What audiences see is sometimes more in their own heads than it is on the screen. When movies were introduced, the projector was called "a magic lantern." The best filmmakers know that the motion-picture camera creates the popular art closest to psychology. The movie audience watching one hour of film actually watches twenty-seven minutes of total darkness which, at sixteen still frames per second, is the total of the darkness between flickering frames. The ratio of image to darkness suggests the proportion of the conscious to the unconscious. Anything could be in that dark the way that gray fear lies in the blur of frames. Occult material is a perfect match to the environment of cinema that flickers in a large dark hall filled with strangers sitting alone together in a maze of chairs where anything can happen. Tales of vampires, witches, and ghosts have been big box office since Dr. Caligari opened his cabinet and put the howl and bellow in Bell and Howell.

If the occult film canon is vast, its source is surprisingly uncomplex. Northern European *technology* facilitated the supernatural film, and Northern European *sensibility*—German, Scandinavian, Anglo-American—

complemented the form with suitable matter. Director Robert Wiene's *Cabinet of Dr. Caligari* (1919), a five-reel silent film, set the visual horror style of German expressionism, featuring distorted perspective and deep shadows signifying imminent danger, forbidden desire, and the approach to a kill.

In 1922, director F. W. Murnau created his vampire classic *Nosferatu* by rethinking the Irish horror novel *Dracula*, written by Dublin author Bram Stoker, whose widow successfully sued Murnau for plagiarism. Murnau's first addition to Stoker's vampire legend was his subtle injection of witch-craft's secret ingredient, homosexuality. (By magic's own secret code, the archetypal demon lover always goes beyond heterosexual acts.) His second was equation of the vampire with Adolf Hitler, who with his "black tooth-brush moustache" loomed like a fundamentalist Puritan who would ban everything. In 1966, Sigfried Kracauer wrote *From Caligari to Hitler* to analyze how in the 1920s early German directors—many of them Jewish—coded their silent films of horror and the occult with warnings to movie-goers about the rise of Nazism.

In the 1920s and 1930s, director Carl Dreyer's *Leaves from Satan's Book* (1921) and *Vampyr* (1931) established the "less is more" horror principle. Dreyer intuited that horror must rely on the offscreen imagination of the viewer: tapping the ratio of conscious to unconscious. In this way, letting the sun actually shine into his lens to create a visual aura, he directly in-volved the gray subconscious of his viewer's innermost fears. Cinematog-rapher Rudolph Mate shot most of the *Vampyr* exteriors through black gauze to create an eerie mist even in sunlight.

In the 1960s and 1970s, American International Pictures, famous for the extraordinary pop pulse of *Easy Rider* (1969), approximated Mate's gauze shots at the climax of its H. P. Lovecraft film *The Dunwich Horror* (1970). Sight, hearing, and sometimes kinesthesia are the prime sensual conduc-tors for film reality. Roger George's special effects for *Dunwich*, however, purposely "designed in" the sense of touch. For the Black Mass sequence in which Dean Stockwell rubs his hands down Sandra Dee's naked thighs, the footage was shot through a textured screen—like a kind of cinema Braille—to visually excite the viewers' sense of touch as much as sight and hearing.

Mate's black-and-white *Vampyr* cinematography, even if it hadn't been necessity in those pre-Technicolor days, suited the psychological placement of Dreyer's script. Since the late 1960s, films once traditionally shot in black and white have been, like *Rosemary's Baby*, filmed on color stock. The economics of TV sale to mass-market network sponsors demanding prime-time color has virtually spelled the end of black-and-white cinematography in the American film industry. In November 1963, president John F. Kennedy was assassinated in black and white; color TV arrived a year later.

The actors famous for their horror roles have exploited names as Transylvanian as their accents. Lon Chaney Sr., in Rupert Julian's *Phantom of the Opera* (1925), Bela Lugosi in Tod Browning's *Dracula* (1931), Boris Karloff in James Whale's *Frankenstein* (1931), and Maria Ouspenskaya in George Waggner's *The Wolf Man* (1941) were the first generation. Vincent Price singlehandedly continued the cottage (and castle) industry of horror primarily peddled by American International Pictures. AIP led the way to the huge popularity of the horror genre which aims blockbuster American Gothic films at the teenage demographic.

Through an almost Faustian pact with AIP, Vincent Price salvaged his career at a time when Hollywood stars of a certain age were well past their zenith in the new youth culture of the 1960s. He ranged from the comedy *Abbott and Costello Meet Frankenstein* (1948) to the first 3-D horror movie, *House of Wax* (1953), to the art-house *Spirits of the Dead* (1969). He hit a Hollywood milestone in 1970 with the release of *Cry of the Banshees*, his hundredth film. Price's popular endurance as a mandarin of the occult was not only his copyrighted appearance, but his taste for what sells. Sears and Roebuck's campy mail-order "Buy-A-Painting" isn't called "The Vincent Price Gallery" for nothing.

When Price wasn't tapping medical fears like "transplanting too much too soon" as in *Scream and Scream Again* (1970), he jumped into the public-domain classics of Edgar Allen Poe. *The Pit and the Pendulum* (1961), *The Raven* (1963), *The Masque of the Red Death* (1964), and *The Tomb of Ligeia* (1965) qualify him as king of the "Poe fright trash." Faithful to his peers—Jane Asher (one-time paramour of Paul McCartney), Joe E. Brown, Lon Chaney, Boris Karloff, John Kerr, Peter Lorre, Debra Paget, and Basil Rathbone—Price milked "has-been" and "whatever-happened-to" reputations for leftover camp appeal. Produced and directed by Roger Corman's pop genius, no Price picture ever lost money at the box office.

By his hundredth film, Mercury Records had contracted the droll Price to record a horror album on how to cast spells and curses. "I can't imagine," he said, "why they asked me." On that album, *Witchcraft and Magic* (1969), Price read five cuts : "Secrets of Magic"; "Magic Revealed"; "How to Make Love Potions, Charms, and Spells"; "Raising the Devil"; and "Witches Sabbath." His readings encouraged Anton LaVey to release his own recordings *The Satanic Mass* (1968), *Strange Music* (1994), and *Satan Takes a Holiday* (1995).

As corporate accountants have made "box office gross" the fiscal definition of popular culture, then Price, who was also the longtime host of *Mystery* on PBS, was a cash-and-scary phenomenon. "I do fairytales," he once said. "My pictures are good clean, wholesome fun. I burn two or three people; maybe hang a girl up by her thumbs. But I've made my pictures into popular staples like only the western used to be. Audiences go to be relieved of tension, screaming and clutching each other; then at least they don't go home and beat the kids."

The straight Price so plied his stock-in-trade camp that he was unafraid to play Butch, the gay hairdresser, in *Theater of Blood* (1973), which also starred his wife, Coral Browne. Asked if he believed in witchcraft himself, Price pointed to the 1970s witchcraft revival and said, not too enigmatically about witchcraft's victories, particularly against attempts to invade England by King Philip II of Spain in 1588 and by Adolf Hitler in 1940, "In the time of the *Armada* the British witches got together and cooked up a storm. They did it again when Hitler was on the way. Enough said?"

As with film director Roman Polanski, most fright films from the serious to the superficial grow from one man's obsession. The widower Polanski believes that good can never beat evil. His filmography includes *Dance of the Vampires*, also known as the camp *The Fearless Vampire Killers, or: But Your Teeth Are in My Neck* (1967); *Rosemary's Baby* (1968); and the terribly autobiographical *Macbeth* (1971), based on the bloody and Satanic Charles Manson murders at the Polanski home. Kenneth Anger, the obsessed whipping-boy genius of American underground cinema, has long outraged audiences with his guru-like homosexuality and his sadomasochistic fetishism. However, behind Anger's surface shock lies his constant spiritism. His "Magic Lantern Cycle" gains theme, symbol, and ritual structure from the magisterial occult of Aleister Crowley. Anger, who changed his name from "Anglemyer," chronicles his challenging and demonic homosensuality in features such as *Fireworks* (a fifteen-minute film shot in 1947 when he was seventeen); *Inauguration of the Pleasure Dome* (1954); and the leather-biker-meets-Jesus scenario of *Scorpio Rising* (1964), which revealed the secret lifestyle of outlaw gay men that Hollywood had cleaned up for Marlon Brando in *The Wild One* (1954).

Kenneth Anger flows in the bloodstream of British and American—and specifically Hollywood—pop culture. He authored the notorious book *Hollywood Babylon* (1958). His art is a pedigree that proves homosexuality is a link to almost everything. Anaïs Nin played Astarte in *Pleasure Dome*. *Scorpio Rising* is dedicated to its own influences: the alienated gay actor, James Dean; the masochistic gay visionary, T. E. Lawrence of Arabia, who died on a motorcycle; the Hell's Angels; and the gay poet Hart Crane, who disappeared (did he jump, or was he pushed by sailors?) from a ship in the Gulf of Mexico. Hart Crane greatly influenced Tennessee Williams, whose play *Suddenly Last Summer* (staged in 1958) was written under the influence of the mid-1950s release of *Pleasure Dome*. The similarity? The parallel? In both Williams and Anger, Bacchus is killed by the Bacchantes, who in modern sexual equality can be wild (gay) men as much as they were classically wild women.

Finally, regarding *Invocation of My Demon Brother* (1969), the sound was composed by Mick Jagger, and the role of Satan was played by Anton LaVey, with Manson Family member Bobby Beausoleil as Lucifer. (It should be noted that Anton LaVey had nothing to do with the Manson Family.) In 1967, Beausoleil, a musician scoring *My Demon Brother*, reportedly stole the negatives and prints from Anger. For a time that material—once recovered by Anger—was hidden in the Berkeley, California, home of legendary gay author Sam Steward who in the 1930s had been an intimate of Gertrude Stein and Alice B. Toklas. Steward in the 1950s and 1960s, working as the tattoo artist Phil Sparrow, tattooed many of the Hells Angels, including founder Sonny Barger. For his part, Bobby Beausoleil has always denied stealing *My Demon Brother*.[11]

Yet beyond such personal vision and sexual obsession, nothing so possesses an artist as his culture. The archetypal films of Carl Dreyer (the witchcraft trials of *Day of Wrath*, 1943) and Tod Browning (*Freaks*, 1932) dramatize how the popular Christian culture of Northern Europe was in conflict with sorcery, witchcraft, and physical deformity. Carl Dreyer's masterpiece *The Passion of Joan of Arc* (1928) dramatized the last day of the "people's saint" Joan, using actual transcripts from her trial, as well as intensifying extreme close-ups, to tell a serious tale of one transgressive woman's murder for her visions. Films of occult horror had an honorable tradition long before Hollywood movies sank to the Satanic drug-ritual B movies spawned by the Manson Family's Tate murders: *Ritual of Evil* (1969); the drug-infested *Beyond the Valley of the Dolls* (1970), written by movie critic Roger Ebert; and *Mephisto Waltz* (1971).

The popular Swedish director Ingmar Bergman built his career pitting good against evil. His classic *Seventh Seal* (1956) questioned the values of a malpracticed Christianity. Bergman's protagonist, the knight Antonius

Block (Max von Sydow), sees religion and society collapsing. A witch (Maude Hansson), a woman outside the pale of church and state, is burned out of Christian righteousness, but not before Block interrogates her. Questioned, she does what witchcraft has always done by adhering to its "anti" values in the face of persecutions by Christians who prove that Nero may have been right about them after all.

As a witch, Maude Hansson mounts the basic attack of witchery: she deflates both Christian dogmatics and Western rationalism, calling them both relative, not absolute answers to human experience. In *The Magician* (1958) Bergman continued the struggle between Christian rules and occult freedom. His 1959 *The Virgin Spring*, which won the 1960 Academy Award for best foreign film, used high-contrast black-and-white film to suggest in the medieval world the polarity that continues into the modern: the battle between Christianity and paganism. Witchery is Bergman's constant metaphor for freedom "puncturing" punishing institutionalized dogma.

Certainly the earliest filmic study of witchcraft is Benjamin Christensen's *Haxan: Witchcraft through the Ages* (1922). This Swedish semidocumentary is full of informational data for students of film.[12] *Haxan* was revived in the 1970s at Greenwich Village's famous Waverly Theater, where between features the Muzak trilled "The Theme from *Rosemary's Baby*." *Haxan* reconfirmed the perfect match made in hell between film and the occult. Janus Films scored the new edition of the silent *Haxan* with a jazz soundtrack mixed with the voice-over of William S. Burroughs reading Christensen's original silent titles.

Except for one Lon Chaney film, director Christensen slipped below the Hollywood radar after this erotic documentary of demonic witchcraft. Because his footage was shot before the invention of safety film in 1930, most of his nitrate prints crumbled to dust. When Janus Films restored this basic cult film, Christensen achieved a permanent place in the expanding universe of occult filmography. Christensen, who played his own Devil in *Haxan*, led a secret Hollywood life nearly as interesting as Christopher Bram revealed James Whale's to be in *Father of Frankenstein*. Bram's gay-themed book became director Bill Condon's *Gods and Monsters* (1998), which won an Academy Award for best screenplay.

Haxan opens with Burroughs intoning an exorcism. (Burroughs often stated that "magic is a gateway to art"; he also revealed that homosexual acts could be performed for magical purposes.) Burroughs reads, "Lock them out and bar the door. Lock them out forever more. Curse go back. Curse go back. Bent with double pain and lack. Silver arrow seek and find."

The ancient witchery of Persian and Egyptian art provides images for *Haxan*'s prologue. German woodcuts and engravings from the Middle Ages to the Renaissance show the growth of the occult in the popular mind. In his first episode, Christensen dramatizes age-old popular stereotypes: crones drop decaying corpse fingers, hopping toads, and snakes into a cauldron. Typically anticlerical and with a studied vengeance, *Haxan* suggests a recipe of "pigeon heart and cat shit" to seduce a corpulent monk. The witches peddling the potions are portrayed as shrewd business people selling the real thing and always getting top dollar.

In the film's most chilling episode, "The Annihilation by Inquisition of the Entire Family of Jasper Le Riem," Christensen sensationalizes the sex and sadism of a repressive Christianity on its circumstantially trapped victims. Long passages dwell on the salacious torture of helpless women. Christensen illustrates their confessions of Satanic commerce with enough eroticism, nudity, and horror to explain the early twentieth-century censorship of the film: naked women are smeared with oil to fly to sabbaths; crosses are trampled by cackling housewives who eat toads and unbaptized babies; women kneel to kiss Satan's hairy buttocks, then run to a neighbor's doorstep to squat and make water for a curse; finally, a kind of pre-Rosemary gives explicit dramatic birth to a Satanic baby. A young friar, sympathetic to a beautiful witch, is scourged by his superior. When the prior ceases whipping the naked young man, the young friar cries in masochistic ecstasy, "Oh brother, why have you stopped?"

The narration in *Haxan* sometimes rises to the screech of Maria Monk, who in 1836 wrote the best-selling and bogus confessional book *The Awful Disclosures of Maria Monk, as Exhibited in a Narrative of Her Sufferings during a Residence of Five Years as a Novice and Two Years as a Black Nun, in the Hotel Dieu Nunnery in Montreal.* Monk, escaping the convent to save her baby, told a tale of convents rife with witchcraft rituals, tunnels, and mass graves for babies born of nuns' liaisons with priests. Christensen, for all his over-the-top tabloidism, knows how to make an appealing pop-culture film. Yet in his artfulness, he seems not too far from Spanish filmmaker Luis Buñuel; or from British director Ken Russell's study of convent and cloister, *The Devils* (1971), based on Aldous Huxley's *The Devils of Loudun;* or from Alejandro Jodorowski, who in his 1971 film *El Topo* raised the whipping of one monk to four naked young monks, as he enlarged the theme of magic.

Haxan says, "Convents in the Middle Ages were hotbeds of flagellation and mortification. Raving mystical lunacy led to sacrilege and erotic behavior." What the superb Stanley Donen film *Bedazzled* (1967) does to the Devil and convents through comedy, *Haxan* does through vivid melodrama: a nun stabs a consecrated host and sticks out her tongue (the wagging sign of Satan, and the trademark symbol of the Rolling Stones) at her Superior; she steals a statue of the infant Jesus and carries it to the inquisitors of the previous episode. "Take me," she screams orgasmically. "Burn me!"

In Russell's *The Devils*, Vanessa Redgrave updated this Satanic *Haxan* nun in her bravura and archetypal performance as the hunch-backed freak Soir Jeanne, a Mother Superior possessed by black magic, and adept in desecrating religious iconography by masturbating with a crucifix. Opposite this Soir Jeanne, Redgrave also starred as the trance-breaking Guenevere in the musical film *Camelot* (1967), based on the white magic of Merlin versus the black magic of Morgan La Faye in the legendary *Le Morte D'Arthur*. A performer who makes outsider choices in art and politics, Redgrave has twice channeled mystic San Francisco dancer Isadora Duncan, in the film *Loves of Isadora* (1968) and on stage in *When She Danced* (1991). She played the matriarch of the empathic family of seers in the film version of the Isabel Allende novel *House of the Spirits* (1993), and has also narrated Peter Maxwell Davies' *Parody Mass, Missa Super L'Homme Arme,* for the art-music group, the Fires of London (1971). Peter Maxwell Davies also wrote incidental music for the film score of *The Devils*. Covering the Salem witch trials, she starred in the film *Three Sovereigns for Sarah* (1985), based on actual transcripts of the trials, and her son-in-law Liam Neeson headlined on Broadway in a 2002 revival of Arthur Miller's *The Crucible*. She continued her esthetic connection to the occult in *The Riding of the Laddie* (2003), the sequel to the horror classic *The Wicker Man* (1974),[13] which was the first appearance on screen of the image of the Burning Man.

At the end of *Haxan*, in a final coda of "redeeming social significance," Christensen waxes moral after all his sensational reportage. His documentary finale explains that women no longer fly to sabbaths on brooms; now they use airplanes. He says, "In 1920 we don't burn old, poor, and hysterical women; we put them in institutions; and if they're rich enough, in clinics where the therapeutic shower has replaced the torture chamber." Christensen's point in naming witch hunting itself as a modern pathology is a significant statement that helps right the long historical oppression of women.

Thirty years after Christensen's definitive work, Director Erik Blomberg's *White Reindeer* (1956) won the Cannes Festival Award for best film based on a mystical legend. Blomberg, like Bergman in *The Virgin Spring*, dipped into medieval folklore to re-create a world of mysticism and witchcraft. Through ancient Finnish folk tales Blomberg noticed a recurring white reindeer. The bewitched animal was a transformed woman who appeared during certain phases of the moon to kill.

> In the northernmost reaches of Lap Land,
> Where the snow and sky seem one . . .
> There's a mythical world of white shadows
> Called the Land of the Midnight Sun.
>
> It is whispered by natives who dwell there,
> Over campfires in voices low,
> That a long time ago to their valley
> Came a stranger who braved the snow.
>
> 'Twas a woman whose pains were of labor,
> And the needs of the birth were filled.
> For at midnight a girl-babe was wailing,
> And the breath of her mother stilled.
>
> But the spell that was cast on that midnight
> Was to live after, one by one . . .
> And each child of that child was afflicted
> With the Curse of the Midnight Sun.

In popular pagan as well as in Judeo-Christian folktales, woman is the constant evil. Neither tradition has forgiven Eden's Eve, who ate humankind out of house and home, nor forgotten that birth itself seems to males a rudimentary rejection by the mother.

Within months of founding his Church of Satan in 1966, Anton LaVey, according to popular legend, cursed the late film star Jayne Mansfield for consorting with companions whom LaVey judged not a worthy match to her role as "female altar" for his Church of Satan. In fact, LaVey explained that he simply warned Mansfield that her lover, lawyer Sam Brody, would come to a bad end, and if she wanted to avoid his fate, she should stay away from him. "It was a very magnificent curse," LaVey said. Not long after, on June 29, 1967, at 2:15 a. m. on a slick curve of U.S. 90, gliding along a foggy swamp twenty-three miles outside New Orleans, Jayne Mansfield's Buick Electra smashed into the rear of a slow-moving tractor-trailer truck, and plowed on in under the big rig.

"The impact," United Press International reported on June 30, 1967, "sheared off the top of the luxury car and shoved it back so that it appeared to be a convertible." Both the chauffeur and Sam Brody were killed. "Miss Mansfield," UPI said, "was decaptitated."

The *femme* was very *fatale*. In the back seat, her three children, fathered by her second husband, Mr. America bodybuilder Mickey Hargitay (from whom she was divorced), survived with minor injuries. In his book *Hollywood Babylon*, Kenneth Anger printed a controversial photograph of Jayne Mansfield's dead dog lying outside the crushed Buick, next to what looks like a blond wig (or a scalp) on the ground. Mansfield's daughter, Mariska Hargitay, age three the night she was in the accident, grew up to be the dark-haired star of the television series *Law and Order*.

Whatever their relationship, the LaVey-Mansfield connection recalls popular notions in films that reduce complicated female psychology to Satanism. Joseph von Sternberg directed Marlene Dietrich in the film *The Devil Is a Woman* (1935), which was scripted—and titled—by esteemed novelist John Dos Passos. (Dos Passos, in his *USA Trilogy*, was the first American novelist to construct fiction that used the movielike material of popular culture—a montage of newspaper headlines, radio broadcasts, and reading cards from silent news reels winding through his narrative—to tell his story.) Von Sternberg's film inspired Luis Buñuel's surreal *That Obscure Object of Desire* (1977), in which two actresses play the same part. Dietrich's conniving gold digger, whose charms destroy men, was a model for Catherine Deneuve, who played a killer of men in Roman Polanski's *Repulsion* (1965).

From Lilith to Eve to Delilah to Lulu to Lola, storytellers from the Bible to the movies cast women as seductive destroyers of men and marriage. For shock value, Mel Gibson cast a woman to portray Satan cuddling a forty-year-old baby during the flogging scene in *The Passion of the Christ*. Women as earth mothers and healing witches come from nature itself. Women as evil witches, vamps, and vampires come, Edward Lucie-Smith assesses in *Eroticism in Western Art*, from "the basic male fear . . . of castration, specifically by the castrating female. . . . The male fear of female aggression is matched, even overmatched . . . by sadistic impulses toward women."[14] In the battle of the sexes, the Inquisition was a skirmish in the age-old gender war in which each side thinks the other the enemy. The archetypal struggle is penis versus vagina and vice versa.

Pop culture's update of the Inquisition is that modern women have taken the *vagina dentata* (the vagina with teeth) and spun the femme fatale from liability to asset. Women were once burned at the stake for being vamps, vampires, and witches. In modern media, vamps star in movies. Vampires have their own television series. Vaginas sing in movies like *Chatterbox*, and star in theatrical productions like *The Vagina Monologues*. Ball-busters get elected to public office. If the Devil is not a woman, the thoroughly modern Ms. Faust seems to know how to make an empowering pact with the Devil. What is true is that the disquieting image of woman as toothsome destroyer demands a demystification if only to put to rest the bewitched, bothered, and bewildered anxieties about women that the hurtful mystique has caused in religion, art, politics, and culture.

The images to deconstruct are endless. In movies and on stage, when the male magician closes a woman into a wooden box and saws her in half, they are ritualizing one of the principle tortures of the Inquisition. The saw, as much as the axe, was used to kill pregnant women and homosexuals who—unlike the smiling woman in the magic show—did not rise up unharmed to thrilled applause. Kim Stanley, in *Seance on a Wet Afternoon* (1964), starred as a dead child's mother, who, posing as a medium, decreed the death of a young girl to give her dead son a playmate in the afterlife. *The Witch* (1955) from Finland, and *The Sorceress* (1956) from France reinforce the 1960s summary movie title *Deadlier than the Male*. In *The Witch*, from Mika Waltari's stage play, the plot is B-movie classic: over the protests of villagers, an archeologist removes a stake from the heart of a three-hundred-year-old corpse; in hours, the corpse rejuvenates into a seductive young girl who casts spells on the village males, and everybody screws and kills everybody else; of course, it's her fault, so the villagers redrive the stake through her vamp heart. Is this archetype or stereotype?

The Sorceress, filmed on location in northern Sweden, shape-shifts the vicious crone into a seductress. This focus on the female as sexual destroyer came even clearer in *Les Sorcieres de Salem* (1957), a French screenplay by Jean-Paul Sartre based on Arthur Miller's *The Crucible*. Sartre spelled out the ideosexual perspective of Miller's witch play more completely, said the *New York Times*, than did Miller himself, who was actually paraphrasing 1950s McCarthyism as a political witch hunt.

Even holy ladies aren't the simple sacred prostitutes they used to be. Luis Buñuel's "Krafft-Ebing" convent in *The Milky Way* (1970) was preceded by Jerze Kawalerowicz's *Joan of the Angels?* (1961). Based on the seventeenth-century trial of Pere Grandier, *Joan*'s source—like Ken Russell's *The Devils*—is the same as Aldous Huxley's *The Devils of Loudun*. The plot is conventional convent coven: the Mother Superior of a convent of Ursuline nuns is possessed by eight demons; the other nuns follow her example, contracting themselves with minor demons; men die by the dozens as a result of these ladies' commerce.

No wonder monsters like *The Fly* (1958), *Konga* (1961), and *Reptilicus* (1962) think they "get the girl." Like seeks like. Folklore has long inferred the theory of "La Pucelle": that Joan of Arc and Robin's Maid Marian, and all the other mystical and magical women who traveled with men, were in fact altars of male covens. Robin Hood himself, woven through myth, is actually a merry prankster version of Satan. When guest-actor Anton LaVey explained his motivation as the Satanic Beast mounting Rosemary in *Rosemary's Baby*, he respun the Christian archetype of the Good Soul coupling in mystical union with Jesus. Prior to Polanski's frankness, personified "white middle-class female goodness" was continually being carried across sound stages by various "black masses" in *Curucu, Beast of the Amazon* (1956) or *Dinosaurus!* (1960). David O. Selznick's bestiality epic *King Kong* (1933) mined the deep psychological vein of race, phallic size, and blonde stereotype. King Kong, the protagonist, was the ultimate African symbol of sexual possession, who, although sympathetic, must die.

In the sex-guilt ethic, the attempt to lay blame for erotic feeling outside the self is as old as Adam accusing Eve. The running joke on the *Flip Wilson Show* (NBC, 1970–71) had the comedian repeatedly decked in drag, exclaiming in a pinched falsetto non sequitur, "The Devil made me buy this dress!" That, during the Watergate Scandal, became the national catchphrase joke for any wrongdoer who got caught: "The Devil made me do it." With similar disingenuous disavowal of personal culpability, the Middle Ages invented the female succubus to explain males' nocturnal emissions, and the male incubus to allay feminine guilt at erotic dreams. The secret tradition of the Western world has long regarded the frolic of intercourse as a horizontal Devil dance: good women merely submit to a necessary evil, and all men are beasts. In 1969, *Succubus*, a grind sexploitation flick, introduced to pop culture the forgotten medieval word of its title more on the strength of its sound than its meaning.

Psychologist Carl Jung often compared his theories of individual and collective memory to the movie medium. Film illustrated his archetypes because the camera is the machine most like the subconscious. Just so, filmmakers, like advertisers and witches, turn to psychology to package their product for maximum bounce.

In 1958, the producers of *My World Dies Screaming* used subliminal perception based on human physiology to increase the shock value of their film.[15] To augment the horror, they interedited throughout the length of the movie the word *blood* so that it appeared on screen for only one-fiftieth of a second. The eye is accustomed to perceive whole motion at twenty-four sound frames per second on 16 millimeter film. Thus the queasy *blood* imposed over star Cathy O'Donnell's face could be perceived only sub-liminally, inducing a deeper, more unconscionable horror. Because terror in any audience's head is an immeasurable variable, another experimenter interedited the 1955 William Inge film *Picnic,* a romantic comedy, not with *blood* but with *Drink Coca-Cola* and *Hungry? Eat Popcorn* at 1/3000 of a second every five seconds. Confection sales, unlike terror, are measurable. With subliminal suggestion, Coke sales at the Fort Lee, New Jersey, the-ater rose 57.7 percent, and popcorn sales 18.1 percent. Producer Hal Roach Jr., planned similar occult subliminals for his film version of Henry James's *Turn of the Screw,* titled *The Innocents.* The presence of his ghosts was to be projected below the threshold of the viewer's conscious perception, much like William Castle's *13 Ghosts* (1960), for which movie-goers were given optional "ghost-viewing" glasses.

The occult has always been sensitive to human psychology. Spiritualists thrive on subliminal access to consciousness. Technology helps mediums and mind-reading mentalists update their settings from smoke and mir-rors to soft subliminals created by film projectors, video, and audio run during the soft psychedelia of sittings. Catholic ritual, in particular, is so dripping with subliminal seduction of the psyche that other religions stand aghast. Reductive Protestantism removed art from its churches; Judaism forbids icons; and both sects have accused Roman Catholicism, which is the most magical of modern religions, of witchcraft. Even Walt Disney makes fun of the magic inherent in arcane Church Latin. His magician in *Cinderella* (1950), singing "Salagadoola mechika boola . . . It'll do magic, believe it or not," parodies the Gregorian chant of Roman Catholic plain-song in the singsong of "Bibbidi Bobbidi Boo." This is jokey satire in the same way that "hocus-pocus" mocks "Hoc est enim corpus meum," the essential line of transubstantiation in the Catholic mass.

These experiments illustrate how easily psychologist, artist, witch, and priest can plunder the human subconscious. The business secret of gen-uine as well as phony occultists is tweaking the hidden fears of their clients. Similarly, the horror film business projects on screen the repressed and subconscious anxieties deep within the viewer's self.

The screen monster most terrifying to an audience is, in the final analy-sis, the well-brought-out beast in itself.

The Lord of the Flies was built dramatically on the premise of Satan worship. The last reel reveals the source of evil was not the pig head Beelzebub (*Beelzebub* translates to "Lord of the Flies"), but was rather the evil in the boys' own selves. Again comes the unavoidable theme, and the horror-inducing existential twist, that the Devil rises from inside humans. Metro-Goldwyn-Mayer's little classic *Forbidden Planet* (1957), a camp retelling of William Shakespeare's *The Tempest*, offered the ultimate horror to the Freudian mindscape: the amok monster, unbridled of superego, turned out to be the id of one of the space travelers. Sold to television, *Forbidden Planet* is sometimes titled *Id: The Creature from the Unknown*, a label that divulges the entire plot.

If any film externalizes the horror of the self acknowledging its own secret mutations, it is Tod Browning's long neglected *Freaks* (1932). Based on the novel *Spurs* by Tod Robbins, *Freaks* is unique in film history. European critics have praised it for the same reasons American distributors have kept it at the bottom half of double bills in grind houses "where your feet stick to the floor and rats run across your shoes." The 1962 Cannes Film Festival Repertory balanced matters somewhat by selecting the thirty-year-old *Freaks* to represent the essential horror film. By the 1970s, the Browning revival of *Freaks* was in full swing.

Mexican director Alejandro Jodorowsky, while he was casting his mystical cult epic *El Topo*, stated that he was emboldened by *Freaks* as much as he was by *Viva la Muerte*, the 1970 film by Fernando Arrabal that began the "panic movement" in cinema that coincided with the first generation of Satanic panic films, *Rosemary's Baby* (1968) and *The Exorcist* (1973). In New York, Lincoln Center's spring 1970 film festival featured Browning's *The Unknown* (1927) with Lon Chaney Sr. and Joan Crawford. By the end of 1970, Browning's *Freaks* was commercially rereleased with Victor Halperin's *White Zombie* (1932). Because Southern Baptists were the first onward-marching soldiers opposing rock-and-roll, rock groups inevitably reacted by hailing religion's foes, Satanism and the occult. They chose for themselves from cult horror movies rebellious band names like Black Sabbath and White Zombie, the latter with its album *Sexorcisto: Devil Music Volume One*.

The difference between *Freaks* (art *changes* its audience) and 1957's *I Was a Teen-age Werewolf* (entertainment *diddles* its audience) is one of essence and surface. The essential horror film goes, like a vampire, for the jugular of the subconscious soul. The superficial fright movie cleverly exploits shock so that kids on a movie date have excuse to grab hold of each other.

The art of horror films is, well, almost seamlessly existential: the terror con-jured (often by being offscreen) is real because it references the endgames of the human condition, like the fact that everyone in the theater will die, horribly slowly, or worse, horribly suddenly, killed before their time. The drive-in fright feature, from advertising to projection, is constructed with its scares onscreen like a ride through a haunted house: no one takes it seri-ously, and, like a magician's act, it easily falls into comedy and camp because the monster/villain/killer—for instance, King Kong—often becomes the hero the audience identifies with and cheers for. Because of the sexual rev-olution, horror movies have mated with soft-core porn and have changed the plot from the creation of monsters who eat cities to the trope of the "young woman in sexual peril trapped in her house." The master producer of horror films, Roger Corman, has revealed some of the secret erotic psy-chology of horror: "In a movie, a house is always a woman's body."

Browning's *Freaks* is the essence of Sartrean existential horror, because everyone in the audience secretly fears their own inner freak, which they hope no one else will notice. Browning, his career shaped by controversial film pioneer D. W. Griffith, earned his aesthetic reputation as "the Edgar Allan Poe of the cinema." His canon includes *The Unholy Three* (1925), *Mark of the Vampire* (1935), and *The Devil Doll* (1936). Never fashionable as camp, and certainly not exploitative, Browning, like Poe and Sartre, took everyday appearances and dealt with the realities that lay beneath. Brown-ing began in the genuine folk world of circus and vaudeville, but matured up and out of the jolly theatrics of the sideshow in the same trajectory that Anton LaVey, on his way to founding the Church of Satan, was a lion tamer in the circus. LaVey, with his exquisite sense of pop culture, gath-ered funds to found his church by appearing on San Francisco's North Beach strip of adult clubs with an act he produced and billed as "Anton LaVey and His Topless Witches Sabbath"—which was as far from serious as Krafft-Ebing is from Kander and Ebb.

Many occultists claim that psychiatrists spend much time curing patients by talking them out of belief in their very real paranatural experiences. Occultists nevertheless fully appreciate artful films like *Rosemary's Baby* and *Freaks*, because they know that the artist, more than anyone else, can popularize paranormal experience. *Rosemary's Baby* did for the witchcraft industry what *Hair* did for astrology. Similarly, *Freaks* changed attitudes.

Apropos *Freaks*, Saint Thomas Aquinas (1225–74) wrote in his Catholic theology texts that "grace builds on nature. The more perfect the body, the more grace is bestowed by God." This very high-school pecking-order notion flips to a Platonic fascism: the less perfect the body, the less the access to grace. Point man Aquinas wrote *Summa Theologica* (written 1265–74), in which he modernized Catholic doctrine by appropriating Aristotle the way that Catholic ritual appropriated white magic. Aquinas, the greatest mind the Catholic Church ever produced—and then did not kill—also wrote *Summa contra Gentiles*, a work directed against Islamic philosophy infiltrating European culture. Aquinas's principle of a healthy soul in a healthy body seems, by comparison, less cruel than born-again Protestants selecting themselves as perfect and saved simply because they themselves say so. Witches, of course, celebrate everybody else—the sick, the deformed, the weird, the queer, the dark skinned, the outsiders—which accounts for witchcraft's strong appeal among teens alienated in high schools; among the young who are estranged from mainstream American politics, religion, and culture; and among homosexual noncitizens in a heterosexual culture in which penetration, breeding, and conception are the basic ritual of human measure.

Out of this body fascism, wherein only the beautiful people of the platonic ideal are full of grace, the Middle Ages condemned congenital deformity. Imperfection was a sign that the person was conceived from Satan's bad seed, which caused the deformity. Looking at this "body fascism" through a glass darkly, witches spin the right-wing Thomas Aquinas leftward. Witches teach that physical abnormality is a natural asset to occult powers. For reasons of dwarfs, bearded ladies, and strong-men contortionists, *Freaks* has become a coven classic on campuses. For the same reasons, audiences squirm when watching the movie *The Bad Seed* (1956), about a very mechanically nice little girl who, disguised in blonde pigtails twisted too tight, is the Devil's spawn.

In his *Satanic Bible*, Anton LaVey, who appreciated blonde Hollywood beauties like Marilyn Monroe and Tuesday Weld, wrote that looks mean a great deal where magic is concerned. A striking appearance, from the beautiful to the offbeat, is a great aid to bewitchment if a person knows how to enhance for enchantment. In his "Letters from the Devil" column in *The National Insider*, LaVey once stated, "If your ears are pointed, you are wise in taking pride in them, rather than feeling embarrassment, as that in itself is a very magical attitude. Whatever you do, don't attempt to cover or conceal them. In fact you might even consider shaving your head to emphasize them!"

This "physical language of magic," particularly the "language of eyes," speaks in oral storytelling and written fiction. Characters are often described as "having a cast in their eye" inferring they possess if not the evil eye, at least an outsider's vision. Serial author Charles Dickens used this short-hand phrase, which his mass audience immediately recognized as meaningful. In *Pickwick Papers* Dickens characterizes the essence of his elfin Nathaniel Pipkin as ". . . a homeless . . . being, with a turned-up nose . . . rather turned-in legs, a cast in his eye, and a halt in his gait." In his ghost story, *The Haunted House,* Dickens summed up the minister in one stroke: "The officiating minister had a cast in his eye." Other popular writers citing the "cast in the eye" as a character-revealing physicality wherein the external body part referred to exposes the interior person are George Eliot in *Silas Marner* (1861), Mark Twain in *Saint Joan of Arc* (1904), and Enid Bagnold in *The Happy Foreigner* (1920). Popular woman's writer Bagnold (1889–1981) was a morphine visionary and the author of the novel *National Velvet* (1935), which as a 1944 movie made Elizabeth Taylor, with her unique violet eyes, a child star.

Roddy McDowell was the longtime friend of Elizabeth Taylor and star of *How Green Was My Valley* (1941), *Lord Love a Duck* (1966), in which he played the Devil, and *Planet of the Apes* (1968). He was at first rejected as a child actor because, according to casting agents, he had a cast in his eye, which was homophobic code that Roddy—who also became famous as a photographer—used his eyes the way gay men roll their eyes to signify secret knowledge, condescension, and irony. People are quite ready to believe that any anomaly undoing the balance of two eyes is evidence of the evil eye. In every world culture, anthropologists have measured faces and have found universally that the more balanced the facial features the more beautiful or handsome that face is considered in every family, tribe, society, and race.

The official distributor's press release for Tod Browning's *Freaks* reads,

Prior to World War II nearly every carnival and circus had its collection of human monsters or freaks—persons deformed in birth or horribly maimed—who were proudly exhibited to the public for a price. Browning assembled the most famous of these performers from all parts of the world and employed them in a story of intrigue in the circus. In its plot, a beautiful "normal" aerialist (Olga Baclanova) learns one of the midgets (Harry Earles) has inherited a fortune. She contrives to marry him, planning to kill him. In one of the many memorable scenes, almost surrealistic in quality, the midget's fellow performers, unaware of the aerialist's intentions, organize a wedding celebration wherein they offer a macabre toast and honorary position to her

with an orgiastic chant of "We accept you . . . we accept you . . . gooble gob-
ble . . . one of us." Later, both the midget and his friends discover the poisoning attempt and, in hair-raising climax, the freaks set upon the aerialist
and maim her.

The maiming scene in the *Freaks* epilogue, where the freaks turn the
"normal" woman into a freak, has been called the most horrible scene in
film history.

Freakiness, as the happy hippie freaks and Jesus freaks demonstrated,
may be relative, and every minority group takes pride in its essential difference from the norm: black pride, gay pride. Anton LaVey teaches, "Everything is attitude." *Freaks* in 1932 paved the way for Hollywood in 1939 to
film an analog of *Freaks, The Wizard of Oz.* In Frank Baum's story of white
witches, wicked witches, and wizards, the magical Munchkin "freaks" accept
the perfect outsider Dorothy (Judy Garland), but they do not maim her.
From *Freaks* to *Oz* is a major jump in pop culture—from the genre of *horror* to the genre of *musical comedy.* What a double feature at the midnight
picture show! When Judy Garland accepted the leprechaun Munchkins,
she could hardly have known that life would imitate art. Her identification with the outsiders was magnetic. For the rest of her career, Judy Garland's core audience was homosexual men who understood the code of
the suffering warble in her nevertheless invincible voice. What witchery
lies in the timing that five days after Judy Garland died on June 22, 1969,
New York City's Stonewall Riots, started by shape-shifting drag-queen
freaks, broke out near midnight on June 27–28, 1969, beginning the gay
liberation movement?

CUT TO

TV

Significantly, *The Wizard of Oz* has become an annual classic on television, where sorcery reigns. So rich is *The Wizard of Oz* that pop-culture
lore insists that the rock band Pink Floyd's concept album *Dark Side of
the Moon* (1973), if started the moment the MGM lion roars the third time,
creates an eerie alternative soundtrack that reveals mystic secrets buried
in the film. Nielson ratings chart the immense popularity of occult programs: the domestic comedy of *Bewitched, I Dream of Jeannie, The Flying
Nun, My Favorite Martian, Topper, The Ghost and Mrs Muir,* and *The
Nanny and the Professor*; the Saturday morning *Archie* cartoon show with

its character, Sabrina, the teenage witch; the gothic stylizations of *The Addams Family*, *The Munsters*, and the actress Vampira; the playful animism of *My Mother, the Car*, and the "lycanthropy" of the talking horse *Mr. Ed*; and the supernatural turns of *One Step Beyond* and *The Twilight Zone*.

I Dream of Jeannie is pop-culture product from ancient Islamic demonology that came to Europe and then America *via* medieval Spain. The grimoire spell books of the time teach how a master can conjure and control the little service-demon called a *jinn* (a *genie*.) In Chicago, the Pontifex Maximus of the Sabaeans, the pagan white witch Frederic de Arechaga, pointed out that Ray Bolger's classic scarecrow in *The Wizard of Oz* is more occult than parents might first believe. The scarecrow in the Old Religion of pre-Christian times was stuffed with straw as a symbol of fertility. "In a sense, it still is, because it is placed in a field to scare off birds and keep them from eating the crops. In this way," Arechaga noted, "it remains a symbol to preserve growth."[16]

The Wizard of Oz fixed the popular stereotype of the good witch and the bad witch. Billie Burke is barely remembered as the good witch Glynda; but no one forgets Margaret Hamilton as the wicked witch of the west. Happy to be recognized as an actress, Miss Hamilton wished she were not remembered only for her iconic role in *The Wizard of Oz*. "It was a lovely picture," she once said, "but I was injured, you know. Not only did I become typed. I broke my ankle. All my disappearances in that cloud of smoke happened because I was dropped through a trap door—pointed hat, broom and all." If Margaret Hamilton could have trademarked her image, Hallmark cards, Disney Studios, and other crone caricaturists could have made her a rich woman.

More overt than the subtle *Wizard of Oz*, the NBC occult soap opera *Dark Shadows* operated five days a week, fifty-two weeks a year, for a total of 1,225 episodes (1966–71). Partly a computer creation, *Dark Shadows* mixed staple soap-opera sudser with popular witchcraft. ABC's evening soap opera, *Peyton Place* (1964–69), introduced to prime time Mia Farrow (who became Satan's mother in *Rosemary's Baby*), as well as the soap cadences of the afternoon: intrafamily tension followed by prolonged critical illness leading to accidental or homicidal death followed by prolonged courtroom drama causing rearrangement of identities, spouses, and heirs to build new intrafamily tensions, illnesses, suicides, murders, and trials. *Dark Shadows* used these staples, but the plot was bounced off the wall of the supernatural.

With existences in "parallel time," no one need stay permanently dead and the villain need not be human. *Shadow*'s lovable vampire Barnabas Collins, in fact, became so popular that Barnabas-actor Jonathan Frid guested at the 1969 White House Halloween party hosted by Tricia Nixon-Cox, who transformed the north portico of the White House into a giant jack-o-lantern guarded by a cauldron and two witches. Inside the Great Ballroom, the Devil played a trumpet and the ghouls danced the night away. This historical fact shows the levity regarding witchcraft that existed in American pop culture prior to hysterical press coverage of the Manson Family. Times have so changed that one can only imagine the horror this Nixonian nonseparation of Satan and state must cause the born-again right wing that has since so demonized Halloween.

Vampire Frid once explained the success of *Dark Shadows*: "Fascination with evil is the whole thing. College kids and matrons are the main ones. People want to meet me for weeks and then they run in utter horror. I haven't studied the occult, but the fascination and repulsion attraction is, I think, rather obvious." Frid, during the interview, gladly and easily slipped in his vampire denture. "A show is a success in this business when it's imitated. ABC copied us with *Strange Paradise* for a while. We on *Dark Shadows* have used every classic horror theme. We're the worst plagiarists going. We've stolen Mary Shelley and Henry James. In fact, I base the whole thing on *Macbeth*. Personally, my interest comes from the old Universal Studios' horror pictures. It's hard to top Maria Ouspenskaya's unforgettable line, 'You bent up the pentagram, young man.' I think the writing and special effects on *Shadows* are about the best in the image business."

Johnny Carson, on NBC's *Tonight Show*, repeatedly featured the mystic shtick of his "Carnak the Magnificent." Carnak, channeled out of vaudeville, was a cartoony Persian guru who held sealed envelopes to his oversized turban, pronounced the answer ("Zazu Pitts"), then opened the envelope to reveal the question ("What do you find in Zazu prunes?"). To the moaning audience Carnak cursed, "May the fairy-god-camel leave a hump under your pillow." Nevertheless, despite the spoofing, Carson often showcased the serious occult (Jeane Dixon) and questioned his more pop-culture guests about their own occult practices. NBC, with an eye to policy, vetoed Carson's wish to feature a séance on his show Halloween night, 1969, two months after the Manson Family murders.

NBC quickly corrected its hypersensitivity and followed its audience's taste for the occult during its last hour of prime-time telecasting in 1969. On that New Year's Eve, the weekly series, *Then Came Bronson*, based on occult imagery, closed the 1960s with Thomas Drake's teleplay, *Sybil.* The Bronson character was played by gay favorite Michael Parks, who had been a peek-a-boo Adam when he and his penis starred in John Huston's epic film *The Bible* (1966). Bronson was not Brando in *The Wild One*: Parks played Bronson as a sensitive motorcyclist loner who magically solved people's problems each episode. In the opening credits, he was identified as the tarot deck's Knight of Cups, announced his sign as Taurus, and painted the All-Seeing Eye in a triangle on his cycle tank. The *Sybil* episode featured "supernatural" cinematography as old as silent film: distortion angles and shots through candle flames; standard "supernatural" dialogue: "Demons we summon you!" "Make a choice, Sybil, the living or the dead!"

NBC cashed in on the occult to capture the Nielsen families, yet the network soothed its sponsors. Bronson's final sermon protested a bit too much: "I believe very much in the spirit. I believe it continues, but I don't believe it's connected to magic, or conjuring, or prediction. I believe a spirit breathes in man. An undiscovered country causes man to run there to cure his ills, to avoid the problems in the one he's part of. I believe you're surrendering *your* responsibility for *your* reactions."

CUT TO

Consumers and Advertising

The media of popular culture exist to capture consumers' dollars. In the dark night of the soul on late-night radio, offbeat stations broadcast occult programs at midnight the same way that talk-radio stations broadcast religious programming in the afternoon. No different than radio preachers selling Protestant books between their gab, the seductive female radio host who bills herself as "Big Witch" broadcasts regularly to peddle her "How to Form a Coven" pamphlet, mailed from her post office box. Even "America's past-time," baseball, telecast from among its billboards and endorsements, has—among all its superstitions of spitting and lucky charms—Pennsylvania Dutch hex signs hanging on the Philadelphia Phillies dugout in Connie Mack Stadium. The combination of baseball and Satanism played for sexy laughs in *Damn Yankees* was immediately understood by fans of this most superstitious sport: never stepping on the white lines, not wearing the number thirteen, and sometimes showering in uniform to wash out the gremlins. The occult is a multimillion-dollar-a-year business. It not only sells itself; it pushes, through media advertising, everything from Ben Gay to Hunt's Manwich Sandwich.

How can witchery prevent exploitation in the merchandising of popular culture? It can't. The marketplace rules. Witchcraft is accustomed to appropriation, particularly by procrustean corporate advertising, which co-opts everything. In the 1960s, when environmentalists suddenly rose up after reading Rachel Carson's *Silent Spring* (1962), Madison Avenue jumped to spin the semantics. Ecologists had claimed many products glorified by Madison Avenue were pollutants. The surprised agencies immediately began co-opting the ecologists' very words to pitch that their products "pollute *less* than our competitors' products."

In a similar fashion, student revolutionaries marching on Washington in the summer of 1970 were called "bums" by the Republican administration. Spinning the Richard Nixon–Spiro Agnew semantics, the students carried prideful signs: "We're all bums on strike for peace." They took their cue from 1960s hippies who had also reversed the semantics of the slur *freak* and turned it to optimistic synonym for *enthusiast* (as in "acid freak," "rock freak," "peace freak," and "freak freak"). Advertising loves co-opting the occult. Casper the Friendly Ghost's friend Wendy the Witch endorsed Pepsi-Cola, and a cute little Devil himself touted Orange Julius as "a devilishly good drink." The 1970 television season saw seventeen Roman-collared clergymen postured with teacups in a rectory drawing room. They had each shaved successively with the same blade, proving that the shaving product advertised would give at least seventeen shaves to a blade. After all, would a room full of clergymen lie? Not any more than the preceding season's Dracula knock-off, "Count von Throat Pain," who told the whole truth about his agency's throat-lozenge account.

Literary mystic T. S. Eliot wrote that "the greatest treason is to do the right thing for the wrong reason." Had astrologers warned him, he might have prevented, after his death, Andrew Lloyd Webber's use of his poetry to create the anthropomorphic—if not downright "lycanthropic"—musical *Cats*. Cats come into magic via Egypt, a kingdom steeped in ancient magic, which also gave name to the Gypsies. While most genuine witches shy away from the limelight, witchcraft as a concept is often eager to sell itself for motives of money, propaganda, and proselytizing. Witchery is not always the unwilling victim of the big sell, no matter that its "right thing" is often subverted by adventurers within the occult as much as by abusers from outside. Witchcraft, in short, has been willfully merchandised into a business by witches as well as by the average Christian bookstore, which at tidy Christian prices sells antiwitch supplies such as holy water, crucifixes, and books "revealing all" about witchcraft. Virtually every village in America has a "religious book store." Occult supply stores in those same villages are more hidden, usually behind the counters of health-food stores, crystal jewelry shops, beauty shops, and women's tiny bookshops and tea rooms.

Walk into a botanica in any major American city and leave behind the perceived sense and sensibility of White Anglo-Saxon Protestant Christian culture. This leads deep into the voodoo world of the 1960 hit movie, *Macumba Love*. This is a noncampy world of spirit. The primary colors rise invocative out of "primitive" cultures. The sensual smells are pure head trip. Folk poets Paul Simon and Art Garfunkel, in the song "Scarborough Fair," hailed the powers of "parsley, sage, rosemary, and thyme." That song has been appropriated by Wiccans, who sing it as a hymn of white magic. Botanicas add cinchona bark, hasp, Devil's shoestring root, Canadian snake root, buckeyes, waahoo bark, Irish rowan berries to ward off bad magic, and graveyard dust. For uncrossing voodoo spells, for financial success, aphrodisiacs, and black artistry, a botanica is the *in*-gredient shop.

Because belief in good spirits predicates a belief in evil spirits as well, orthodox religion should not be surprised to see the traditional picture of the "Sacred Heart of Jesus" on aerosol cans marked, "Blessed Spray, Matthew 2:11. Contains Genuine Frankincense and Myrrh Oil. Caution: Contents under Pressure." Nor should the fainthearted be shocked to see the Sacred Heart itself beating in a pulsating plastic sculpture lit from within, or bloody statues of saints who died rapturous deaths of sex and violence like Jesus himself hanging on a crucifix of bones and chicken feathers. In botanicas, "Saint Anthony" candles in quart-size vigil glasses promise to "find lost people and lost things." Next to them stand candles of "Saint Christopher, Patron of Journeys," in a row of multicolored vigil lights painted up for each astrological sign, and next to them, the "Death unto My Enemy" vigil lamps deliciously "guaranteed to burn." The great American philosopher Peggy Lee, who summed up existentialism in her song, "Is That All There Is?" also summed up the theology of witchcraft in her "Fever! (What a Lovely Way to Burn)."

Witch Elisa in the Bronx devotes the enterprising length of her bathtub to the burning of *chango* candles that are wax *fith-fath* figures of men or women whom she wishes harm. To neighbors who have curse-or-bless candles and no place to burn them, Elisa rents tub space at a dollar a week per candle. For that fee she tends up to a hundred candles and adds reinforcing curses and prayers of her own. How is her tub different from the banks of votive candles lit by millions of believers, and burning night and day in every Catholic church in the world?

The botanica, long a staple of Hispanic culture, crossed over during the hippie 1960s to mainstream popular culture. George Agee, who operates a Detroit boutique/botanica says, "The hippies are able to feel unfavorable vibrations, and they must seek some power to offset them." Anton LaVey has observed that middle-class people are tired of invoking a God who does not hear them. They prefer a more providential Satan who does hear them, and actually intervenes. To contact God or Satan, or any of the saints and angels and spirits in between, seekers need candles, incense, and mojos. Classified ads offer plenty of guidance:

> Call Prophet Smith. This God-sent man can help. No case beyond help. Are you troubled or unlucky?

> Reverend Dr. Anthony Burns. Witchcraft, spells, evil annoyances removed. By appointment only.

> What is your trouble? Love-crossed condition? Advisor for home, marriage, or success.

For the people who consult the advertisements of this spiritualist sub-culture, the botanica serves as a convenient drugstore. A reader named "Edgar," who calls himself "the dean of the Chicago botanica owners," sent a Cuban family back to their spiritualist because the quantity of laxative recommended had not been specified. Botanica owners, to a person, tend to be close-mouthed. The "House of Candles and Talismans" on Stanton Street in New York City caters largely to Puerto Ricans. The Irishman who manages the store knows his Catholicism from obeah. (*Obeah*, often invoked by Tennessee Williams in plays such as 1957's *Orpheus Descending*, is necromancy, conjuration of good or evil spirits and magic—the same rituals Anglo-Saxons do when they sleep on wedding cake, knock on wood, or throw spilled salt.) Yet making his distinction, this Irish-named botanica manager will answer no questions, tired as he is of curious tourists and wary as he is of police, reporters, and his widening Anglo-Saxon clientele. The U.S. Food and Drug Administration likewise watchdogs botanica wholesalers, like Oracle Laboratories in New York, as well as the Prayer Candle Company and the Universal Botanic, both of Brooklyn. Wholesaler and retailer alike carefully note on much of their packaging in as small letters as possible: "Sold as a curio."

Botanica shelves seem to be stocked by two main product lines: "So-Called" and "Alleged." In the "So-Called" line there is "So-Called Holy Oil Double Strength with Alleged Lucky Roots," "So-Called Essence of

Murder" (Universal Botanic), and "Alleged Dove's Blood Oil." For suburbanites too sophisticated for the friendly Hispanic botanica, "Genuine Dream Oil Fortune-Teller Spray" can be mail ordered.

International Imports of Prescott, Arizona, offers from P.O. Box 2505 their twenty-fifth anniversary mail-order catalog. The list contains thousands of occult book titles, herbs, and oils (four dollars for four ounces, and up), opium pipes, red satin Satan's capes and Devil's hats (all-rubber pates with horns and pointed ears), crystal balls, imported straw voodoo dolls (red for love, black for hate, green for money, yellow to counter evil, and pink for success; each includes voodoo pins to stick in the doll), stereo recordings of the actual Anton LaVey and of the impersonated Marquis de Sade, tarot cards, "psychedelic" black lights, an *Illustrated History of the Horror Film*, as well as peace symbols, slave chokers, and Saint Christopher medals. International Imports notes, "All items are sold *as curios only*. We do not guarantee nor imply any supernatural qualities attributed to any of our products." A coiled snake on the catalog cover spits: "Warning! This book is dangerous—to ignore."

With all the finesse of a Coco Chanel, Los Angeles Witch Rita Norling advertises her white-magic aromatherapy with a high-fashion brochure: "Rita Norling has conjured up a remarkable new bath oil . . . astrologically formulated . . . The Rita Norling Mystique . . . Step into the Magic Circle of Rita Norling's world." In a voice accented somewhere east of Zsa Zsa Gabor, Rita says, "One of the main reasons I got into this business was because there were so many swindlers dealing through the mail. I always give the customer exactly what he wants." (Rita Norling, interview with the author). Some of what Rita's customers want are bone of black cat, heart of swallow, bat's heart, hog's heart (all wrapped in plastic baggies), petrulli root, oils, and candles. She caters primarily to the matron trade, who would faint in a botanica.

Botanicas of one kind or another are everywhere, including hundreds of over-the-top religious art and curio shops outside the four major Virgin Mary shrines at Lourdes in France, Fatima in Portugal, Guadalupe in Mexico, and Knock in Ireland. In the United States, mainstream shoppers flock to botanica boutiques that are West Side Puerto Rican, or African American, or universal hippie, or gay sex shops selling very insertable priapic sculptures, oils, and aromas such as amyl (butyl) nitrite, which by lowering the body's blood pressure causes out-of-body experiences that feel like flying. A botanica is a business built on dreams and fears. Because the

First Amendment to the U.S. Constitution protects witchcraft in its many forms as a religion, the only monitor of the brisk trade in "snake oil" is through consumer protection by the Food and Drug Administration as well as the Better Business Bureau. Neither can do anything about the efficacy of products "sold as a novelty only."

Whether it be "Alleged Aerosol of Love" or "Zodiac Charm Bath," the fact is that most of the herbs, charms, aromas, lotions, and potions are shipped to all major American cities from Louisiana, which as culture, location, and port is the point of entry for occult goods from all around the world, particularly the Caribbean with its gris-gris, Macumba, and Santeria. Gris-gris, pronounced "gree-gree," are amulets, bangles, and charms worn to conjure luck and conquer enemies. Macumba is a Brazilian trance cult of possession with human transformation into jaguars rather than werewolves. Santeria is one of the many combo religions of the African-Cuban diaspora combining evangelical Catholicism and even more evangelical blood sacrifice traced back to the Aztecs. Even in jurisdictions with antique laws against the occult, the bunko police try to keep the dealers on their guard. Because the occult is defined as an alternative religion, often tied to review-proof ethnicity, what separates the legal from the illegal is a shadow.

Cities, with problems more pressing than occult practitioners, allow the botanicas, the palm readers, and the mystic healers to keep their doors and post office boxes open as "doctors," "reverends," "fathers," "daddies," "mothers," "prophets," "madams," and "bishops." These counselors are small-business people who collect five to five hundred dollars for their services. Who dares say that their skills emerge from the blind faith of clients clutching at last straws? What is the difference between voodoo, the power of positive thinking, and the miraculous cures caused by the Virgin Mary at her many shrines worldwide, including her house of curative waters in Ephesus, Turkey, venerated by Muslims and decorated with Arabic quotations from the Koran about the Catholic Virgin? The mainstream success of a Jeane Dixon or of a Peter Hurkos, the spiritualist who unmasked the Boston Strangler and almost revealed the Manson Family, causes even the skeptic to begin to suspend disbelief. Popular medium John Edward—whose clients gladly join a three-year waiting list for a reading—has carried the psychic torch to the twenty-first century with books such as *Crossing Over* (2001); CDs, *Developing Your Own Psychic Powers* (2000); and television, particularly his show, *Crossing Over with John Edward.*

Christianity, Judaism, and Islam are absolute dogma. The occult is relative ambiguity.

Buy "garlic amulets with prayer sheets" for gambling success and to fend off evil spirits. Buy "Black Cat Jinx Remover" and "Chinese Floor Wash" to keep evil out of the house. Buy black candles to affect enemies; blue candles for healing; red candles for seducing; white candles for contacting spirits. Buy a gold needle to stick in an enemy's black candle. Buy *The Master Book of Candle Burning*, by Henri Gamache (1942), which has sold nearly two hundred thousand copies. Buy imported seed necklaces from Haiti. Buy in a botanica; buy in a Wiccan boutique; or buy by mail. The magic word is *buy*.

Botanica marketing has made a triumphant entrance into commercial popular culture. In 1970s television advertising, Miles Laboratories, amid lightning and thunder, suggested that Mr. Hyde, who "wasn't feeling himself," drink Alka Seltzer to change back to good old Dr. Jekyll. The TV genre of the wizardry sell surfaced first in the 1960s with "Wanda the Witch" shilling Hidden Magic Hairspray. Wanda was quickly joined by the Ajax White Knight, the Man from Glad, white doves (Dove dishwashing detergent) and white tornado omens (Ajax liquid cleaner), and the disembodied Ultra-Brite Toothpaste kiss mystically bussed to a young man's cheek.

In television ad lore, eating bread topped with Imperial margarine magically puts a crown on the bread-eater's head. Hertz lowers clients into their rented cars via an invisible magic carpet. Keebler Cookies are made by elves who front themselves with factories "because people believe in factories, not elves." Popular personalities like Ruth Buzzi of *Rowan and Martin's Laugh-In* costume themselves in witchcraft drag to pitch mainstream products. Chicago's Marshall Field department store sells antiques spiritedly in *The New Yorker*: "Of other voices, other rooms, in antiques brought together now in grand design for more than a shade of their former selves. A spirited and splendid collection. . . . The rarest of 18th-century craft in an entity of past, present, And future? . . . At Field's in Chicago. . . . Our new Trend House has everything but ghosts."

Playtex, with its "Living Gloves," has a strangle-hold trademark on the shape-shifting "Living Bra," which is a sexy animism akin to the hair of Medusa. Cannon towels' TV spot features an invisible girl wrapped in a shapely terry cloth towel sarong, with the voice-over saying, "When a girl can't be seen, it's important what she be seen in. Available at your favorite haunts, to liven your spirits." Vaudeville comedian Bert Lahr, dressed in a red union suit playing the Devil, tempts for Frito-Lay Potato Chips. His Devil-with-chips subway poster appears in the film *Dutchman* (1966), written by Beat poet LeRoi Jones, now Amiri Baraka. Cashing in on his *Frankenstein* image, Boris Karloff, in a mad-doctor laboratory, recommends, "A-1 Sauce: Experiment with it!"

Bigelow Carpets has conducted the largest national astrology promotion. Carpet stylist Barbara Curtis travels nationwide to Bigelow dealerships to conduct "Astrology Carpet Clinics" that forecast carpeting color and pile according to the natal signs of the customers who line up in droves for the seminar. Full-page Strega liqueur ads picture the black-hooded face of a seductive neowitch, with the copy, "Every woman needs a little unfair advantage. If you have your eye on the future, serve him Strega, the spirit with a past. Explain that this ambrosial liquid was created centuries ago in Italy by the beautiful witches of Benevento. Whisper the legend of Strega—that when two people share the golden spirit, they are united by the Love that Lasts Forever. Will the legend work its magic?—Supernaturally! But don't share it with just anyone—forever is a long, long time. Strega, 80 Proof."A similar siren shills for the spirits of Lang's 8 Scotch Whiskey, claiming, "My name is Nadine. Call me collect. Learn what the Zodiac says about your future. If you're planning an affair for a hundred people or just two, tell me your birth date, and I'll tell you what your horoscope promises. And remember, any affair is more successful when you serve Lang's 8 Premium Scotch. Give my brand a try, and call me collect in Los Angeles at (213) 787-2840."

To figure out who reads a magazine or who watches a TV show, look at the advertising. Ads reflect the audience demographic. Daytime TV sells to women wanting "miracle cleaning" products for the house, and seductive botanicals like "vanishing creme," "Black Magic Shampoo," "Hidden Magic Hair Spray," and "aromatherapy bath-oil beads." The wizardry sell is a constant theme, because the consumer wants things to change, and magic promises to effect the change. Glidden Paints advises, "When your house begins to haunt you, use Latex Spred Paint." Madison Avenue commercially confirms American belief in the occult.

With such confirmation, Western Culture has come full circle. Deuteronomy gave the ancient rules for witch-testing. Modern witches are no longer tested. Popular witches endorse every kind of marvelous, magical, and fascinating product.

CUT TO

The Newsstand

MAD Magazine cover: *Rosemia's Boo-Boo*
Everyone is talking about the recent movie that has shocked the nation. (Not
THIS nation . . . Upper Slobovia!) We're referring to the picture that has sus-
pense, witchcraft, sorcery, religious fantasy, and most important of all—a
couple of shots of naked ladies . . . all of the elements necessary for good
"Box Office" today . . . mainly, bad taste! This picture obviously was intended
to offend people . . . you're sure to be offended by our *MAD* version of
Rosemia's Boo-Boo.

MORT DRUCKER AND ARNIE KOGEN, *MAD Magazine*, January 1969

Long before *Rosemary's Baby* became a popular book and movie, pub-
lishers from *Summis Desiderantes* on knew that the occult was a cash reg-
ister. *The Old Farmers Almanac* has been making a profit out of white magic
since 1792. Some of its imitators are successfully into their own second
hundred years. *The Moon-Sign Book*, one of the more recent (not yet a
century), sells steadily by defining "dates for breeding and setting eggs"
and making "astro-guidance for romance, homemaking, farm and garden,
fishing and hunting." Such agrarian panaceas sell next to the sexually desperate *How to Find Your Mate through Astrology: The Bachelor Girl's Practical Guide to Locating, Landing, and Loving Her Man.* While Bachelor Girl
is interviewing, she might purchase the *Zodiac Sign-In Book*, advertised as
"fun at parties, birthdays, and seances." By the time she lands her fish she
will likely need *Your Baby's First Horoscope.* And the baby may need *You
Were Born on a Rotten Day.* Occult titles hide in plain sight in the "self-
help" section in stores afraid of having an out "occult" section.

Nothing, however, is financially less risky than the risqué. Sex always sells.
Witchcraft has always been the code word for sex. The porno occult has
come out from under the gloriously funky counters of the late, lamented
42nd Street porn shops documented (and causing latter-day nostalgia) in
Midnight Cowboy (1969), *Taxi Driver* (1976), and *Cruising* (1980). In the way
that water always seeks its own level, occult erotica has flowed out to clean,
well-lit suburban drugstores and supermarkets. At magazine and book
racks where *Fate* magazine once stood alone with innocent articles about
UFOs, customers take to the coded occult genres like Rosemary stroking
her baby. Barry Cuff's *Damned Spot* (1969) is frank porno witchery. Wilson Tucker's *The Warlock* (1967) reveals what everyone "always knew": that

the CIA is into the occult. Heinrich Graat's *Revenge of Increase Sewall* (1969) could easily trade promo blurbs about an evil-shadow-overhanging-a-town's-unspeakable-rites with Elizabeth Davis' *Suffer a Witch to Die* (1969). The popularity of 1970s occult novels, such as Anne Rice's *Interview with the Vampire* (1976), is porno-Gothic enough to frizzle the hair of Nancy Drew. What essayist Erica Jong did for sex with the platonic ideal of the "zipless fuck" in *Fear of Flying* (1973), she did for women and sex in her provocative *Witches* (1981).

Joseph R. Rosenberger's *The Demon Lovers: A Psychosexual Study of Witchcraft and Demonology* (1969) is as porno pop as it is pop scholarly. Rosenberger alternates historical documentary with erotic "sociological" reportage. Rosenberger cannot be lightly dismissed. If he writes non-fiction, he reports too well the dark side of suburban demonology; and if what he writes is fiction, he sells too well to be dismissed. He represents the new diverse scholarship that must be considered by critics of both witchcraft or popular culture.

Rosenberger's chapter on the Great Beast Aleister Crowley (1875–1947) recounts with delicious prurience Crowley's "Raising of the Devil" through ritual sodomy, fellatio, and sadism with his opium-head friend, Edward Allen Bennett. "As Crowley wrote years later, in his masterpiece, *Magick in Theory and Practice*, 'Satan appeared in the triangle, but only for a moment or so; yet he did appear, as a very beautiful boy with golden curls, a naked, handsome boy with a sexual organ that was shaped as a trident.' It was a terrible experience for Edward Allen, however. He screamed and fainted when he saw Satan."[17]

Like the Crowley-Bennett ménage à trois with Satan, the literature of demonology is often inverted, erotic, and sadomasochistic. Number 22 California statute 16603 defines the horror comic book as "Any book or booklet in which an account of the commission or attempted commission of the crime of arson, assault with caustic chemicals, assault with a deadly weapon, burglary, kidnapping, mayhem, murder, rape, robbery, theft, or voluntary manslaughter is set forth by means of a series of five or more drawings or photographs in sequence, which are accompanied by either narrative writing or words represented as spoken by a pictured character, whether such narrative words appear in balloons, captions on or imme-diately adjacent to the photograph or drawing."

If the legal definition of *horror* and *comic* mixes, then the lurid photos and print of the mass-circulated tabloids are the "fun" horror comics of the adult occult. In comparison to *Screw, Pacer, Tattler, Gay, Midnight,* and other pop-sex sheets, the *National Enquirer* is the granddaddy of junk journalism, which often means it has revealed embarrassing human truths polite people don't talk about. The *Enquirer* loves the occult, and so does its huge readership. Available in supermarket checkout lines everywhere, the *Enquirer* has the largest circulation of any weekly paper in America. Before the *Enquirer* "righted" itself with religion and Republican politics in 2000, a typical week's issue often carried four or five occult articles under teaser headlines like:

Movie Star Eddie Bracken's Occult Experience: Spirit Message from a Dead GI Leads Eddie Bracken to the Soldier's Grave

After 11 Years, Man Is Fired Because Handwriting Expert Says He Is Not Suited for the Job

Doctors Confirm that Woman Dying of an Incurable Disease Recovered Completely after Seeing Vision of Pope John XXIII

Witch Sybil Leek Says Horoscopes Can Help Men and Women Choose Right Careers

Tennessee Williams, writing in *Esquire*, August 1975, called the original-recipe *National Enquirer* "the finest journalistic review of the precise time we live in."[18] In volume 44, number 42, the *Enquirer* editorialized how its staff created its content: "During his twenty-three years with the Newspaper Enterprise Association syndicate, Hollywood reporter, Dick Kleiner, has talked to hundreds of stage, screen, and TV personalities. Kleiner tabulated that seventy-five out of every one hundred actors have had psychic experiences and he tells of these dramatic experiences in his book, *ESP and the Stars.*"

Even as one generation of actors descends to the next in the tabloids, some things never change. Michael Jackson made an autobiographical film titled *Ghost* that debuted (and mysteriously disappeared), Halloween 1996. The singer Sting and his wife, Trudy Styler, claim their home has a ghost, as does Dan Ackroyd, the star of *Ghostbusters*. Uma Thurman moved from her home because of ghosts. Nicholas Cage has seen a ghost in the attic of his uncle, Francis Ford Coppola. Keanu Reeves, star of *The Devil's Advocate*, saw ghosts as a child, and Paul McCartney has sensed the ghost of John Lennon.

The Enquirer has run millions of mystic classified ads:

Fortune Telling Cards. Amazing Deck with Instructions. $2.00. New York.

"Your Horoscope and Your Dreams," Book of Deep Insight into Self, with Astrology. Louisiana.

Computerized Horoscope. Personalized, Fifteen Pages, Startling revelations. Love, Career, Forecast. Send $5.00, Birth date, Birth time, Birth place, Sex. California.

Become an Ordained Minister, and Doctor of Divinity. Degrees issued immediately. Donation: $5.00. Vermont.

Where Witches and Warlocks Abound! Write to The Psychic Club. Ohio.

Witchcraft! Genuine Herbs, Roots, Oils, etc. Free List. Instructions. California.

WITCHCRAFT LIVES! Hexcraft-magic-occult headquarters. Books, supplies, curios. Sorcerer's Apprentice Manual: 25 cents.

Voodoo doll kit $2.00. Cult Handbook illustrated, $1.00. Arizona.

Every serious reader of the contemporary occult knows of the two famous books by Anton LaVey: his theoretical *Satanic Bible* and its practical companion volume, *Satanic Rituals*. In the age before LaVey reinvented Satanism for modern urban culture, Lewis de Claremont had written the two best books of ritual: *Legends of Incense, Herb, and Oil Magic* (1936), and *The Ancient's Book of Magic Containing Secret Records of the Procedure and Practice of the Ancient Masters and Adepts* (1940). *Legends of Incense*, as a kind of list, details the materials needed for ritual, and *The Ancient's Book*, as a workbook, details the form for mixing the materials, particularly those sold by its publisher, Oracle. Catharine Yronwode of the Lucky Mojo Curio Company has noted that *Legends of Incense* was "basically European and Medieval in orientation, but it has from the first been packaged for sale to hoodoo practitioners in the African-American community. It has proven consistently popular and has never gone out of print, despite the fact that in 1966 an important chapter [chapter 10] on seals and talismans was eliminated by the publisher."[19]

Both Lewis de Claremont books are controversial. Fans feel the books give access to deep secrets. Critics argue the books are a mail-order sales gimmick. Could they be both? Pontifex Maximus Frederic de Arechaga, in interview at his Babylonian-style temple in Chicago, said that while de Claremont reveals some worthwhile information, the books are profanations of old Sabaean texts which should themselves be published without de Claremont's mass-media dilutions. De Arechaga founded his Sabaean religious order in Chicago in 1968 when he took over his mother's occult supply store, El Sabarum, on Sheffield Street. (Pontifex de Arechaga's original 1969 interview appears in the final chapter of this book.)

Despite controversy, for a novice needing a ritual primer, or a basic catechism, de Claremont's tidy manuals give access to otherwise inaccessible and out-of-print texts that, perhaps, the person writing under the name "de Claremont" might have learned in some thereafter lost oral tradition. Times change, and stories die out. Of course, Lewis de Claremont may have been a supremely talented creative writer expressing what his imagination told him. He would have fit the grimoire pattern of copying and recopying secret mysteries and rituals. Gerald Gardner, who claimed he inherited the *Book of Shadows* in fragments during his initiation in 1939, was also accused of being the author of his "found" book. Anton LaVey frankly authored his *Satanic Bible* out of many "found" texts which he made his own. Tracing solo authorship always reveals the same fact. The beating heart of nearly all secret, ancient literature—including the Bible—is the rhythm of a multitude of voices speaking in whispers under the roar of the world.

De Claremont, Gardner, and LaVey are three voices crying in the centuries-long wilderness caused by the occult holocaust of torture, murder, and book burning that has kept the hereditary craft of witchcraft, both white and black, oral and written, underground. Debunkers may declare de Claremont a fraud, Gardner a plagiarist, and LaVey a huckster; but the student of the occult will read these authors and glean from them as much of the hidden history of the occult as possible.

CUT TO

SNAPSHOT: Abbot's Magic Company, "Magic City," Colon, Michigan, 1970.

In Colon, Michigan, the local gas station attendant hops on his motorcycle. He roars past a bearded Amish man who leads his three barefoot boys across the cracked pavement of Blackstone Avenue. On the opposite curb, the boys' mother smiles at her family from under her plain bonnet. The sound of the cycle fades. The family regroups and enters the Magic City Hardware. Every day of the year, the 1000 residents of the village live quietly. But four days every August, Colon lights up to what it is: "The Magic Capital of the World." Each summer's end, nearly one thousand international magicians double Colon's population for "Abbott's Magic Get-Together." The elementary school becomes a gigantic showroom, and the high school hosts "Four Gigantic Stage Shows" by professionals. Registration is $20 per person.

Colon got magic by association. Outside of town, on Sturgeon Lake, is the island where the famous Blackstone the Magician (1855–1965, born Henry Boughton in Chicago) built his first summer retreat, "the one that burned to the ground." Millie Bouton (changed from *Boughton*), the wife of Blackstone's brother and stage double Pete, still lives in Colon. But the grand times are gone. Sally Banks, the wife of Blackstone's stage manager, is now Colon's Avon Lady.

Businesses like "The Magic Carpet Bar" and "The Magic Pocket Pool Hall" anchor the two blocks of Main Street where true showbiz lives. The town theme is everywhere, but the town's essence stands behind a new supermarket in two black buildings painted with white skeletons and ghosts. This is the Abbott Manufacturing Company, the world's largest manufacturer of quality magic.

Abbott is its own perfect museum of the popular culture of commercial magic. It was founded in 1927 by Australian magician Percy Abbott, who came to Michigan one summer to visit Blackstone. Abbott's memoir is *A Lifetime in Magic*. Owner Recil Bordner claims a mailing list of ten thousand names. *The Wall Street Journal* lists Abbott's annual take at $200,000.

The genteel Bordner, who resembles actor James Stewart, readily admits to the commercialism of demand and supply. "We're in show business," he says. "We manufacture what our customers want. In 1966 we built the magic illusions for the touring skating show *Holiday on Ice*. Our shops were clogged for months. Several of the illusions were so big we had to assemble them in the streets."

His Abbott Publishing Company prints undated titles like *A Magician Goes to Church: A Guide to Gospel Magic*, by Jim Dracup of the Fellowship of Christian Magicians, and *Lessons in Scripture: Magic Trick Patter*, by the Reverend Donald Bodley.

Of fundamentalist Bible magicians like Andre Cole, who is sponsored by the business entity Crusade for Christ, Bordner says, "Many of them are excellent illusionists. Their magic makes the Bible miracles quite graphic for youngsters. So they're very popular with churches throughout the country.

I personally think they're defeating their purpose trying to duplicate scriptural miracles. If a man can do the same miracle as God, God must seem a little less. But if they want it, we'll supply it. If they write a book, we'll publish it. I don't think it's best, but I'm not my brothers' censor."

Bordner, in fact, distributes many monthly periodicals of magic like *Genii: The Conjurors' Magazine* from Los Angeles, and *The New Pentagram* from Peter Warlock in Britain.

The Abbott showroom is a fascinating study in nostalgic carnival color. A stage jammed with floor models emphasizes the vaudeville-show atmosphere. Red and black paint enliven the exhibits. Mandarins, rabbits, and genies decorate illusions like "The Girl-without-a-Middle Cabinet" ($650), and Andre Cole's "Chinese Chopper" for the head and wrists ($95). Levitation illusions range from $77.50 to $1500. Magic wands cost $2 to $6. Crystal balls—glass from England, plastic from the USA—cost from $7.50 to $20.

"Never leave your crystal ball in your auto," Bordner warns. "Several of our magicians' finest tricks have been sending their cars up in flames. They catch the sun, you know."

The Abbott catalog likewise cautions, "Be very careful in selecting merchandise. . . . A valuable part of every magical effect is its secret. Once you have learned the secret, we cannot exchange or refund money on tricks or books unless there is a flaw in materials or workmanship."

"When we ship internationally—even to our one Russian who deals through West Germany," Bordner says, "we declare only half the list value because half the price is for the sharing of the secret, and they can't tax that intangible."

Bordner points with pride to a magician's table. "I cut the stencil for that design," he says. "You saw it in the Tony Curtis film *Houdini* [1953]. Paramount Studios borrowed quite a lot of equipment from us for that movie."

In the Abbott cellar, Arturo, a prized craftsman among Bordner's twenty employees, explains, "Hollywood paid me to use both my name and my straitjacket escape for *Eternally Yours*. That was around 1939 with Loretta Young as the wife of magician David Niven."

The books as well as the "restraint-and-torture" equipment of guillotines and such in the main showroom could be perverted to a bondage fetishist's delight—particularly the setups, but not the solutions, of a manual called *Escapes: Secret Workings for Handcuffs, Ropes, Boxes, Bags, Chains, Padlocks, Strait Jackets, Wrist Stocks.* On the cover is a rather alarming fetish-like photo of a uniformed cop handcuffing a boy in swimming briefs preparatory to the youngster's underwater live burial and suspense-filled escape.

Bordner realizes his products can be appropriated to anyone's fancy or fantasy. He has, in fact, received requests for botanica ingredients as well as farmers' requests to remove curses from oat crops. One woman caller, a self-identified witch, left disgruntled that Bordner supplied materials for popular stage magic, but not natural magic. Bordner muses that while he carries tarot cards, his doves—alive and cooing at six dollars a pair—are for the stage, not the stew.

In point of fact, hard-core occultists amuse the Abbott firm, which goes no farther into dogma than stage magic. At least, that's what Bordner says founder Percy Abbott said; but where there's smoke, there's usually a trick, and behind it a trickster.

The Abbott Manufacturing Company has a monthly magazine, *The New Tops*, which at $7 a year does not lack a sense of humor. In its news items, *The New Tops* was happy to see the media-savvy witch Louise Huebner stump the TV panel, who could not guess her occupation on the television show *What's My Line*, May 4, 1970.

The ceiling of the Abbott showroom is plastered with a fortune in original posters of the magicians Thurston and Harry Houdini, as well as of the circuses of Ringling Brothers and Barnum and Bailey.

A portrait of Percy Abbott hangs glowering on the wall, with Satan looking over his shoulder.

"It's melodramatic, isn't it?" Bordner says. "Some say he had the Devil in him. He and Blackstone were both very temperamental."

Over Bordner's head, an old and peeling poster reads:

GEM THEATER: CASSOPOLIS MICHIGAN
10 PM SHOW TIME
The Spirit of Sir Arthur Conan Doyle
presents
SAX—ONA
in his Sensational Spiritualistic Seance
and GHOST SHOW
No Children Admitted
Ladies Must Have a Male Escort
Doctor and Nurse in Attendance

In a nearby showcase stands a magician's gag sign. It reads: "Applause, Please."

Cut to

Inner and Outer Space, Apollo 13

Because the occult seems to answer questions in areas of human experience where the only real answers are increasingly intelligent questions, consumers will use, wear, read, and view anything to open the mysteries locked within themselves.

"Houston, we have a problem."

The Marathon Oil Company's *Apollo 13* drinking glass commemorated more than that damaged moonship's desperately shaky return to Earth in 1970.

It proved humans will buy amulets, crucifixes, and filling-station glassware to exorcise their innermost fears. Owning the popular "*Apollo 13* Safe Return" glass was like owning some kind of team chalice for a magic toast. "If the astronauts made it, so can we."

The news knew.

Everyone knew.

The very return of the ill-fated moonship, astrologically named *Aquarius,* was a miracle.

Numerologists had warned the National Aeronautics and Space Administration not to launch *Apollo 13* on Wednesday, April 11, at 13 hours and 13 minutes (Houston time), carrying the 12th, 13th, and 14th men to the moon, because the spaceship would be traveling on Friday the 13th, the date the explosion actually occurred.

What of this numerological coincidence?

Titanic was launched in 1911, on April 1—April Fool's Day.

I give people Ayn Rand with trappings.
—HIGH PRIEST ANTON LAVEY,
CHURCH OF SATAN

CHAPTER 3

Sex and Witchcraft

ꝕ

Puritanism is the haunting fear that someone somewhere is having a
good time.

—H. L. MENCKEN

P*URITANS FROM HELL, Black Masses, Anton LaVey and*
the Church of Satan, Hell's Angels, homosexuality, leather
sadomasochism, Saint Priapus, magic Christianity, gender
witchcraft, muscular paganism, Sylvia Plath, fith-fath voodoo
dolls, the withering of the witch, and sex in a vat of Velveeta

Fear of Satan has driven America to sex and violence, censorship and
racism.

When Pilgrims, Puritans, Protestants, and Catholics weren't quoting the
Bible they were reciting the imported theologies of Calvinism and Jansenism. In the popular culture of Europe, where future American colonists
were being minted, the twin theologians, Protestant John Calvin (1509–64)
and Catholic Cornelius Jansen (1585–1638) were rock-star preachers. They
poisoned human psychology. They taught that human nature was totally
depraved, that there was no free will, and that only the predestined were
saved. That chosen elite, announcing that God had told them they were
born again, embraced an austere piety and a Puritan morality, and mixed
religion into politics to exclude those who weren't pious, Puritan, and
predestined. Free will was no more than a temptation from Satan, who
seduced souls to express their depraved human nature.

In New England, the religious colonists perched on Plymouth Rock were desperate survivalists. Afraid of the American forest, of the Indians, and of each other's sexual urges, these refugees—from a Europe terrified by inquisitional witchcraft—transplanted the Calvinist-Jansenist split between body and soul into a kind of sexual schizophrenia of good versus evil. From their founding on religious tolerance, they turned in fear to a rigid Puritanism. Even good humans had lewd bodies. Pleasure was wrong. Art was immoral; music, forbidden; clothes were plain, not fancy. Yet the colonial ideal was civil liberty and personal freedom. That meant trouble, because where there's free will, there's a witch. In 1636, Anne Hutchinson, an upstart wife new to Boston from England, was accused of heresy and witchcraft, because women met in her home, where she challenged Puritan teachings on moral conduct and piety. For voicing principles of religious freedom and civil liberty later written into the Constitution of the United States, the transgressive poet was banned in Boston, driven out of town on a rail, and forced to live on the frontier where the First Church of Boston figured the Indians would—and did—kill her.

Jonathan Edwards, in his sermon "Sinners in the Hands of an Angry God" (1741), preached masochistic resignation to a sadistic deity whose "providence" was more to curse than to bless, if it even bothered to curse. Denied God's intervention, the Puritans, in their totally harsh environment, created the first alternative American underground, because God's failure to answer their prayers made freethinker Roger Williams's naming of Providence, Rhode Island, ironic. Theological irony always leads back to Satan, the original ironist. If God fails to respond, the Devil is open for business. Irony is the Devil's tool. God created the world, but Satan designed it.

Driven by circumstance, some settlers turned to witchcraft for the comfort theology denied them. As with witchery's late-twentieth-century revival, it was the children who fostered the colonial cults. It was the young who danced on May 1, 1627, around Thomas Morton's priapic maypole at Merrymount colony in New England—before the Puritans chopped it down. It is the physically hardy who understand Anton LaVey's savvy 1966 axiom that Satanism is, in essence, "libido out for a romp." In 1697, as a swipe against ever-increasing Satanic practices among the freethinking settlers, the fundamentalist Massachusetts Bay Colony, equating sodomy with bestiality, made all three—Satanism, sodomy, and bestiality—capital crimes punishable by death. They had so few livestock they resented young men, playing with their food, having sex with the animals. Since Salem, witchcraft has become a religion, and sodomy and bestiality, because they are nonprocreative sex acts, remain "crimes" fought over in the courts.

Born in Salem, July 4, 1804, Nathaniel Hawthorne, one of America's first novelists, wrote best-selling tales that often used witchcraft as the window into psychology that it actually is. In his house, he personally felt the guilt of the race-and-sex sins America was committing against Indians, African Americans, women, and sexual nonbreeders. His great-great grandfather, Judge John Hawthorne, who presided at the Salem witch trials in 1692, had executed 13 women and 6 men—the sum total murdered of the 54 confessed and the 144 accused. In the history of gender witchcraft, it is likely that most of the 6 men Judge Hawthorne killed were homosexual, because straight men are rarely accused of witchcraft, which is perceived as a feminine sin.

What family doesn't have its ups and downs? Young Nathaniel Hawthorne, the sensitive artist, rebelled against his blunt Puritan heritage. In *Twice Told Tales* (1837, 1842), he took delight in writing about the Thomas Morton dancing scandal in "The May Pole at Merry Mount." He advanced to issues of choice and preference and freedom and nature in *The Scarlet Letter* (1850). In this first American novel of psychology, his heroine, Hester Prynne, wearing the scarlet letter *A* as punishment for adultery, had to choose between custody of her child and the personal freedom of meeting with Mistress Hibbins's coven in the forest. Hester's was the same choice the California courts gave Charles Manson's women in 1969. When the police raided the Spahn Ranch where the Manson Family lived, they "took all the babies. And this is one point, one main point. Every time they take a baby from his mother, they dangle it in front of her. What it breaks down to is that they tell the mothers to get back into the world *they're* in—or else. That is the tactic they used on Susan Atkins."[1] In contemporary America's divided society, as in Hester's and Hawthorne's times, the straight establishment judges the occult underground with a sex-envy paranoia that is not unlike the racial hysteria that occurs when race riots break out in city after city in America.

Arthur Miller, in his drama *The Crucible* (1953), exposed the Salem witch trials as a village squabble over sex and property. Additionally, the Salem landlords tried to control rebellious girls and old women who were influenced by the black outsider, the slave woman Tituba. This automatically made the witch trials about race, age, and gender. Arthur Miller equated the witch hunts in Salem to the House Un-American Activities Committee witch hunts in which Senator Joseph McCarthy sniffed out domestic communists. Just so, the young in Salem also stand as archetypes prefiguring the rebellious youth culture of the 1960s and 1970s. College students fighting on the liberation fronts wanted to stop war, racism, and sexism as much as they wanted sex, drugs, and rock-and-roll.

SNAPSHOT: Andre Cole, Campus Crusade for Christ, Western Michigan University, Kalamazoo, 1971.

This activist youth culture makes religionists crazy. The Crusade for Christ, obsessed with disobedient youths on campus, sponsors a magician named Andre Cole, billed as "America's leading illusionist." Campus crusader Cole has appeared on more college campuses than any other lecturer in America. His advance fliers, on which he gestures hypnotically like the cartoon-strip *Mandrake the Magician*, suggest he may be able to effect the onstage return of John F. Kennedy and Martin Luther King. He has spoken in forty-three countries on five continents. He has appeared on national television in thirty countries. His stage is set with scarves, top hat, and a screen with a fire-breathing dragon of the kind sold by Recil Bordner at Abbott's Manufacturing Company in Colon, Michigan. His taped music includes Herb Alpert and the Tijuana Brass for hip cool, and Richard Strauss's *Thus Spake Zarathustra* for the space-age mystery of the film *2001: A Space Odyssey* (1968). He charges a dollar at the door, and goes "on public record against frauds." Cole is an icon of "magic Christianity." He takes center stage the way that born-again bodybuilders preaching "muscular Christianity" appear, heaving and sweating onstage as "strong men for Jesus."

Cole's slick lecture is more slight-of-head than sleight-of-hand. He is a professional opponent of anything occult, "except for Jesus, the only dead Man who ever returned." He rejects the popular Fox sisters, Margaret, Leah, and Catherine, who from their home in Arcadia, New York, had in 1848 a million followers of their spiritism that—endorsed by the controversial New York newspaper editor, Horace Greeley—remains a psychic milestone of women's liberation. Cole also discounts the famous Harry Houdini (born 1874, died Halloween 1926), and thinks to disprove the whole world of the paranormal because Houdini was a stage-and-film magician who used tricks to escape from bondage.

To proselytize for Christianity, Cole reduces all witchcraft to magician's stage trickery. As if it somehow makes a theological point, he reveals the secrets of stage magic that Recil Bordner wishes he would not. Cole's own pietistic patter, in fact, is more illusionist than his stage magic. At an appearance at Western Michigan University, Cole was booed by his campus audiences, who resented his "false advertising." His posters promise magic: "ESP, Witchcraft, and the Supernatural: Do the Dead Return?" They don't promise sermonizing. Apparently, students so often heckle Cole for his misleading ads that he has built a "moment" into his act so the audience stampede to the exit looks like an "intermission."

Cole's worst is not his contending with faulty logic that because some occultists are frauds, the occult is fraudulent; it is not even his pitch to convert Jews or his hawkish militarism. Cole fires his rudest brimstone, when as a latter-day Jonathan Edwards, he assaults the young audience with accusations of their Calvinist depravity. Cole lifts a frosted cylindrical shade from around a blinding light bulb. He demonstrates that the body (the shade) is separate and apart from the bulb (the soul). "The real you," he says, celebrating the sexual schizophrenia of Western culture, "is, like this bright bulb, the soul inside."

As entertainer, the tricky Cole leaves himself open to real reviews, college boos, and witch's curses. His twentieth-century medicine show graduated from hick towns to the college circuit. Cole may preach whatever Jekyll-Hyde dualism he likes; but his attempt to turn a college audience into a religious congregation is a magic trick beyond his powers. He promises "the truth" about communication with the dead, transcendental meditation, and the Bermuda Triangle, but his truth often lands on the side of government agencies like the U.S. Federal Trade Commission, for whom Cole worked to stop the spread of psychic healers in the United States.

Cole's advertising ethics aside, his body-versus-soul theology continues the Calvinistic confusion about "depraved human nature" that college students neither want nor need. Cole's Campus Crusade is simply the latest inquisition of witchcraft. In the age of flower children, Cole seems not to understand that if the popular occult does anything, it unifies body and soul. As Anton LaVey explains, "The reason there is so much interest in the occult today is that people are tired of depending on 'God' for a crumb of mercy, and seek ways and means to get what they want while eliminating God as the middleman. It might be said that magic is a sort of 'Do-It-Yourself God Kit.' The big reason sex has always been associated with Satanism is that Christianity considers sex as wrong as Satanic worship."[2]

Christianity's body-guilt tension has created its own Frankenstein's creature: the sexual masochist who can be of any sexual preference or gender. Riddled with guilt because he has natural urges he has been acculturated into believing immoral, the sexual masochist resolves the erotic tension between his internal drive and its external prohibition. He seeks orgasm while suffering punishment. In his mind, the pain compensates God for the devilish pleasure. In effect, the atoning pain becomes part of the have-your-cake-and-eat-it-too sensuality. From this readily available whip-and-chill group of masochists, a certain New York homosexual coven secures its ritual participants.

True or not, it's a legend—as ancient as urban—that all homosexuals are bewitched. On the numerologically perfect sex date of 6/9/69, gay parties and orgies occurred throughout the world. One invitation was to a sadomasochistic Black Mass to be celebrated in Manhattan's Greenwich Village. Satanic ritual often inverts Christian symbols. The Lord's Prayer is read backwards, or the crucifix is hung upside down, or the penetration is anal. Naturally, homosexuality, which doctors once identified by the term *sexual inversion*, was at the core of this chic Black Mass. The coven of "inverts" was exclusively male, and their interests were as sexual as they were demonic. Their altar was a young man, nineteen or twenty years old. He was by birth a Christian, by taste a sensualist, by resultant tension a sexual masochist. He was neither of the coven nor a probationer. The coven's magus had met him through a personals ad in the *East Village Other*, which like the *Berkeley Barb*, the *San Francisco Oracle*, and the *Los Angeles Free Press* carry alternative classifieds giving opportunities for Satanists and Wiccans to advertise and meet. The youngling eagerly agreed that what was expected of him was actually his fantasy. He would be ritually showered, tortured, and made the sexually subservient altar to thirteen men.

When the guests arrived, the young man was caged in a corner of the loft apartment. The *dominus limini* (the porter, the keeper of the door) counted as the core-coven and their guests assembled. The coven wore black leather garments ranging from loose medieval robes to motorcycle gear. The blindfolded boy was draped in a floor-length black leather poncho with a hood. After the invocation of the spirits and the inverted Lord's Prayer, the boy was led into the center of the coven's circle to be purged by torture. He was stripped, tied by the wrists to an exposed beam, and mercilessly whipped a ritual thirteen lashes by each of the thirteen members. Periodically, during the 169 blows, the young man eagerly inhaled, through a ventilated gag, amyl nitrite to increase his endurance and submission while making him feel as if he were flying. When the *Magister Templi* (the Master of the Temple) cut the boy down, he was stretched out to be the coven's altar. He was shackled face down and cruciform. Once the young man was secured, the High Priest carved the pentacle on the boy's already bloodied left buttock. The *left* side is, in Latin, *sinister*, and in the occult, the sign of Satan. Finally, a consecrated host, obtained during a communion service at a Catholic Church, was anally inserted into the willing young man who was then sodomized by each of the thirteen members. Afterwards, tea cakes were served.

Homosexuality gets down to the basics of its sacred path, the satirical Route 666, which is a one-way street. The carefully scripted edge-play of ritual whipping and cutting is little different from the physical disciplines of the early Christian mystics who lived on top of pillars of stone, or tied themselves to trees, and whipped and mutilated their flesh to control concupiscence, in order to see visions of God. Gay ritual is also older than the druids, whom the civilized Julius Caesar described as rejoicing in burning huge wickermen with live men tied inside for sacrifice.

Long before he was the wizard headmaster in two *Harry Potter* films, the young actor Richard Harris was hanged by his chest muscles from the top of a teepee in the big-box-office film *A Man Called Horse* (1970). The film revealed to sadomasochists how American Indian shamans use the physically grueling Sundance Ritual to alter consciousness. The ritualized body pain and hallucinogenic drugs lift the warrior-initiate into spirit images of bravery and sex. Native Americans have never stopped practicing this ritual, even on reservations next to casinos. This kind of magic has been kept most alive in white culture in the underground of homosexual S&M, which can be variously interpreted as "sex and magic," "sadomasochism," or "sensuality and mutuality."

The nightbreed who conjure spiritual magic on the "tortured" body are led by shaman Fakir Musafar, founder of the modern primitive movement and author of *Modern Primitives* (1986). Fakir Musafar has brought the Sun Dance and muscular paganism, as well as ritual bondage and body suspension, tattooing, branding, cutting, and scarification up out of hidden world cultures to the popular fringe culture of the American young, hip, straight, and gay. His influence as a teacher, repairing the damage of Christian doctrine that divided soul from body, has grown from the film *Dances Sacred and Profane* (1985), as well as through his worldwide lecture-demonstrations and appearances on mainstream television news shows curious about Fakir Musafar's intellectual defense of self-mutilation as a creative discipline of personal expression, spiritual exploration, and healing of the body-soul schizophrenia. There is substantial erotic appeal in

Fakir Musafar's use and redesign of his own body, and in his performance art of primitive rituals involving groups to whom he teaches his ways.

Denied the societal privileges that come from "simply being straight," the victimized in American society—particularly homosexuals forced as children to be raised in the solitary confinement of closets—find Fakir Musafar's spiritual gain through physical pain to be a way to focus their own magic and rebuild personal identity. Who can rebut his logic? He hardly seems bizarre in a world filled with everybody else's even more bizarre theories about homosexuality. The study of the psychology of people coming out has only recently become a discipline of psychoanalysis, which, of course, arrives better late than never into a scene where homosexuals for years, against all odds, have had to come out, repair themselves, and create lives insulated against discrimination, insults, and hatred. The journeys of gay liberation, women's liberation, and occult liberation are nearly identical.

Gay witchcraft and S&M rituals, inverting the Christian Penitentes who, in New Mexico, Mexico, and the Philippines, whip and crucify each other to deny concupiscence, actually *celebrate* concupiscence, honor the body, and dissipate guilt carefully taught to them by parents, siblings, and society. Los Angeles artist Cavelo, in his gay S&M "Inquisition drawings" of monks and hunks, erotically appropriates historical scenes from the Inquisition. By focusing on the Inquisition's male-on-male torture, Cavelo's hardcore drawings expose, in his *Gentlemen's Quarterly* style, the soft-core subtext of eroticism that has made middle-class "histories" of the Inquisition best sellers in popular culture for centuries. Gay witchcraft, coming out of its own special closet, particularly on the ever more openly gay feast of Halloween, and claiming its spiritual place and gender rights and phallic rites, shocks even liberal witches and covens who have never suspected that they themselves in their doctrine were homophobic or heterosexist.

The truth of homosexual inversion is that gays invert symbols not to get stuck in the inversion, but to move on through the act of inversion to new actions that are not merely reactions to what was inverted. In human folklore, the magic of homosexuality is so strong that one act of homosexuality can turn a straight person gay, whereas a thousand acts of heterosexuality can never turn a gay person straight. In erotic witchlore, for instance, a witch of any gender who can gain physical access to a person can overpower any man or woman by working a nipple spell, in which hypnotic fingering and pressure makes even the most dominant person submissive.

Similar to the earthquake that rocked the Catholic Church during the second Vatican Council (1962–65), which debated sex issues of marriage and celibacy, the modern sexquake rocking witchcraft has its epicenter in the sexual liberation movements of women and gays both redefining traditional gender notions of witchcraft and Wicca. Who can be an altar? Who can be a priest? Are there fecundities other than the heterosexual female planted with male seed? What of male-male conjuring and female-female rituals? Is witchcraft somehow Inquisition-bound to the strict teachings of Saint Thomas Aquinas that all sex acts must lead to conception? Are the yin-yang polarities thought necessary for conjuring magic found only in the man-woman combination, or are the male-female *berdache* polarities present in each person, as Carl Jung says? Are the male-female polarities even necessary? Who penetrates whom? What other power is conjured through the penetration of the male by a man or a woman? Do gene-splicing and cloning mean that the old yin-yang polarity is no longer even necessary for creation? Have Wicca and witchcraft, historically considered free of sexism, actually been too patriarchal? Or too matriarchal? Because matriarchy in witchcraft is as lopsided a sexist hegemony as patriarchy, wouldn't something in between work better than either pole to make magic even more powerful?

What of the special intuition and knowledge of homosexuality that has survived as a secret culture as old as witchcraft itself? In biblical myth lies a time line of witchcraft. Adam was a patriarch to Eve, and they gained knowledge by eating the apple from the Tree of Knowledge. One of their two sons, Cain, in line for Adam's patriarchy, killed his younger brother, Abel, because Abel, who had gained his own secret knowledge from the tree, was made magical by that secret knowledge. The scenario is this: Abel, with his queer eye, saw through his brother, Cain, and laughed ironically at his brother's patriarchal demands, because Abel's secret knowledge made him the first seer, the first witch, the first gay man on the sacred path, and the first "bashed" queer. As valid as any private interpretation of the Bible, this alternation of the archetypal story balances the apocryphal Jewish myth that Adam had a wife before Eve, and her name was Lilith, whom he (ever the patriarch) left because she was a witch.

Both stories illustrate one continuing point. Women and gay men, like magic itself, exist to inject irony into the linear half-lives of the patriarchy as well as of the matriarchy—each of which is as oppressive as the other.

Occult sexuality in all its diversity is coming out of its own closet, because modern mass media demand full disclosure of all secrets, particularly the erotic. Witches-by-night can be as uptight and middle-class as their by-day backgrounds, particularly when sex rears its ugly head. No one should be confused by the sheer white noise of white witches denying they use black magic. Many American witches, acting out their peculiar cultural Puritanism, live in denial of both sex and the black arts, claiming that they only know about nonsexual practices and white magic. This makes practitioners of black magic and Satanists laugh the way audiences laugh at white witch Mary Poppins saying, "I never explain anything."

Less cynical observers figure that such white witches often prevaricate about sex and Satan because they fear reprisal of the historical kind that always ends up with someone burned at the stake. Sabaeanist Pontifex Maximus Frederic de Arechaga puts the feet of witches to the fire when he says, "If they don't admit to at least bisexuality, they aren't the witches they think they are." He adds that "homosexuality and heterosexuality are both queer because they each lack the other; both are equally degenerated, and," he emphasizes, "unpardonable."[3] Anton LaVey says that in the reality of Wicca, sex, and Satan, these so-called white witches "know what side their bread is buttered on." The famously straight LaVey, who was no heterosexist, does not honor the ancient code of the "Silence of the Sphinx" who knows all and tells little. LaVey, speaking like the Wiccan Walt Whitman of the body electric, trumpets sex in magic; he values both straight and gay members in his Church of Satan, because, as a maverick himself rebelling against the traditional sexism of much esoteric teaching, he finds both sexual paths to be sacred paths with spiritual validity. Practitioner Adrian Kirch maintains that "while sexuality is often overrated in both black and white magic, many believe that a homosexual is granted special powers."[4]

Anton LaVey, as doctrinal teacher of the Church of Satan, concurs that mention of homosexuality is missing from many occult books because the writers were self-censored by the homophobic mores of their time. For instance, when Gerald Gardner just barely managed to get Wicca legalized as a religion in England on June 22, 1951, the brilliant national hero Allan Turing, who had saved England by breaking the Nazi Enigma Code, was being tortured by the British government—which had also tortured Joan of Arc—with chemicals that affected his hyper-aware brain because Turing had made passing mention that he was homosexual.

In that homophobic climate, Gardner, who like Turing had repelled Nazis, was not about to jeopardize his crusade for the legalization of Wicca by admitting that homosexual energy was one of the many components of Wicca. As it was, his phone was tapped. Gardner and his Wiccans remembered why Oscar Wilde had been done away with, and, in their own day, they saw the British government drive Turing to "gay suicide." Destroying Turing's homosexuality was more morally important than honoring both his defeating the Nazis and his part in inventing the first computers. His genius had to seem separate from homosexuality and not a coefficient of the homosexual outside eye. "Gay suicide" is a rarified "suicide," because it is self-murder usually engineered by others as a way to be rid of the hyperaware homosexual who breaks codes and injects irony and "weird otherness" into straight-line culture. When it comes to punishing modern gay witches, "gay suicide" has often been the subtle new "burning at the stake," which has been perfected, some contend, by the government-created virus useful to the ongoing inquisition against gays, people of color, and women: HIV.

In the same way that terrified gay people have historically destroyed their own writings and art, Gerald Gardner counseled in his handbook for witches, *The Book of Shadows* (ca. 1939), "Keep a book in your hand and write . . . but never let the book out of your hand and never keep the writings of another for if it be found . . . they well may be taken and tortured. Each should guard his own writing and destroy it whenever danger threatens. Learn as much as you may by heart, and when danger is past, rewrite your book if it be safe."[5]

With the onset of gay liberation in 1969, *The Gay Grimoire: A Book of Spells* surfaced in the under-underground of gay subculture. In the 1950s, gays queried sexual identity out of *The Wizard of Oz* with the coded expression, "Are you a friend of Dorothy?" In the 1960s, seekers into gay witchcraft asked, "Do you know Garry Grimler?" Always handwritten, *The Gay Grimoire* was often copied into the kind of freestyle book popular among gay hippie craftsmen: a one-piece leather cover, folded in half, with parchment pages bound together by a rawhide thong drawn up through the two holes of the back cover, through the paper, and out the two holes of the front cover where the thong was tied into a witch's knot. Whoever possessed a copy of the book could authorize another person to copy out another manuscript, in handwriting only. Thus *The Gay Grimoire* is always alive, because, with each copying, the text breathes, and changes, precisely like the Bible being scratched out—in both senses of the term—by medieval monks, or revised by King James. Even the most careful copyists add phrases, or omit spells, moving between white and black magic. Creative magicians interpolate their own material—specifically gay or pink magic—

which the next copyist might change again. The private interpretation of witchcraft is as free and legitimate as private interpretation of the Bible—which was democratic Protestantism's main contribution to Biblical exegesis that had been totally controlled by the Catholic Church. Born-again Protestants thumping the Bible with the glories of private interpretation of Scripture should appreciate their mirror image in witches coming out tub-thumping their private interpretations of their grimoires.

The Gay Grimoire counsels that such "pouring of the fluid text" from "goblet to goblet no more hurts its truth than the pouring of water into cups keeps water from seeking its own level in the pitcher from which its is poured." In the rede of things, whatever *Grimoire* was "handed to the seeker" was the *Grimoire* that "the seeker needs at that time, place, and circumstance under the stars." Advice is given: "To make a straight man spit, cruise him with a look. Straight males usually spit to avert what they think is the gay evil eye that they know will divert them from their task. If a straight male does not spit, he might be available. Either way you may collect a conjure drop of his juices: spit or semen." The most interesting gay spells invoking love, or protection from danger, are recipes of self-love or self-protection using one's own bodily fluids of blood, tears, sweat, and semen; or requiring collection of clothing, semen, sweat, blood, and excreta from the man who is the object of one's desire—or the enemy who is the object of one's hate; or the collection of sexual juices, seed, urine, hair, cuticles, and fetishes of clothing of straight men "known for their potency," particularly men in authority such as protective lawmen and soldiers, "to whose true north we are drawn." *The Gay Grimoire* is as explicit as the *Kama Sutra*, and as instantly flammable as Gardner counseled in the *Book of Shadows*. Even though "Gary Grimler" rarely shows up, he once advised, "More than one gay witch has lain in wait, in the bushes along a [straight] lovers' lane, waiting to collect the condoms of seed thrown out the car windows." All real witches understand the difficulty of collecting fresh ingredients for spells and potions.

Only Aleister Crowley came close to such boldness. With Gerald Gardner and other traditionalists, the omission of homosexuality in the liberation of mid-twentieth-century witchcraft was a white lie told more out of self-protection than real bias. Antiwitchcraft prejudice through the ages had burned so many magic books, and killed so many witches, that even fewer occult books would have survived if the writers had revealed how often homosexuality was used to raise the cone of power. The history of witchcraft is virtually the same as the history of homosexuality. Analog to *The Gay Grimoire* is the anthology edited by Mark Mitchell and David Leavitt *Pages Passed from Hand to Hand: The Hidden Traditions of Homosexual Literature in English from 1748–1914* (1998).

In tandem with the modern rise of women priests in covens is the visible rise of gay men in the craft who apply their experience gained in gay liberation to the liberation of witchcraft. Gay theorist and activist Leo Louis Martello, founder of the Witches Anti-Defamation League and the author of the groundbreaking *Witch Manifesto* (1968), invented the template for legal suits seeking reparations for Native Americans with real-estate title claims, for African Americans descended from slaves, and for minors molested by Catholic priests. In his good humor, Martello combined two liberation images, the homosexual closet and the witch's broom, in his militant chant: "Out of the broom closets, and onto your brooms!"

Years before the permissive society that gave context to Martello, the brilliant Aleister Crowley, ever exalting in his bad-boy code name "Beast 666," took a quantum step forward when he dared admit to a certain bisexuality and ritual sodomy in his conjurations to raise the Devil. For his efforts, he was denounced by the famous Dion Fortune, who spent her 1920s and 1930s denouncing homosexual occultists and homosexuality. Best-selling author Fortune, like Madame Helena Petrovna Blavatsky and other "reverse sexists," perhaps protesting a bit too much, dismissed the homosexual quotient of Crowley's erotic revelations as personal lunacy caused by drugs. Crowley's enemies enjoyed reminding the public that royal British Customs officials burned eighty-three of the one hundred copies of the 1898 edition of Crowley's erotic-magic poems, *White Stains*, because of its insinuating politics of homosexuality, sodomy, bestiality, and necrophilia. *White Stains*—each of the hundred covers glazed with the white pearls of Crowley's own semen—was published by Leonard Smithers, who showed the power of small occult presses when he dared also publish Aubrey Beardsley and Oscar Wilde, who preferred to sign rather than stain the first hundred copies of their books.

Crowley was a sex-and-magic pioneer. Sixty years after he announced the power of ritual sodomy, gay witches further liberated both homosexuality and witchcraft. They took their own quantum leap forward when they declared that the receptive role of the penetrated male was neither "passive" nor "feminine," but was a new kind of "male power" that activated formerly impenetrable male mysteries and masculine energy in a creative and sensitive way. Masculine men who actively open themselves to the initiatory rite of penetration unlock a magic and a power and a knowledge that is unreleased in masculine men who have never experienced another body inside their own body. Some people believe in this newly uncloseted primordial male power the way they had always believed there existed an ancient female power.

Like being female or black, being homosexual is also not an aberrational way to be human; homosexuality is an *additional* way to be human. The more completely human a witch is, the more powerful the witch's magic is, because, paralleling the insights of both philosopher Thomas Aquinas and film director Tod Browning, witchcraft builds on the human nature of one's sex, gender, and race. Witches who deny sex—in any measure of Alfred Kinsey's "sex arithmetic"—are heretics to the occult because sex energy is the essence of magic, which cannot confine itself to middle-class mores. How can anything sexual be shocking to occultists who range from Wiccans who trust that "everything in nature is sacred" to Satanists who pant that "sex with Satan is the ideal"? People who claim to be witches can be tested with this rede: if they are sexual Puritans, they are not really witches.

In 1900, Crowley was already the perfect "1960s radical." Why has he been reviled by both the government establishment and the Wiccan establishment for his invocation of sex, drugs, and music? Actually, Crowley the humanist outed one of the deepest sexual secrets of the occult: the ability for practitioners, in the name of craft, to shift the shape of sexual magic from procreational sex into free-ranging recreational sex. This runs counter to the puritanical gender dogma of most established religions, and it certainly runs counter to Christianity, which was the most puritanical of all the Near Eastern religions fighting it out when Christ was born into a world so consumed by magic, sorcery, and witchcraft that the Magi (the magicians) followed a star to Bethlehem, and Christ—who often spoke with the Devil—grew up to be the greatest exorcist of his time.

After all, if witchcraft isn't about natural joy, maypoles, guilt-free sprites, magical fairies, sexual freedom, and ritual sodomy (with a bit of necrophilia), then it's just another religion similar to Catholicism, whose priests—instead of being principal conjurors and fertile phallic practitioners—are sworn to an antisex celibacy. For all its personal sacrifice, the minimalism of priestly celibacy really leads nowhere. Celibacy actually diminishes the magic of Catholicism invoked in all its bells, books, candles, incense, holy water, holy oils, burning of palm branches, and sprinkling of salt. When Catholicism loses its magic, the core doctrine of transubstantiation flies out the stained-glass window. Transubstantiation is the one thing that makes Catholics different from everyone else. Transubstantiation is not metaphor; it is not symbol. The magic word *hocus-pocus* is witchcraft's ridicule of the Latin words the priest says to transubstantiate the bread into Christ's body: "Hoc est enim corpus meum." These are the words Christ said in the New Testament to his thirteen apostles (including Judas's replacement, Matthias) at the Last Supper: "This is my body."

"Conjuring on Christ's body" is an analogue of the body-conjuring practiced by white-magic Wiccans and black-magic Satanists. Some Wiccans, such as Gerald Gardner and sometimes Alex Sanders, defining Wicca in their own image, limit acknowledgment to heteroconjuring body rituals only. Because both magical leaders are male, straight and sexually submissive, they have motive to invest the highest authority in the Goddess. This Goddess doctrine—given a wink-wink by male lust—is, some say, a come-on to attract women into the coven where they join in as willing partners with men they'd otherwise never look at. Such parleyed female consent insures beta-male access to alpha-females, socially and sexually. Some cynics say that the male in charge of the coven, like a Hollywood casting director, takes his privileged pick of priestess to reflect the Goddess. Whatever the motivation, such "God-Goddess" chauvinism reflects only heterosexual lust and not the human celebration power of the personal self, which is Anton LaVey's main teaching.

The hetero-occult being what it is, one thinks of British poet laureate Ted Hughes. His mother taught him Wiccan arts, mind control, and the tarot, which he introduced to his American wife, the poet, Sylvia Plath. On their first meeting at a Cambridge party, she had drawn his blood by biting him on his cheek. Hughes, expert at mesmerism, often hypnotized Sylvia to move her from despair to creativity, until finally Sylvia famously committed suicide, because no matter how much a husband hypnotizes his wife he still can't make her believe he's faithful. White magic does not exist to control women.

Satanists are rather more "perversatile;" they know that sex is an intrinsically shape-shifting event. What "God-Goddess" there may be is, like the angel-devil Satan, a shape-shifter, and—never forget—a trickster. Gone is the day when sexism did not allow women to be magicians, but only "magician's assistants" in scanty clothes. In the same way, Neanderthal are the occultists who protest too much that homosex is not often useful to invoking parallax power to boost human magic that is actually limited by being heterosexual only. Countering the bias of heterosexist witchcraft, Crowley leapt into the trenches of the gender wars whose avant-garde has always been—*mais oui!*—witchcraft. If there can be a valid female witch-craft, there can be a valid male witchcraft. If there can be a valid feminist witchcraft, there can be a valid gay witchcraft. All converge in humanist witchcraft.

When the militant occultist Madame Blavatsky (1831–91), founder of the Theosophical Society, was asked if she were married, she replied, "I am a widow . . . and I thank God! I wouldn't be a slave to God Himself, let alone man." So why did she thank a male God? Was Blavatsky advo-cating polar lesbian magic? Blavatsky made her anti-God, antimale and antigay declaration of independence in her virulent reaction to Aleister Crowley and his magic "lifestyle," which she feared would overtake her brand of spiritualism. Blavatsky was mimicked in 1967 by Valerie Solanas, founder of the Society to Cut Up Men and author of the *SCUM Manifesto*, published in 1968, the year that she shot and nearly killed Andy Warhol in virulent reaction to his being a man, she said, having too much control over her life. The times were violent. Solanas shot Warhol two days before Sirhan Sirhan shot Robert F. Kennedy on June 5, and only sixty-one days after Martin Luther King Jr., was shot. At this same time, the years 1968–69, the more submissive Manson girls—none of them as crazy as cult-heroine Valerie Solanas—were, according to *McCall's* reporter Jean Stafford, at times sadistically abused within the sexual rituals of the (Manson) Family.

In *Esquire* magazine, Tom Burke interviewed a nationally popular girl singer. She told of a Hollywood party where "you went in and there were three altars. On two of them, these boys were tied with leather thongs. They were sobbing. These two faggots dressed as nuns—one had a *goatee*—were beating them with big black rosaries. On the middle altar there was a very young girl. This guy wearing a goat's head had crushed a live frog on her privates. When I came in, he had just cut a little cross on her stomach. . . ."[6] The January 18, 1970, *National Tattler* carried a front page headline: "Why Women Crawled for Madman Manson: They Bore His Children, They Licked His Feet." The February 9, 1970, issue of *Spotlight* illustrated a "Pay-for-Pain Girls" article with a picture of a bound girl stretched across an altar under a pentagram. The caption read, "Women like this stage weird sadomasochistic orgies that often end in bloodshed."

The sadomasochistic underground—a nationwide pansexual network typified by the American Eulenspiegel Society, founded in 1972—may be a bastard child of Christianity, but is adopted sibling to the occult. The essence of sadomasochism is ritual, and this ritual finds ready match in occult procedure and coven. Sadomasochists are extremely caste conscious.

When a master appears in public with his slave, certain behavior becomes them both. Slavery has not been abolished in America; it has merely gone into the sexual underground. When it occasionally surfaces with a Charles Manson, mainstream America reels at its different morality.

In the summer of 1969 at Indio, California, a farm commune operated by a cult called Ordo Templar Orientalis, which in one permutation counted Aleister Crowley among its members, reportedly chained a six-year-old boy, Anthony Saul Gibbons, in a sweatbox for fifty-six days. Eleven commune members, including the boy's mother, were accused of torturing the boy by burning his fingers with matches; the boy's punishment was discipline for a fire he had started that had destroyed one house and injured a group of goats. When the October 31, 1969, *Washington Post* Halloween edition carried this UPI item, the public morality was outraged by the cult's private morals. Private discipline and contemporary servitude, like witchcraft, are, however, a psychic reality more frequent in American culture than an occasional news item about corporal punishment might indicate.

Minority sexuality is always a measure of pop culture. "Sex has always been a weapon of the *avant garde*. Sexual imagery," Edward Lucie-Smith wrote in *Race, Sex, and Gender in Contemporary Art*, "has been one of the quickest and most direct means open to any artist who wanted to establish his or her credentials as a transgressor against established bourgeois systems."[7] In the same way, when the sex is couched in witchcraft, the mixture galvanizes culture between the equally seductive poles of attraction and repulsion.

Robert Marasco's Broadway drama *Child's Play* (1970) theorized that the curse that goes with the diamond of a permissive society is society's backlash cry for discipline. Some people have the will to power; others have the desire to serve. The underground premise holds that in a free and permissive society, just as some people submit their wills to religious dogma and tithing, others ought to have the right to sell themselves into slavery to a sadistic cult or demonic coven. Consequently, much underground activity concerns contracting for servitude, temporary or permanent. As chronicled in Geoff Mains's *Urban Aboriginals: A Celebration of Leathersexuality* (1984), the underground press is cross-listed with masters, slaves, and occultists in search of one another. It is a truth of popular culture that "classified ads" by their sheer numbers and demographic themes reveal human truths of behavior and desire. Seekers can find classifieds offering evolutionary groups for conjuring gay magic as well as reactionary groups for invoking anti-Christian blasphemy.

"The Sanctuary of Priapus invites gay men to express their own private sex rituals of masturbation in a group setting that releases gay imagination, gay power, and gay magic through ecstatic drink, drugs, dancing, and sex." While Satanic blasphemy is certainly not a gay activity per se, one private party invitation made this pitch: "The Brothers of Blasphemy offer a group for gay men who blaspheme and get off on blasphemy and sacrilege against the Nazarene and all that is associated with the false X-tian 'God,' and any other false 'god' that gets in your way. We offer a haven from self-righteous religious fools, and a place to indulge and share blasphemies, and encourage others in their pleasure."[8] The Sons of Satan advertised in the leather S&M magazine *Drummer*.[9] The Fist Fuckers of America, philosophically led by the mystic Peter Perusha Larkin, author of *The Divine Androgyne: The Tao of Hindu Gay Consciousness and Rectal-Hand Coordination* (1981), advertises, "Cry out for the God of the Fist! Magic through penetration." A computer service matching gay masochists with gay sadists is called "The Order of the Sixth Martyr." The computer-membership fee of ten dollars is sent to the Order of the Sixth Martyr, c/o ANVIL, P. O. Box 38326, Hollywood, California 90038.

SNAPSHOT: FeBe's Bar, Folsom Street, South of Market, San Francisco, 1970.

The cult of masculinity is alive and well at the famous FeBe's Bar, located on Eleventh Street at Folsom Street in San Francisco, where phallism is coded in the night-time uniform—and ritual vestments—of tailored leather pants with detachable codpiece, and the phallic peak of black leather caps smartly designed by Muir Cap and Regalia of Toronto. In gay culture, the male gods rise and rise again triumphant, because phallic worship is coded into gay art, writing, photography, and culture in the masculinizing fetishization of clothes (leather and denim); tools and weapons (knives, swords, guns); drugs (amyl-nitrite snifters shaped like silver bullets worn on a rawhide thong around the neck, needles, cigarettes and cigars smoked invocatively as in rituals of Santeria and the Bohemian Club); and combustion engines (motorcycles, trucks).

At FeBe's, the Satyrs Motorcycle Club (founded in 1956) and the Warlocks Motorcycle Club park their Harleys, and sadists match with masochists. Established in 1968, FeBe's Leather Bar explains its name and purpose through occult detail in its newsletter: "FeBe (Gr. Phoebe) was the Greek Goddess of the chase and patroness of hunters. . . . She became Goddess of the night and the underworld, later becoming associated with Hecate, the Queen of witches and warlocks. She was also the stern Goddess of punishment when any offended her or violated her laws of virginal chastity. Telephone: Masochism 19450."

The innuendo of FeBe's newsletter leaves little to even the mainstream imagination regarding erotic congress in which full-frontal bondage and pain are common rites of inducing altered states of consciousness in rites of sexual magic. At FeBe's shop, called A Taste of Leather, customers can buy a conjure idol in the form of a two-foot-tall statue of Michelangelo's *David* recast in 1966 by sculptor Michael Caffee, in white plaster, with a biker's cap and jeans in the leather fashion of Marlon Brando. In *The Wild One* (1954), the masculine gay world found its muscular pagan archetype, which Kenneth Anger perfected in *Scorpio Rising* (1964). A townsman asked the swaggering Brando, "What are you rebelling against?" Brando sassed back, "Whatcha got?" Lucifer himself, confronted by God, must have answered exactly that way with those words. So would most liberated gay men.

Caffee's aggressive *Leather David* statue, referencing also the swooning masochism of the gayest of martyrs, Saint Sebastian, symbolizes erotic dominance and submission. It is a phallic conjure *fith-fath* (any doll used for casting a spell) as specified in FeBe's newsletter, of occult leather rites of the kind popularized by black magister Kenneth Anger in his sacrilegious, blasphemous, and Satanic underground art films. Director Michael Zen reflected similar shape-shifting gay fantasies in his very popular and seminal film *Falconhead* (1972), in which a bodybuilder wearing a falcon's head uses a magic mirror to transport men into the "other dimension," where they perform their most secret fantasies. In the endlessly inventive camp-voodoo of gay culture, several toy dolls made by Mattell—particularly the macho G.I. Joe more than Barbie's vanilla friend Ken—not only often double as fith-fath voodoo dolls, but they have sired a best-selling line of hyper-masculine gay dolls that are often used to cast love spells, hexes, and blessings.

The music played on the collage audiotapes mixed especially for gay leather bars like FeBe's incidentally reflects occult themes in pop culture. The range of album cuts features:

- Led Zeppelin, whose lead singer Jimmy Page owned one of the largest occult bookstores in England, bought Aleister Crowley's Loch Ness mansion Boleskin, and often quoted Crowley's rede, "Do What Thou Wilt";

- Alice Cooper, who, spelling on a ouija board, jumped across gender and named himself after a seventeenth-century witch;
- Ozzy Osbourne, once of Black Sabbath, invoking Crowley on his first solo album, *Blizzard of Ozz* (1980), in the song, "Mr. Crowley";
- the Doors, whose lead singer Jim Morrison, riding the "King Snake" dressed in black leather, featured a bust of Crowley on one of the band's album covers, and in 1970 married the self-proclaimed witch Patricia Kennealy in a Wiccan hand-fasting ritual;
- the Beatles, who admired the freethinking rede "let-it-be" that Crowley introduced into pop culture;
- the Rolling Stones, who through singer Mick Jagger were connected to Crowley's heir, Kenneth Anger, whose "magick lantern" films are often screened in gay leather bars.

By the beginning of the 1970s, *The Real Thing* (1968), an epistolary novel by William Carney, had risen from the gay subculture to pop-culture notoriety. Unlike the comparable straight *Story of O* (1954) by Pauline Reage, this American gay *roman noir* dictated norms of ritual, caste, and costume appropriate to sadomasochistic ascetics.

Black magic is the source of Carney's dress code and psychic preparation for ritual scenes. For the sadist, Carney's leatherman's handbook advises, "Mere nakedness is nothing . . . some element of the uniform must always be retained. . . . only the Victim was completely naked. . . Live like an athlete . . . wear colors sparingly. . . . The rule for cloth is up tight. Snug. . . . Boots proclaim the man. . . .Chains? Yes. . . . Choose your belt and buckle with care and wear them as they should be worn: . . .left side is *sinister*, sadist, top man, teacher, master, shepherd, S; right is *dexter*, masochist, bottom man, boy, slave, mutton, M. . . . Deliver words and blows with a minimum of effort and a maximum of effect. . . . Finesse! finesse! . . .Begin gently and let the violence take hold of you bit by bit."[10] For the slave, Carney advises the proper ritual behavior: "If you are the Victim you will, naturally, be passive. But you will not be merely passive. You will take care to respond in a manner which is both proper to your role and adjusted to the particular Master who is working on you. . . . The acceptance of another session is a prior acknowledgment that it will go further than the last one did."[11]

Carney quickly became the first best-selling international oracle on S&M cult and culture, paving the way for the widely read *Leatherman's Handbook* (1972) by Larry Townsend. The mystical orders Carney has codified complement the hierarchy of coven. The ethos of the S&M Way, comparable to the minor orders of the Catholic Church, contains four orders: oblates, purists, exemplars, and the perfect. Carney tolerates the oblates as uninitiated dabblers in cult; their involvement is the sensational pastime of bar boys, and not an art. The purists are cult fetishists; their kick is ritual involvement with costumes, ornaments, and conducive setting. The exemplar is a dedicated high-priest sadist who, like the title character in Tennessee Williams's eucharistic short story "Desire and the Black Masseur" (1946) is "devoted to the task of breaking the victim he confronts in the manner of the priest who creases and splits the Host. He contemplates his victim, worshiping him with studied savagery, and the victim, broken, is consumed. The lives of these uncorrupted Exemplars are oriented toward the attainment of such singular moments of transcendence. . . ."[12]

Finally, the perfect are latter-day anchorites. They are venerated and feared; they are more abstracted than the exemplars. Their presence at an S&M session—like the raising of Satan at a Black Mass—insures the perfect rite, the ultimate scene, where the sadist's agonizing hand on the masochist's body transforms mere gesture from transitory effect into transcendent eternal moment.

This gay sadistic spiritual hierarchy has its source in occult ritual. Each regimen inverts the symbols of Christianity. As the Latin-American Penitentes during Holy Week in the American Southwest torture one another with scourges and ritualized simulated crucifixion to honor Christ's Passion, so do demonic ritualists torture to negate Christ's salvific act. Sadomasochists, such as the members of the gay Hellfire Club founded in Chicago in 1971, torture to affirm the pleasures of the flesh through pain that changes consciousness. White magicians, even those descended from Gerald Gardner, use ritual pain, often of the velvet kind, wherein whips are made of silken threads. Tennessee Williams pointed out a huge psychological "hang-up" in western culture: Christ on the Cross. In *The Night of the Iguana* (1961), Williams defined what he meant when he laughed at the defrocked priest tied up in a hammock and said that some people are jealous of Christ because he endured the original crucifixion. Their S&M "imitation of Christ" relates to the hanged man of the tarot. Begun in 1970, a journal of mystic adventure in San Francisco included this documentation of a gay crucifixion scene:

> Ryan tied Kick's huge arms wide open on the cross. . . . He watched his lover strain and flex like a muscular Olympic gymnast performing the crucifix on the double rings. . . . His loincloth fell away. . . . He hung, by his massive

arms, crucified, head back and haloed by the shine of the tracklight. . . . The moment grew mystical as Kick struggled, flexed, relaxed, flexed, and endured against the hard wooden Cross. It started as night games: heroic sculpture from drawings and movies. It became some ritual else. Their separate fantasies meshed in the flesh, then separated in their minds, coming back together. . . finding the Energy, the Entity conjured between them. . . . Kick was the bodybuilder crucified. . . . Ryan was his . . . lover, his priest. . . . He hit them both with popper. This was no Imitation of Christ. This was real. Kick was more than an *alter Christus*. He was the incarnation of the real Christ Himself. Kick, throbbing with the tension of the muscle bondage, glistened. His whole body tightened down into a cruciform Most-Muscular position. . . . Ryan looked up lovingly at his crucified Savior. He could feel the power rising in the crucified's body. Then suddenly, the white clotted rain shot like saving grace. . . . "Oh, my beautiful God."

The next day Ryan's best friend, Solly Blue, said on the phone, "What you gayboys won't do to have fun."[13]

The journal, covering twelve years, was published as the "faction" novel of sex magic, *Some Dance to Remember*. (Truman Capote defined *faction* in terms of his 1966 book *In Cold Blood*, as a new genre mixing fact with fiction.)

Gay dramatist Tennessee Williams may be correct about the erotic influence of the stripping, whipping, and crucifixion of Christ, which is the main image of Western art, because painters, sculptors, photographers, and filmmakers, such as Mel Gibson, tend to portray the Christus as a young naked athlete suffering gloriously. In 1900, photographer F. Holland Day pictured himself as the crucified Christ in a series of self-portraits that reflect not so much narcissism as the gay existential condition. Delmas Howe, an anchorite painter living in the New Mexico desert, painted a *Golgotha* series of large canvases depicting gay men suffering the Passion and death of Jesus. Christ's magical sex appeal on the Cross is analogous to the erotic appeal of Saint Sebastian, whom hypermasculine Roman soldiers tied naked to a stake and slowly shot to death with arrows. Derek Jarman, set designer for *The Devils*, wrote and directed his gloriously louche version of the gay legend in his homomasculine classic *Sebastiane* (1975). Jarman's was the first feature film with dialogue all in Latin, and was produced thirty years before heteromasculine Mel Gibson's Roman soldiers spoke Latin in the equally louche *The Passion of the Christ* which in 2004 became an instant cult favorite in gay S&M culture.

George Lois created quintessential pop iconography for the 1960s on the covers of *Esquire* magazine. Ever provocative, he photographed Muhammed Ali for the April 1968 *Esquire* cover posed as Saint Sebastian, as suggestively tied to a stake as any witch for burning. The handsome, muscular Ali, dripping with sweat, blood, and sex appeal, stands stripped to the waist in white satin boxing trunks against an all-white background of the absolutely inquisitional photo titled *The Passion of Muhammed Ali*. His head is tilted up in the attitude so familiar from photographs of lynched black men, and his muscular arms seem tied behind his back. Five arrows pierce his pecs and torso, and another arrow is shot into his right thigh. Lois canonized Ali as a pop-culture martyr-saint, because Ali had been stripped of his heavyweight boxing championship title for one reason: he was a black man vocally opposing the Vietnam War, which was being fought by drafted black soldiers.

Lois' strong image of Ali became an instant holy card of S&M and phallic worship as well as racial fetishism, particularly among gay men worshiping black men. This cover greatly influenced the photography of the twenty-two-year-old Satanist Robert Mapplethorpe who, studying at the Pratt Institute (where Lois also studied), wanted to break the white taboo against photographing the bodies and phalluses of black men. Akin to Mapplethorpe lounging among his bronze statues of the goat-footed Satan, Lois lives—with his longtime wife—in Greenwich Village in an apartment filled with African virility and fertility cult objects that bespeak folk art if not witchcraft. Lois collected his best covers, advertising, and political images into his book *Sellebrity* (2003). The book includes his famous shape-shifting May 1968 *Esquire* cover of a corpse-like Richard Nixon—the trickster criminal president known as "Tricky Dicky"—having his "vampyr" face disguised and masked to look alive with lipstick and cosmetics just like the Mascarae.

Pop culture is everything to homosexuals.[14] So what can be made of the pop culture when these leather men and gay artists were growing up? In 1959, *Toys and Novelties* magazine carried an advertisement for "the line with something for everyone." The toy was an "Assemble-It-Yourself Plastic Crucifix." The child had simply to cross the beams and then nail down the plastic Jesus. The rest of the copy for this camp collectible read, "Inspiring. Beautiful. Authentic. Faithfully scaled from a famous masterpiece, this easily assembled crucifix reflects the serenity and beauty of the original. . . . A prized, welcome, and tasteful addition to any Catholic home." Does anyone actually think that the original torture-murder was serene and beautiful?

Making himself legendary, photographer Mapplethorpe, always a self-referential Satanist, shot, for the cover of issue number 7 of *Creatis: La Photographie au presant*, a self-portrait in an outstretched cruciform fashion. He was presented as a leather Satanist to the leather community in "The Mapplethorpe Gallery (Censored)" in *Son of Drummer* (1978); he shot the dark-themed cover of *Drummer* magazine's issue number 24 (September 1978); and he was mourned in "Pentimento for Robert Mapplethorpe: Fetishes, Faces, and Flowers of Evil," in *Drummer* 133. He often referenced Satanism, priapism, muscular paganism, and Christ's magical passion in his S&M photographs of leather, bondage, urine rituals, penetration by fist, and transcendental torture by razor blade and needle. In the early 1970s, Mapplethorpe was constructing his photographs on the Catholic rituals and iconography of his youth. He knew that Satanism was the ultimate trump card. The young artist, who groomed himself to look like the Satanic love child of Mick Jagger and Jim Morrison, told the art world of galleries, critics, rich collectors, and the terminally hip, "If you don't like these images, you're not as avant-garde as you think."

He photographed muscular naked black men for their phallic magic and to reference the African magic he felt inherent in their flesh. He shot himself as a Dionysian satyr with horns, as a gender-shifting trickster in mascara, as a black-leather gangster with a gun standing in front of a pentagram, and, in his most famous signature portrait, as a crouched Satan with a scatological black-leather tail curling from a bullwhip handle poked up his rear. Because of these creepy Crowley images, he was hired to illustrate a pricey edition of the poet Arthur Rimbaud's *A Season in Hell* (1986). His goddess-muse, whom he photographed through the years in a kind of ghostly Kirilian camera style, was the punk poet and singer Patti Smith. He photographed bodybuilder Lisa Lyon as a fanged vampire.

He finished his brief life with a ghost-portrait of himself (*Self Portrait,* 1988) that could be titled *Death with a Death's Head Cane*. The Hamlet-Yorick photograph looks like a still from *Vampyr* as much as from the elegant Ingmar Bergman film *Persona* (1966). That film, whose stark images by Sven Nykvist reflect the complete iconography of the psychological horror film, is an unspooling succession of the kind of perfect black-and-white frame composition Mapplethorpe epitomized. His photography so outraged the Puritan religious right that United States Senator Jesse Helms, a southern Republican from the poisonous tobacco-funded state of North Carolina, launched a federal government inquisition against his Satanism, his homosexuality, his sadomasochism, his black penises, and his so-called child pornography. The 1990 Mapplethorpe "witch trial," dramatized in the film *Dirty Pictures* (2000), was held in Cincinnati, and contributed to a Puritan government victory that virtually destroyed the National Endowment for the Arts.

Mapplethorpe contemporary Andres Serrano, raised in a devout Catholic family, plunged a crucifix into a vase of urine and caused a furor with his photograph of it, *Piss Christ* (1987), which Serrano said was religious art while critics screamed blasphemy. Winston Churchill's granddaughter, Edwina Sandys, in her large bronze crucifix sculpture titled *Christa* (1975), reversed the male nude of the crucified Christ to that of a nude woman crucified. Has art merely exposed the inherent erotic power of the crucified Christ? Christian mystics for centuries have conjured their magic on the four-pointed star of the cross and its phallic cult-hero, always a magnificent Jesus, dying from his lifelong combat with Satan. Mapplethorpe's bloodiest series of photographs are the quintessence of the phallic Christ crucified as they are simply reductive pictures of a male phallus nailed to a board, as if they are botanica holy pictures to be hung over the altar in the Church of Saint Priapus, who is really Jesus in pagan drag.

Magic-sex ritualist Yukio Mishima, the gay right-wing militarist and internationally renowned poet, often photographed himself nearly naked in erotic S&M scenes, sometimes pierced with arrows (eros), sometimes cut with swords, and always dying a languid gay martyr's death, which he finally fully acted out when he committed a shockingly public hara-kiri on November 25, 1970. "Yukio Mishima," Edward Lucie-Smith notes in *Eroticism in Western Art,* "described, in his semi-autobiographical book, *Confessions of a Mask,* a youth's obsession with the sado-masochistic fantasies suggested to him by Guido Reni's painting 'St. Sebastian.'"[15] Mishima's book of muscular paganism, *Sun and Steel: A Personal Testament on Art, Action, and Ritual Death* (1970), reveals his rituals of male identity and self-integration through hero worship of the Sun God and the fetish worship of male muscle pumped by iron weights. Mishima is reflected by the artists Goh Mishima and Gengorah Tagame in drawings of muscular Japanese men tied up in ritual postures of transcendent, heroic suffering. Anti-Puritan, "Bodybuilding is a rebellious, Faustian, Luciferian act."[16]

Mishima wrote that the "cult of the body and a mighty nihilism" always relate to the "cult of the hero," particularly in people who internalize the muscular sufferings of the mystical Christ. No group internalizes by rote the magical mystery tour of Christ's suffering muscular body better than Catholic homosexuals who are, in an ironic way, the most dedicated

worshipers at the pagan roots of muscular Christianity. Gay S&M Catholics are the latest manifestation of some historic mystics, like Saint Francis
of Assisi (1182–1226) and Padre Pio (1887–1968) who, according to Mishima,
so idealize the "enfleshment of Christ" that they sometimes create in themselves the stigmata of Christ, bleeding from real wounds, psychically caused,
in the palms, feet, and side—and sometimes bleeding from real wounds
that are physically caused. Stigmata is mainly a Catholic phenomenon,
usually Latin or Mediterranean, often occurring in the hands and feet of
reformed pleasure seekers. Because he famously wrote that flesh was beautiful, and that bruised flesh was more beautiful, Mishima is the patron saint
of athletic gay men and S&M aficionados. He taught, lived, and died conjuring the shape-shifting magical power of the male body, whose essence
is phallus.

Herein lies a principle. Homosexuality should come out of its largest
closet and defiantly declare itself an ancient religion—the way that witchcraft defended itself by a declaration of religious freedom. Homosexuality
is a natural religion. In the way that Protestant ministers declare themselves ordained reverends, gay men might pronounce themselves priests
and ministers of natural gay churches, and thereby be legally protected.

Religions change. Revealed religions, in particular, change. Mysteriously.
Usually in synch with politics, power, and money. Intuitive religions such
as Wicca and homosexuality, both anchored in nature, change far less.

In the year 313, Emperor Constantine legislated that the sect of Christianity, which had been outlawed in the Roman Empire for nearly three
hundred years, was not only suddenly legal, but was the state religion.
Constantine's "combo plate" of church and state lasted from 313 until 1776,
when the founding fathers of the United States separated church and state
"à la carte" in order to preserve personal rights.

Something personal in gay men understands Satan, or at least the Faustian pact with Satan that underlies Oscar Wilde's *The Picture of Dorian
Gray* (1891). Author Mart Crowley, in his Broadway and movie hit *The
Boys in the Band* (film version, 1970), revealed the quintessential Satanic
truth that there was not a gay man alive "who would not trade his immortal soul for a half-hour of skin-deep beauty." *The Boys in the Band* was
produced by Dominick Dunne, the society author obsessed with sex and
murder, and directed by William Friedkin whose next films were *The Exorcist* (1973) and the very controversial leather S&M film *Cruising* (1980).
That script outed a gay heart of darkness. Outraged homosexuals who were
not into sadomasochism and who feared backlash from this dark media

image, broke a sweat marching in the streets to stop its location shooting. Meanwhile, leathermen eagerly lined up to play extras in the Mineshaft bar scene. Early on in the exuberant brawl of defining gay identity, gay liberation in the Titanic 1970s achieved ecstasy of the kind described in the memoir-novel *Some Dance to Remember* (1990).

> The intensity of male Energy, he [Ryan] was convinced, was religious. They were men, as bonded as ancient priests, assisting in the reincarnational birth of a kind of homosexual religion that existed millennia before Christianity. . . . "Eons have passed," Ryan wrote, "waiting for this specific convergence of so many old souls to worship the Old God who predates Christianity. Our spirits have been harvested from time older than time, collected here and now out of all the uncounted ages of men for this reincarnation in unison. . . . Never on this planet have so many men of such similar mind gathered to fuck in the concelebration of pure, raw, priapic manhood. If the mythic Saint Priapus has never been canonized by the Catholic Church, then he has been made a saint in San Francisco. . . . in the temples of our conjoined bodies, tangled in passion, slick with sweat, and glazed with seed."[17]

In a San Francisco neighborhood not far from Anton LaVey's Church of Satan, the Church of Saint Priapus celebrated in the 1970s the magic cult of homomasculinity at 583 Grove Street, near the hippie Haight-Ashbury and the gay neighborhood of the Castro. *Phallos: The Saint Priapus Church Newsletter* details the phallic worship of this homosexual cult of masculinity. The main tenet of this white magic—sometimes called "pink magic"—is how spiritual access comes through the body electric. Homosexuality is the tell-tale heart beating out the rhythms of human ambiguity hidden by the straight life. Certainly, priapic worship reveals that there is a power outside of humans that humans can only try to control. Because a penis can harden or soften beyond the control of its owner, it is a sign that forces outside the person are operating inside the person. The Devil, according to priapic monks, will often make a man impotent with his wife, in order to test him with other women with whom he is not impotent, and with men with whom he is never impotent, because—magically—impotence rarely occurs in the refreshment of homosexual sex. As an independent symbol of irresistible power, the shape-shifting phallus becomes a magic object of worship and conjuration. The wand waved by magicians at the transubstantiating moment of "presto change-o" is, of course, a pure phallic symbol of what in less Puritan rituals was the pointing and waving of the erect penis showering its magic.

Long before Richard Knight wrote his *Discourse on the Worship of Priapus* (1785) and Ryley Scott wrote *Phallic Worship: A History of Sex and Sex Rites* (1966), the gospels of Priapus trickled down from antiquity. Mythic Priapus, born erect—and erect he remained—was the pug-ugly son of Aphrodite with several possible sires, including Hermes. A kind of dirty old Devil more ancient than the Greeks, Priapus was popular among the Romans who put him, erect, for luck atop stone markers called *herms* marking boundaries, in order to put a "no trespassing" scare into enemies and to guide travelers. Ever into gesticulation, the Romans also made the Sign of Priapus by putting the thumb between the forefinger and middle finger to ward off the evil eye. The Sign of Priapus is akin to the Sign of the Cross used by Christians to fend off evil.

During Nero's bloody reign, Petronius wrote the seminal priapic story, the novel-like *Satyricon*, spinning the sex adventures of Encolpius following his dick through decadent Rome, tricking and being tricked in the Temple of Priapus, with his two boyfriends, Ascyltos and Giton. *Tricking* is the main code word for gay anonymous sex. Before the ancient Encolpius escapes from the Temple of Priapus, he is tricked—literally—and sodomized. The same year that the modern Encolpius was rear-ended in *Fellini Satyricon* (1969) the cast of *Hair* was singing Broadway's second-most pagan hymn, "Sodomy, Fellatio, Cunnilingus, Pederasty." Perhaps the most priapic was the song, "I Have a Noble Cock," from the bawdy musical comedy based on Chaucer, *Canterbury Tales* (1968).

In this lineage of erection and sodomy, the modern Church of Saint Priapus reaches back to Priapus and assumes hereditary witchcraft status from ancient paganism as well as the historic magic rituals of the Knights Templar. Founded in the twelfth century by Hugh of the Pagans, the Knights Templar practiced priapic and scatological witchcraft rituals centered on pledging allegiance through the kissing of penis, anus, and mouth, as well as group orgies of male bonding expressing fraternity through bondage, flagellation, coprophagia, and seed exchange. Petronius might have cheered the fan club of his notoriously pornographic novel as well as the 1969 film version, *Fellini Satyricon*. Oscar Wilde was accused of many things, not the least of which was an alternative translation he is rumored to have made: *The Satyricon of Petronius Arbiter*.

According to the dogma of Saint Priapus, gay anonymous sex is fundamental priapic worship. A particularly popular "kneeling" ritual is anonymous fellatio, performed through "glory holes" cut in walls of confessional-like booths, through which the penis alone "appears" as if magically disconnected from the body on the other side of the wall. Catholics once venerated a more modest Saint Priapus, until the Second Vatican Council in 1964 purged him and dozens of other "saints"—some of whom, like Priapus, were pagan demigods who had tiptoed into Catholic devotions on their own Nijinsky feet while Christianity was busy appropriating other bits it chose from paganism.

The way Christianity co-opted Wicca, witchcraft had long before co-opted phallic homosexuality by using its conjure power, which it kept as secret knowledge. From time immemorial at men's bathhouses, and particularly in modern gay baths, drugs and warrior-sex conjure ancient feelings. In an erotic epiphany, the Irish-American protagonist of *Some Dance to Remember* connects the dots of ancient ritual during a "séance" in a 1970s gay bath house, the Barracks, in San Francisco. "He [Ryan] was high and certain these men knew they were, all four of them, concelebrating priests of a man-to-man ritual in the old discipline. They were shamans, more ancient than the Druids, invoking priapic Gods, congregating among profane men, who themselves, remembering or forgetting, it mattered not, tripped the corridors of the Barracks with motives as ancient as lust. The four were in perfect alignment. Under a hit of popper, Ryan fell down the violet tunnel with the black spot at the end. He was sure the spot was the moon in full eclipse viewed through a sacred tunnel of rune-covered stones."[18]

In the services of Saint Priapus, foreskins (very much attached to bodies) are also worshiped after the fashion of Christians venerating the phallic Christ's foreskin, which was the only part of his body that did not ascend into heaven. In witchcraft, foreskin piercing, like the piercing of the head of the penis, is an adornment that, like rings on the fingers, adds the energy of precious metals to body gestures. As the phallus has always been a force against the evil eye, the gold ring through the phallus head or shaft, or through foreskin helps blind the evil eye. In medieval times, the *Malleus Maleficarum* (1486) pointed out that the penis is the Devil's organ. The Devil himself lives under the foreskin, which was the crown of Satan. The smegma under the crown was Satan's communion, feared by many, prized by others, and at modern orgiastic Sabbaths is spread like cheese from a vat of Velveeta.

In the privacy of craft, there is much more sexually unlabeled woman-to-woman ritual, and much more man-to-man ritual, than is suggested by Wiccan publicists touting heterosexual rituals meant to advertise, popularize, and recruit. The sweep of gay literature is virtually defined by the priapic coming-out novel: the protagonist first shifts his own shape, worships, and conjures. In fact, the genre exists on that magical archetype. Its plot turns when a self-realizing boy changes from thinking he is straight to knowing he was born gay. Raising the cone of power on his phallus, he sees the vision of another boy he begins to worship from afar. He continues to conjure on his own penis, in solo masturbation, on the image of the young god worshiped until, in the denouement, he kneels before the athletic god's phallus and is accepted or rejected, loved or killed. Typifying this, the remarkably "perversatile" Marco Vassi, in *The Metasex Manifesto* (1976), wrote a story of a young man whose coming out metamorphosed him into "an utterly superior human being" whose salvific acts of sex "soothed the soul" of his partners. Called "Fist Fucker," the story ends telling of a photo of the young man "suspended from a crossbeam" being "lowered onto two men" who double-fist him. "A Buddhist monk, seeing the picture, was heard to exclaim, 'That is a man who has attained Nirvana.'" This semicrucified Christ figure is killed, buried in a field, and, in the last line of the story, "Several members of Troy Perry's Gay Church subsequently began an official movement to have him proclaimed their first saint."[19] Marco Vassi had a history of dipping into popular culture with his exploration of kinky sex, drugs, and cults in America's underground in *The Stoned Apocalypse* (1973).

Muscular Christianity, which the YMCA and straight churches use to recruit boys, is a perfect analogue of gay muscular worship. Thomas Hughes, author of *Tom Brown's School Days* (1857) tub-thumped Victorian "force" into a "bicep-ual" cult of manliness. In 1899, Reverend G. P. Horne, in *Sandow's Magazine*, Bible-thumped an essay titled "Muscular Christianity" that equated becoming spiritual with being physically strong: "*Mens sana in corpore sano:* a healthy mind in a healthy body." In this vein, the sanctuaries of church, gymnasium, and coven connect muscular bodies to muscular character. In 1993, the first "Lord's Gym" opened in Cincinnati, and in 1997 a Christian corporation opened several "non-sex" "Lord's Gym" locations across the Bible Belt. However, no men more than gay men focus directly on literal body conjuring to invoke spirit. Muscular witchcraft is part of muscular paganism, which is a part of masculine magic, which is part of gay magic, which is part of human magic.

Gay male witchcraft, "coming out" as priapic worship or leather sadomasochism, is simply reclaiming the roots of its ancient identity in both white magic and black magic. This principle is declared explicitly in *Some Dance to Remember.* "Kick is a wizard. All us faggots are wizards, you know. . . . I mean we're all wizards, descendents of the Druidic priests of the old phallic religions that predate the Goddess religions of virgin-mothers. . . . Read that part of . . . the *Masculinist Manifesto*, Chapter Three, 'Magic: Homomasculinity as the Old Religion.'"[20]

Adam and Eve ate the apple to gain knowledge, but gained only limited knowledge and lost Eden. By archetype, their son Abel, a witness to their loss, learned from their rebellion. Ancient homosexuality was the original repository of secret knowledge. In order to establish itself as a religion, modern homosexuality needs to develop a real theology. That would require theorist theologians who would not get bogged down in, for instance, sex, gender, and politics.

A queer-theory theologian might debate that whatever "God the life force" is cannot be circumscribed by gender, particularly if that life force is transcendent, omnipresent, and omniscient. Projecting gender on a life-force God is anthropomorphism, like projecting human qualities on Bambi, Mickey Mouse, and Smoky the Bear. Greek and Roman mythology is an exercise in which humans try to picture the life-force God in their own image, even as they try to address human psychology. John Ruskin called such attribution of human qualities to nature "the pathetic fallacy." Blaming the life-force God for gender problems of patriarchy, or trying to recast religion, Wicca, or witchcraft as matriarchy, might say quite a bit about human problems of gender relations, but it does no justice to the life-force God.

In fact, gay witchcraft that chooses to be matriarchal is as weak as witchcraft that chooses to be patriarchal. The horizon of witchcraft is not gender. Magic is stronger than femininity or masculinity. The horizon of witchcraft is power. That power is not male power or female power, or gay or lesbian power, but human power unfettered by limits of any of the thousand genders.

Gender magic, which is one kind of primitive tribal magic that celebrates itself in gender, can be straight or gay or lesbian. One straight male, or one straight female, or a straight couple, or groups of straight people can raise the horn of straight gender magic. Lesbian gender magic can be invoked by one lesbian woman, or a lesbian couple, or a group of lesbians. Gay gender magic can be raised by one gay man, or two gay men, or groups of gay men. The 1969 Stonewall Rebellion, which ignited the modern gay liberation movement, for instance, was judged demonic by many people, but was actually an act of gay faerie magic, according to gay pioneer Harry Hay.

Even so, gender magic is only one kind of human magic. The history of witchcraft itself is a warning against practitioners becoming lured by coven or cornered by enemies in gender. Witchcraft through the ages has been severely hurt by the battle between the sexes fought in villages, churches, and nations, including the most gender-driven terror of all time, the Spanish Inquisition. To control outsiders—Jews, Muslims, women, and homosexuals—the inquisitors canceled the pluralism of traditional folk magic.

Cherchez la femme. The Spanish Inquisition was begun by a right-wing woman, Isabella of Castille, "La Catolica," who had become queen in her own right. To unite Spain, she married her cousin, Ferdinand of Aragon, whom she herself crowned king. Their daughter, Catharine of Aragon, was famously divorced from the phallic King Henry VIII who, in a Tudor sex scandal, broke from the pope of Rome, established the Church of England, and married Anne Boleyn, whom he later claimed had a sorcerer's "extra finger" and a "third breast," and had "bewitched him into the marriage" that produced Queen Elizabeth I, who had her own royal astrologer, John Dee. In 1478, Queen Isabella enacted the Inquisition, with approval of Pope Sixtus, and named her own priest-confessor, Tomás de Torquemada, grand inquisitor and chief torturer. To retrieve the purity of Spanish blood and Spanish identity, Isabella and Ferdinand exercised their power three times in the watershed year of 1492. They used military force at Granada to defeat the Islam of the Moors; they expelled all Jews—even the Marranos, who had converted—because Jews were perceived to be taking over Spanish culture through the Spanish economy; and the king and queen, initially believing that the world was flat, sent Columbus to the New World to spread Spanish culture and Christianity. Under the umbrella of witchcraft, the Inquisition focused on race, sex, and gender. Its purpose was to end diversity, because diversity (which is a code name for democracy) is difficult for autocratic governments to control.

In all their gay pluralism, the Church of Saint Priapus, Frederic de Arechaga's Sabaeanist Temple, Wiccan radical faeries, gay witchcraft, leather sex magic, and the Metropolitan Community Church are various examples of homosexuality working its way through mysteries of sex, gender, and politics toward belief systems. And why not? In January 1990, *Drummer* magazine editor Joseph Bean devoted the entirety of issue 136 to "Leather-sex Fairies" and "The Spiritual Dimensions of Submission." Mark Thompson, author of *Gay Spirit* (1987), wrote in *Leatherfolk: Radical Sex, People, Politics, and Practice* (1992), "In America, where growing up gay or lesbian usually means to exist on the outer limits of a conventional life, there is little choice but to explore the edges. At some point in our lives, through exclusion by others or self-exile, we are deported to an archipelago of things that are left largely unspoken. Human sexuality, in all its diversity, is contained in this faraway place, as if keeping it out of sight will also keep it out of mind. Small wonder, then, that erotic discovery is important to gay people. In fact, having been primarily defined through sexuality, we're adept explorers of it. And leatherfolk are the most expert investigators of eros of all."[21]

Eros, of course, is the soul of witchcraft. The growth of the penis from soft to hard is the essence of shape-shifting, and the semen, mysteriously delivered in a stormy paroxysm of body quakes, vocal thunder, and head lightning, is a potent fluid that actually is fertile and alive. Even to flat-earth fundamentalists ignorant of poetry or metaphor, the physical orgasm certainly seems to have something like God behind it, because the fundamentalist God is always making proclamations about it. As the authoritarian God and the authoritarian Satan fight over who owns orgasm, it is the indulgent Priapus who rules sex worship of the penis, particularly the communion of fellatio and its load of seed-bearing mana, which is analogous to Christ saying to his apostles, "This is my body. Take you and eat."

When witches claim that black magic or white magic require the male god to penetrate the female goddess, their theory collapses. At night, in covens, out on the cold heath where so many wait to be penetrated, why is Satan famous for having an ice-cold penis? Because the penetration is not hot male flesh into hot female flesh. The penetration is by "a widow's comforter," a dildo—chilled by the night air—that is inserted into warm flesh, fore or aft, because Satan traditionally has a two-headed penis able to penetrate anus and vagina simultaneously.

Once something (a dildo) is substituted for the actual thing (a penis), then ritual (a dramatization of reality) literally begins.

Because—as William Blake wrote—witchcraft is creativity, it is always inventing itself, freely switching one thing for another. Witchcraft has always improvised. In the world of magical relativism, is the penis more powerful when it's a dildo? Is an old crone more powerful when she's a drag queen (with a secret penis) or a mime-faced male nun from the Sisters of Perpetual Indulgence (with a satirical satyr's penis)? Witchcraft exists in every culture and has survived longer than Judaism, Christianity, or Islam because it is personal, not authoritarian. If sexuality is an archipelago, witchcraft is the sea. If religions are islands, witchcraft is the ocean. And sea-level is forever changing.

The phallic dildo is conspicuous in primitive sculptures. It is also a best seller in contemporary boutiques, botanicas, and gay bars. It gives women power to penetrate, and homosexual satyrs satisfaction. Archeology proves that the most ancient religions—at least the ones with the best vases—depict males worshiping males with phallus and dildo. Is it any wonder that, as fecal readings are used in Washington, D.C., to predict politicians' futures, gay witchcraft personals offer "phallic readings to predict the lengths to which the owner will go for love, health, happiness, and money." To check the magic power of the phallus, simply go to a public place—a street corner or a gallery—and raise up a home-made sculpture of "a dildo on a stick" to begin a situation comedy of police, priests, and art critics. Camille Paglia, herself perhaps a bit of an Italian strega, addressed the freak-out power of the penis in her books *Sexual Personae* (1990) and *Vamps and Tramps* (1994), as well as in her cultural analysis of the penis on the British Channel 4 special *The Penis Unsheathed* (1994).

Immediately after the June 1969 Stonewall Riots, signaling the beginning of the most priapic of all liberation fronts, Priapus rose rampant. Greenleaf Classics published the first anthology of contemporary erotic gay literature, *In Homage to Priapus* (1969), edited by E. V. Griffith. Edward Dahlberg wrote *The Sorrows of Priapus* (1970), parts of which were published in the *Chicago Literary Journal*, alongside pieces by Jack Kerouac, Gregory Corso, and William S. Burroughs. In the same revolutionary climate, the repeal of the United States postal laws forbidding photographs of frontal male nudity opened the door for the phallocentric rise of the gay erotic presses, such as Guild Press in Washington, D. C., which published a fully illustrated volume, *The Phallus in History and Fact* (1969).

A few miles northeast of Los Angeles, a certain gay sadomasochism ranch holds an annual "Easter Flagellation" to celebrate the male body. William Kloman, writing on the "Banality of the New Evil" (*Esquire*, March 1970) tells of "one young Hollywood leading man [who] still carries a scar where his hand was nailed to a cross in the course of a recent Hollywood party game." In 1967, a motorcycle gang crucified a girl, eighteen-year-old Christine Deese, on a tree in Florida. Each of these incidents takes in common the major Christian symbol, the Crucifixion, and inverts it for one reason or another like the silver cross hung upside down over the crib of Rosemary's baby.

William Carney assesses all American violence as a popular style of sexual aggression that has become institutionalized in recent aggressive American wars. Americans, he contends, have made cruelty an internationally enviable virtue. He writes, "One of the things which distinguishes Americans from other nationalities is their ability to turn theory into practice. . . .

Consider the Germans and the English, who are our closest rivals in this (sado-masochistic) work: they fall far behind us. The former lacking subtlety and flair, and the latter vigor. The Teuton is deficient in imagination and the untransplanted Anglo-Saxon forever skirts the epicene. The American's command of sadistic gesture, authority in appearance, and skill in procedure are the envy, if not the delight, of the world."[22]

On Good Friday, 1970, American artist Carlin Jeffrey reconstructed his award-winning sculpture *Living Crucifixion* at an elaborate townhouse party on New York's East Side. For four hours Jeffrey was crucified nude to a cross in the brownstone's gothic chapel. His living sculpture, designed as a tribute to homosexuals who died in American wars, was a variation on the inverted-Christianity theme of black magic. Jeffrey was crucified (chained) backwards, face to cross, buttocks mooning the gallery. After his four-hour gesture-comment, Jeffrey descended from the cross, collected his thousand-dollar fee, and three days later was back at the popular New York Gallery of Erotic Art, crucified by appointment only. Jeffrey's backward positioning of the crucified victim typifies the inversion of Christianity common to homosexual algolagnia (sexual gratification from giving or receiving pain) and the demonic occult.

In 1969, at the Cordier and Ekstrom Gallery, Manhattan sculptor Nancy Grossman first exhibited her life-size severed heads. These astonishing artificial sculptures, hooded and wrapped tight in black leather with laces and zippers and flaps, reveal mouths and teeth in anguish. Should one call in the censor or bring out the censer? Art is by essence a shape-shifting event that sometimes moves the art object away from the intent of the artist. In Hebrew and Celtic tales, mummified heads, real and shrunken or artful and carved, serve as speaking oracles. In modern times, "Exhibit A," serial killer Jeffrey Dahmer, judged insane and guilty, kept severed and decorated heads in his refrigerator; "Exhibit B," brilliant American photographer Joel-Peter Witkin, famous in the art world and made a knight by France, cuts dead human heads in half, photographs them, and sells the prints to museums and collectors, who hang them in their studies next to the clichéd human skull affected by scholars who think they're Hamlet. In white and black magic, corpse heads are often used for divination, in the way that preserved bodies (and body parts) of dead saints, like Saint Vincent de Paul laid out in glass caskets in Catholic churches in Paris, are prayed to for miracles.

Myth, religion, and the occult, like television, are full of talking heads. In Arthurian Camelot, Sir Gawain, wearing a pentacle on his armor, beheaded the Green Knight, who kept on fighting because his vital magic came from sorcerer Merlin and witch Morgan La Faye. In New England, Washington Irving—who was once the lover of *Frankenstein* creator Mary Shelley—retold the biblical tale of Satan being "Death on a Horse." This tale became the German folktale, which became the American gothic tale, "The Headless Horseman of Sleepy Hollow," in *The Sketchbook* (1820). Whatever Nancy Grossman intends with her beautiful beheaded sculptures, the Satanic quotient of her existential decapitations exerts a dynamic voodoo pull. Rich, gay, New York leather men particularly respond to her severed male heads in bondage, as if the sculptures are the "speaking oracles" of some kind of leather fith-fath. Prized by private collectors, her leather-bound heads are, frankly and frequently, the centerpiece of leather sadomasochistic orgies of the blackest magic, the darkest sex, and the dirtiest coprophagia.

Sadomasochists and the new occultists are, in fact, people in search of one another. Both groups circulate among themselves a vast quantity of otherwise unpublished erotic literature reproduced via all the modern means. No one story has any one author. The chain-letter narratives change as anonymous individuals—before computers—successively retyped with carbon paper while editing, rewriting, illustrating, and amplifying the episodic plots. These sadomasochistic stories, long steeped in every conceivable taste and fetish, found their 1970s interpolations to be additions of occult phenomena: succubi, incubi, diabolical bestiality. These porno-occult addenda, like the sexual, are geared to be "masturbagenic"—that is, facilitating masturbatory activity, which is the point, obviously, of all pornography.

Here for the first time out of mimeograph is part of a questionnaire compiled and circulated by several sadomasochism groups across the country. The directly occult questions are interpolations made by a Manhattan coven, which uses the form for recruiting auxiliary members and victims for altars. This questionnaire, circulating underground in the 1960s, formed the basis of Larry Townsend's 1972 sadomasochism bible, *The Leatherman's Handbook*.

In S&M psychodrama I dig the following scenes with related gear and torture.

Check your choice:

Soldiers ( ) Firemen ( ) Cyclists ( ) Sailors ( ) Marines ( )
Airmen ( ) Coast Guard ( ) Nazi SS ( ) Policemen ( ) Inquisition ( )
Witch Trial ( ) Executioners ( ) Black Mass ( ) Cowboys ( )

Wrestlers (   ) Truck Drivers (   ) Witches Sabbath (   ) Construction (   )
Surfers (   ) Leather Types (   ) Doctors (   ) Satanic Coven (   )
Crucifixion (   ) Hot wax (   ) Piercing (   ) Hanging over flames (   )
Choking (   ) Dunking (   ) Pressing (   )

This participatory sadomasochistic underground, circulated by first-class U. S. mail, has its mainstream counterpart. Even the most learned academic (and religious) witchcraft books delight in detailing the tortures attendant upon the inquisition and punishment of witchery. The very popular *Encyclopedia of Witchcraft and Demonology* (1959) by Rossell Robbins, fellow of Britain's Royal Society of Literature, insures interest and sales with its lurid detailing of "A Typical Day's Torture: A Verbatim Report of the First Day's Torture of a Woman Accused of Witchcraft at Prossneck, Germany, 1629." The popular taste for "respectable" porno-violence has always relied on the literature of witchcraft as polite excuse for masturbatory erotica. In fact, inquisition literature has flourished for centuries, because the books are such juicy meditations on sex, women, men, genitalia, pain, race, and power.

In a way, sadomasochism is Christianity's gift to witchcraft. Puritanical Christianity denied the natural, physical body to redeem the soul. Witchcraft celebrates nature to redeem the body and its soul. Had Saint Paul not perverted Christ by attaching guilt to physical pleasure, witchcraft would never have had to exorcise that guilt through pain to restore that pleasure. Men's magazines such as *Argosy, Saga,* and *Man to Man,* with nearly-nude women bound and gagged on their covers, are popular literature written as a result of confused Judeo-Christian morality. Adam continues to punish Eve for leading him into temptation. Human nature being what it is, witch-baiters fighting witchcraft seem to get off on the erotic details. Gay witch Leo Louis Martello says that the 1968 film *Rosemary's Baby* is about the dark side of Christianity; so is sadomasochism in the contemporary occult. Scratch the surface of a gay Satanic leatherman, and get a Catholic.

In a mid-twentieth-century analysis of the state of the occult, little about witchcraft was what it used to be. Prior to twelfth-century Christianity, witchery was a rather innocent vestige tolerated as a pre-Christian folk way, a harmless country quirk. Not until Saint Thomas Aquinas defined Christianity as "the Good" were witchery and women downgraded into "the Evil." The Dark Ages were passing. As the modern world was beginning to organize its medieval mind, all the bits about witchcraft were codified into the *Malleus Maleficarum*. Scholastic Christianity, building on the rhetoric of the early Church fathers, more or less caused the invention of black magic, and outlawed female gender magic and gender healthcare.

In the evolution of popular thought, scholastic philosophy was a closed system based on absolute causality. It needed a villain to explain the evil that God (the good prime cause) could not cause. Whereas the Scriptures loosely called any but the Hebrew God a *Devil* (literally a *slanderer*) or a *Satan* (literally an *adversary*), scholastic hermeneutics united the galloping pantheon of these many once-relative tribal divinities into one Christian Satan. And like God, supreme over the great chain of being, this newly defined Satan ruled as well over his own chain of evil spirits and wicked women, homosexual men, enchanted animals, and magic vegetation that could be turned into lotions and potions. In this way, Christianity, confronting the universal problem of evil, set the Western-world stage for the bipolar hysterias of possession and exorcism by "needing" a Devil to explain evil and illness as well as to define the otherness of outsiders.

Religious and political fundamentalists fear occult ritual the way they fear art. They tunnel their vision in on their own fantasies of child sacrifice and orgies of bloodlust. Witches might also react with prejudice if they stood in the rear of any suburban Catholic Church on Good Friday. Robed men, altar boys, and altar girls lead processions of incense, candles, and bells down the aisle to the altar. A lector reads aloud about a glorious torture-murder of a handsome God. A man in a white robe shoulders a huge wooden cross down the aisle. The convened congregation of single parents and seniors cries out on cue, "Crucify him! Crucify him!" Then in two lines the Catholic faithful wind their way to the altar so that each participant can kiss the wooden cross and eat, under the appearance of transubstantiated bread and wine, the real body and blood of Christ, the crucified murder victim. This transubstantiation is literal. Catholics believe that the wine and bread, which is to be swallowed and not chewed, are turned into the actual blood and body of Christ and all that remains of the bread and wine is its appearance. All Catholic children have been warned by nuns about the seven-year-old girl who bit the wafer of bread at her First Communion and began screaming as her mouth filled up with blood.

Witchcraft, like theater and art, has had to survive Puritan censorship.

One theory of censorship is that the censor is simply fighting in others' lives and in others' art the thing he most fears in himself. A censor of things Satanic is, by that theory, simply announcing that he has seen Satan in himself and is so terrified he can only stamp out Satanism wherever it might appear to tempt him. Anton LaVey peels back this basic truth basic to reveal such popular Calvinism: "Each time a Satanist performs a ceremony, he worships the Devil as an externalization of himself."[23] Is this only an inverted, positive restatement of Calvinism's negative doctrine of man's essential depravity? Is it a truism that Satanism can really occur only in a theistic society? Belief in good spirits predicates a belief in evil spirits as well, a fact many theists forget. Can an atheist be a Satanist? Can there be a world where only Satan exists with no notion of any God?

The connection of good people with evil spirits is evident in one of the most popular texts of twentieth-century Catholicism; *Moral Theology* (1961), translated from the German of Heribert Jone and adapted to the laws and customs of the United States by Urban Adelman, opposes everything from séances, ouija boards, and palmistry to divination and sorcery. Advertised as "a quick and convenient means for rendering decisions in questions of conscience," the pocket-size edition offers itself "to Pastors, Seminarians, and the Educated Laity . . . to help them . . . in solving many of the minor problems of conscience that occur in their daily lives."

As with good-spirit Christianity in general, Jone/Adelman forbid commerce with evil spirits on the premise that evil spirits really do exist. In the explication of the First Commandment, the authors posit,

> *Divination and sorcery* are in themselves very grave sins, since they contain an explicit or implicit invocation of the Devil. One may sin by engaging in these practices oneself or by causing others to do so, e.g., to tell fortunes or have one's own fortune told, provided he himself or the other person is serious and not merely jesting.
>
> *Implicit invocation* of the Devil is also a grave sin. Even though one protests against the influence of the evil spirit, one still invokes him by using evidently inadequate means to produce some definite effect. If there is a possibility that the effect is the result of some unknown powers of nature, one may use such means if he protests against any diabolical influence. Such a protestation is unnecessary if one is certain the effect is produced by natural causes, even though the respective natural powers are little known, as happens, for example, in the use of the divining rod for the location of water or veins of metal. At times there will be only venial sin, or no sin at all in the implicit invocation of the Devil because of ignorance, simplicity or error, or because one does not really have faith in the questionable practice or because one engages in it more or less as a jest and provided no scandal is given. It will likewise be a venial sin or none at all if one does or omits

something indifferent in itself because of certain information received, being prompted not by a belief in fortune telling, dreams, etc., but rather by some indefinite fear or by curiosity.

One may practice superstition also with the aid of *religious objects*, e.g., using the paten as a mirror and expecting thereby to recover from an illness; so, too, if one copies prayer leaflets and distributes them in order to obtain certain effects; furthermore, if one ascribes an infallible efficacy to a certain prayer or picture, etc., as frequently happens in the case of chain-prayers. Simplicity generally excuses one from sin in such cases.

Rotating tables may be connected with phenomena . . . put into motion by purely natural powers. It is impossible, however, for such powers to manifest absolutely hidden things. Some authors believe they may reveal things that are known to at least one of the persons present. Such practices (e.g., the use of the ouija board) are, however, always to be discouraged, since they easily lead to superstition. . . .

Spiritism claims to be able to communicate with the spirit world and endeavors to establish such commerce with it. Although spiritism is *for the most part* fraud [emphasis added], still the intention alone to enter into communication with spirits is gravely sinful. Therefore, it is *mortally* [emphasis added] sinful to conduct a spiritistic seance or to act as a medium, even if one protests against all communication with evil spirits. It is also forbidden to attend a sitting as a mere spectator, even if one thoroughly discredits spiritism. Merely witnessing a seance may be gravely sinful because of scandal or because this would imply a promoting of spiritistic practices. Apart from scandal, a scientist does not sin by attending seances for the purpose of studying the nature of spiritistic phenomena.[24]

This popular guide of Catholic moral theology scares up as real a belief in the powers of darkness as anything in the 1973 film *The Exorcist.* The Church teaches that spiritism is "gravely sinful." To all Catholics, this means a sin serious enough to merit an eternity of punishment in the Devil's hell. Therefore, Catholic and Satanist believe the same doctrine. Psychologists say the line between neurosis and true religiosity is thin. The similarity between acts of occult and religious ritual is thinner. Both need believers.

Satanism fits sex like a condom. It celebrates humans' natural instincts. Satanism is the ultimate Freudian product. Its earthly delights sell like burgers and fries to the young and potent. In two of his "Nine Satanic Statements," in *The Satanic Bible,* the thought-provoking Anton LaVey amps Satan up as an extension of human carnality. He praises the Seven Deadly

Sins, which Christianity teaches are offenses against love: Pride, Lust, Envy, Gluttony, Anger, Greed, and Sloth:

> 1. Satan represents indulgence instead of abstinence! . . .

> 8. Satan represents all of the so-called deadly sins, as they all lead to physical, mental or emotional gratification.

He should know.

Anton LaVey is the lightning rod of twentieth-century American Satanism. He had a face that captures the imagination. In the turmoil of fact, fiction, and fantasy that surrounds him, LaVey was an artist who was a pervasive pop-culture force as an author, a theorist, and a personality. He founded the Church of Satan in 1966 and was the author of several books, including:

- the rock of American Satanic philosophy, the best-selling *The Satanic Bible* (1969), and its companion, *The Satanic Rituals* (1972)
- *The Satanic Witch* (1989) formerly, *The Compleat Witch; Or, What to Do When Virtue Fails* (1971)
- *The Devil's Notebook* (1992), his compendium of humor, rants, and wisdom, with an introduction by psychedelic Satanist Kenneth Anger
- *Satan Speaks* (1998), his essays, with an introduction by Reverend Marilyn Manson
- *The Secret Life of a Satanist: The Authorized Biography of Anton LaVey* (1992), by Blanche Barton, who is also the author of the history, *The Church of Satan: A History of the World's Most Notorious Religion* (1990)

His first record album is *The Satanic Mass*, in part recorded live September 13, 1968, at the Church of Satan, with twelve tracks including, after the Black Mass, "The Hymn of the Satanic Empire," as well as LaVey reading from *The Satanic Bible* a chapter he limned into a new synthesis out of Ragnar Redbeard's controversial book *Might Is Right* (1896).

After his second album, *Strange Music* (1994), his third, *Satan Takes a Holiday* (1995) features eighteen selections including "*Satanis* Theme." He plays and recites—in his inimitable voice—the lyrics of five vintage songs of sentiment and magic like "Golden Earrings." Five other vocals are sung by director Nick Bougas. Two more are intoned by Blanche Barton. She bounces her vocal on the title track "Satan Takes a Holiday" into a sweet burlesque romp that hints with nostalgia at the "spotlight and feathers" that club-goers in San Francisco's North Beach enjoyed during LaVey's 1960s night club act "Anton LaVey and His Topless Witches Sabbath." His films include:

- *Rosemary's Baby* (1968), for which, besides acting the part of Satan mounting Rosemary, he also served as technical advisor to director Roman Polanski
- *Satanis: The Devil's Mass* (1969), sometimes titled *Succubus*, a documentary of Satanic rites, including a ceremonial Black Mass, interviews, and ritual (female) nudity with whipping (of a man)
- *Invocations of My Demon Brother* (1969), an underground film directed by Kenneth Anger in which LaVey plays the horned man; often screened as double-bill with *Satanis*
- *The Devil's Rain* (1975), starring William Shatner, Ida Lupino, Ernest Borgnine, and a young John Travolta, featuring LaVey as the Satanic character, with sets designed by LaVey to reflect the actual interior of the sanctuary of the Church of Satan
- *Doctor Dracula: Svengali's Second Coming* (1977) starring veteran horror actor John Carradine, with LaVey as consultant
- *Death Scenes* (1989), a documentary of police crime photos, 1930–50, presented and narrated by LaVey
- *Speak of the Devil: The Canon of Anton LaVey* (1993), a 90-minute documentary of the Church of Satan and how LaVey founded it; directed by Nick Bougas.

Anton LaVey laughs at the commercial marketing of God and Satan in his Ninth Point: "Satan has been the best friend the Church has ever had, as he has kept it in business all these years." The Christian evangelist Billy Sunday, in a self-revealing quip, said, "I know the Devil exists. There are two reasons. One, because the Bible says so, and, two, because I've done business with him." What is true of Satanism is equally true of sex—particularly homosexuality. The mere mention of either "a witchcraft agenda" or "a gay agenda" in a fundamentalist Christian newsletter raises a flood of cash income to churches fighting one or both of the hot-button threats. In this way, Satanism and homosexuality fund Christianity, a point that was also made in the film, *Bedazzled* (1967), which starred Peter Cook and Dudley Moore, featuring Raquel Welch as "Lust."

Anton LaVey defined his images of pop lust in his dedication of *The Satanic Bible* to a list of Hollywood blondes. His celebration of voluptuous sexuality is far from Christian magician Andre Cole, and closer to Andy Warhol. Through a parallel to the very reclusive Warhol, one can measure how the rather secret LaVey also continues to captivate American pop culture. Both contemporaries are separate, but similar, pop-culture phenomena. Warhol, who changed his name from Andrew Warhola, worked out of his Factory in New York. Anton LaVey, who was born Howard Stanton Levey, worked out of his Black House in San Francisco. Andy Warhol and Anton LaVey, each in his own way an icon of their times, are pop artists working the American psyche. Both are self-inventing enigmas with cult followings. Both exist where cult converges with culture. Both made pop culture. Both *are* pop culture. Both deployed images of women to float their messages. Warhol, employing New York fashion photography, featured Marilyn Monroe and Elizabeth Taylor. LaVey, coming out of Hollywood burlesque, touted Jayne Mansfield and Tuesday Weld, and claimed a two-week affair with Norma Jean Baker before she shape-shifted into Marilyn Monroe.

Warhol created paintings and experimental trance films like the phallic *Empire* (1964), and produced horror movies such as *Andy Warhol's Frankenstein* (1974). LaVey created rituals, wrote books, and participated in experimental art films and Hollywood horror movies. Warhol sold art, hedonism, and drug magic. LaVey purveyed theology, hedonism, and black magic. Puritan religions condemn them both for their carnality. Warhol allowed drugs to cause his actors to become their raw selves in front of the camera. LaVey disapproved of drugs because drugs cause people to lose control of their will. The gay Warhol, wearing a dust-mop wig, surrounded himself with the charmed circle of his trickster superstars. The straight LaVey, with shaved head rampant, hosted his Magic Circle, at which the infamous mixed with the famous to discuss the occult. Warhol pronounced that "everyone will be famous for fifteen minutes." LaVey proved that Warhol's limited estimate can be extended by a pact with Satan: "After all, Satan can get it for you wholesale."

Both lived lives the tabloids love and need. Warhol was shot and nearly killed by Valerie Solanas. The paparazzi constantly shot Warhol consorting at trendy clubs with the slumming rich and beautiful who sometimes appeared in his films. LaVey, with his always-flexing muscular Satanism, was always good for a slow news day at the tabloids. The curious death of Jayne Mansfield made LaVey a star. The Church of Satan gave him high profile, as did the urban legend of his Hollywood connection to Roman Polanski, the director made widower by the Manson Family. It made good copy when the Black Pope denounced the Manson Family, because of his two perceived connections to them. LaVey had once hired Susan Atkins, later a murderess in the Manson Family, as a dancer in his act. (Atkins's memoir, *Child of Satan, Child of God* [1978], never blames LaVey for the lifestyle to which she turned.) LaVey also had worked with Kenneth Anger on the gay magic film *Invocations of My Demon Brother*, with Bobby Beausoleil, who became soon after a convicted torturer/killer in the Manson Family. Art magazines published images of Warhol and his naked superstars. Men's magazines published photos of LaVey and his nude female witches.

In 1966, Warhol produced his own traveling stage show, *The Exploding Plastic Inevitable*, with Nico and the Velvet Underground. Early on in the 1960s, LaVey was billed at a North Beach nightclub in San Francisco as Anton LaVey and His Topless Witches Sabbath. LaVey based his night club act on his admiration for women in the noir world of burlesque. He moved from "Satin Doll" to Satan's dolls. No one has ever noticed that LaVey's act was a direct homage to Aleister Crowley, who toured with his own vaudeville act billed as, with a musical-and-menstrual pun, the Ragged Ragtime Girls.

LaVey once told *Velvet Hammer* e-zine interviewers Michelle Carr and Elvia Lahman, writing for the Velvet Hammer Burlesque Company, how burlesque politicized him, noting, "The world is full of creeps. [In clubs] I've had my fill of it night after night with these guys. I'm playing my heart out. The girls are working hard, dancing away, and some guys jerk off through their popcorn box. I started thinking like the girls: it's us against them. That was the very beginning of my becoming a Satanic High Priest, just negative feelings about people. There's nothing wrong with sex and fetish, but some people are just disgusting cretins. . . . Creeps and assholes are just good for target practice. So many people are."[25]

Bit by bit, the legendary LaVey invented himself out of his knockabout experiences as an emcee in burlesque, as a lion tamer in the circus, and as an organist playing the mighty Wurlitzer in theaters and keyboards in clubs. His imposing physical look, his piercing eyes, goatee, and shaved head, caused many people sitting in his lectures to imagine for him a fantastic past. And why not? On the other hand, his Satanic look suggests to strait-laced people the ambiguous self of the trickster. Anton LaVey, Gerald Gardner, and Alex Sanders have all been accused of plagiarizing their ideas—and their personas—when all they were doing was rethinking ancient traditions and lore to bring them into modern culture. As LaVey modestly mentioned in a private conversation, "About my studies, I can only repeat Isaac Newton, who wrote, 'If I have seen further, it is by standing on the shoulders of giants.'"[26]

Astrologically, LaVey was born in 1930, the same year as were born the globally famous *Apollo 11* crew, which comprised Michael Collins, the captain (born on Halloween), and Neil Armstrong and Buzz Aldrin, the first two men to walk on the moon on July 21, 1969. For LaVey, like Sabaeanist Pontifex Frederic de Arechaga, the moon, as a female symbol with men walking across its face, presaged a tidal surge in popular culture's attitudes about witchcraft that occurred twenty-one days later on August 9, 1969, when the Manson Family's Tate murders took over the headlines and made everyone in America suddenly believe in murderous cults, sexual evil, and scary Satanism.

Like a foil to the clean-cut astronauts, the menacing LaVey shows up on the covers of magazines and in newspaper features. He was a performance artist whose greatest creation is himself. The private LaVey animated the public LaVey. He knew how to give the public the thrill it wanted. *The Satanic Bible* has never been out of print, and is published in Russian, German, and Spanish editions. LaVey was serious, but seemed not to take himself seriously, making jokes about his lifelong predilection for some of the very stuff of popular culture: the Hollywood films of Boris Karloff, comic books, and fast cars. With pleasant honesty, he termed himself a romantic "cornball." In the way the Romantic poets Lord Byron, John Keats, and Percy Bysshe Shelley worshiped nature, LaVey was a kind of "Romantic Satanic Wordsworth." His Satanism can seem quite Wiccan. He sacrificed neither children nor animals; instead, he invented Satanic baptism for children, and officiated at the first such ceremony for his daughter, Zeena, whom he baptized onto the left-hand *widdershins* path on Friday, May 23, 1967. LaVey once wrote, "The Satanist recognizes animals and small children as the natural magicians of the world. They do not deny their natural instincts and can perceive things that the average adult human can never hope to. The Satanist realizes he can learn much from these sacred creatures. They have not learned to deny their natural indulgences. Man must learn to properly indulge himself by whatever means he finds necessary, so long as it hurts no one who neither deserves nor wishes to be hurt. Only by so doing can we release harmful frustrations, which if unreleased can build up and cause many very real ailments. The Satanic Church advocates and teaches *INGULGENCE!*"[27]

The Satanist rede of Anton LaVey bears repeating: "Hurt no one who neither deserves nor wishes to be hurt."

LaVey is interesting because he feels that nearly all of Western culture is "just good for target practice." He takes aim carefully. He is America's Devil's advocate. Inside Catholicism, the Devil's advocate is the critical thinker who tells the Pope all the reasons why some nominee for sainthood should not be canonized, or why some idea should not be turned into doctrine. In the upheaval of the 1960s, LaVey was one of the fresh voices criticizing the establishment, and sorting out the old conformity to bring in the new pluralism. He was an original thinker who, as a scholar, visited ancient and modern texts to give classic bones to his original body of thought. In his thesis, he combed the past of Aleister Crowley, the Knights Templar, and Ragnar Redbeard and absorbed their books, built on their rituals, and made them his own so he could give the wisdom away. In his antithesis, he considered the needs and desires of modern humans to be free to celebrate the self. Rubbing together his "thesis" and "antithesis," LaVey sparked his progressive "synthesis" in *The Satanic Bible*, using the past and then improving upon it.

Theorizing makes Anton LaVey valuable. Intellect makes him dangerous. Transgression makes him scary. Wit makes him fascinating. The middle name he gave himself was "Zsandor." No one has ever pointed out that *Zsandor* is an anagram for *Andros Z* which means, in Greek, "the last man," or "the ultimate man." Also, with its announced *A* and Z, *Andros Z* is a backhand slap at God, who in the Bible is called the alpha and omega, the beginning and the end. LaVey worked in layers.

To counterattack Western culture's repression of the physical, LaVey told his initiates, "As a Satanist, you will be encouraged to indulge in the so-called Seven Deadly Sins, as they lead to physical or mental gratification." Pushing the edge of female consciousness, LaVey made an offer to each female postulant, "Would you consider being an altar?" Jayne Mansfield apparently said yes. Satan may be the end, but women are the sacred means to the end. LaVey's one-time blonde consort Diane Hegarty was partner and high priestess; her good humor levitated some of the seriousness in their home, where the front parlor contained an altar, the coffee-table was a tombstone, the divan was Rasputin's sleigh chair, and bookcases swung out to reveal doors that led down secret passages.

LaVey's *Satanic Bible* is quick to point out that the Church of Satan is no orgy cult comprised of sex perverts, drug freaks, and social misfits. In fact, he carefully devotes several pages detailing what his Satanists do *not* do. The nearly ten thousand international members of the Church of Satan have undoubtedly all shouted "Shemhamforash! Hail Satan!" and made the "Conjuration of Lust"; but none has celebrated—at least not under LaVey's doctrinal aegis—the historic sexual excesses of the Black Mass, where among other inversions urine is asperged like holy water. LaVey's rituals, actually, tended more toward a sensual exotica that ended in Irving Berlin's "rubdown with a velvet glove."

LaVey, although on the left-hand path of the occult, tended toward the right-hand path of politics. He was a strong supporter of the U.S. Constitution, because only fifteen years after Gerald Gardner declared Wicca a religion in Britain, LaVey took his cue from Gardner and declared Satanism a religion in the United States. LaVey's was a daring, culture-shifting qualitative leap. Gerald Gardner justified white magic. Anton LaVey constitutionally justified black magic. In the summer of 1966, Anton LaVey corrected the course of American history that had been incorrect since the Salem Witch Trials of 1692. The U.S. Postal Service has put people on stamps for contributions less than LaVey's.

Nevertheless, LaVey threw fans and critics, equally, off kilter and into a moral panic. He was a meat eater. He loved guns, and had a fetish for gun-packing strippers. He wanted law-and-order cops. He welcomed gays. He kept wild animals as domestic pets. Proving Satan is a trickster, LaVey admitted he once voted for that old devil George Wallace in the 1968 presidential election, for political reasons other than Wallace's views on segregation. The Church of Satan has always been "open to all children of Satan."

LaVey, the former lion tamer, insisted that his Church of Satan was not simply a reaction to Christianity. As a satirist, he had been known, however, to promise his "lions just a taste of a Christian or two." His is more than a "self-help" philosophy. He was a cultured libertine who mixed the lore of witchcraft with the lure of self-indulgence. He made one feel that there is nothing wrong with self-indulgence, if one has a self worth indulging. Speaking of his followers, Anton LaVey told Kim Klein of *The Washington Post*, "I give them Ayn Rand with trappings."

LaVey entered iconic rock-star status on August 24, 1971, when he appeared in full color on the cover of *Look* magazine, hovering above a skull. Letters poured into the Church of Satan in San Francisco. To people seeking to join, Magister LaVey sent out a "Questionnaire for New Members" profiling their pop-culture IQs:

What is your idea of enjoyable music? What type of food do you like best? Do you own an automobile . . . what kind? What was the name of the last book you read? Do you own books on occult subjects? How many? What is your favorite form of alcohol? Name four motion pictures which you consider to be among your favorites. As a child, did you read comic books? Which ones? Do you like horror films?

Anton LaVey collected people. So do all religions. So do practitioners of craft. West Coast spiritualist Bishop West once claimed Vice President Hubert H. Humphrey as his client. San Francisco astrologer Joan Quigley counseled Nancy and Ronald Reagan. Singer Sammy Davis Jr., accepted an honorary membership in the Church of Satan on April 13, 1973. LaVey claimed that his guest list was as elite as his membership list. By location alone he was believable. San Francisco is traditionally an "open city," and the home of the secret and elite Bohemian Club, which caters to the powerful and privileged of politics, business, and society. "On the drive to the Bohemian Grove, let's pop by *chez* LaVey!" The Church of Satan's first Satanic wedding on February 1, 1967, caused a media sensation because the groom, John Raymond, was a well-connected journalist and the bride, Judith Case, was a New York socialite from a good family. Naturally, the higher the status, the more there is to lose, and the more there is to protect. LaVey, the guardian angel of darkness, offers help. Question 39 of the "Questionnaire for New Members" asks, "Do you feel that there are any people or forces working against you?"

Once accepted, the new member of the Church of Satan found, in 1970, when the Church was young, that the twenty-dollar initiation fee included a one-year subscription to the church's exclusive bulletin, *The Cloven Hoof,* whose content was instructive and entertaining, with essays on Satanic philosophy and Satanic magic, pronouncements by High Priest LaVey, announcements of coming events and press coverage, notices of the church's growing press clippings, a letters-from-members section, and an Inter-Membership Communication Roster for concelebrating with brother and sister Satanists. LaVey's one caution was that the church and its bulletin would not become a pen-pal and personal-ad service like that of the Canadian sadomasochism magazine *The Justice Weekly.*

Anton LaVey was stylishly McLuhanesque. He massaged his media messages in the manner of Canadian communications theorist Marshall McLuhan, the guru of media pop culture, who wrote the influential book *The Medium Is the Massage* (1967). McLuhan proposed an original theory about retribalizing the human race in a *global village* (a term he coined) where people are united by "hot" and "cool" media of technology. He punned on the terms *mass age, massage,* and *message,* and on the simultaneously technical and magical word *medium.* McLuhan's belief, like many spiritists who read auras and chakras, including the Catholic philosopher Teilhard de Chardin, is that electricity extends the central nervous system. McLuhan contends that electronic civilization is a giant leap forward to connect humans into closer contact with the spiritual; he also points out, as a good thing, that television has broken up the linearity of human lives, human thinking, and human religion. Certainly, in this electric leap against linearity, Anton LaVey is a most interesting mid-century figure in the spiral of popular culture.

Witchcraft is a retailer's wet dream. Consumers will buy anything, but, mostly they buy publications on alternative subjects ranging from astrology to yoga and Zarathustra. In pop culture, sales measure popularity. A fortune is made in the publishing of occult magazines and books that equals the huge fortune made in publishing religious books. Call them "occult" or call them "self-help." The books can be "pro-occult," like *The Satanic Bible* or *Rosemary's Baby* (published in 1967) or "anti-occult" like *The Exorcist* (originally published in 1971) or the millions of other antioccult titles sold annually by Christian and interfaith bookstores that thrive in every village in America. Ironically, these religious cautionary tales often serve as "introductions to the occult" for readers who otherwise would never have heard that "a person could actually—like, you know—*live* a Satanic lifestyle." When Christian authors warn that Marlon Brando's father and grandfather were Theosophists who followed Madame Blavatsky, they inadvertently add magic to Brando's already appealing image as outlaw rebel in *The Wild One* (1954) and well-buttered sodomist in *Last Tango in Paris* (1973). Is there an ironic, maybe even honorary, place in hell for preachers who introduce teens to Satan?

In Britain, Anton LaVey's contemporary Alex Sanders made origami folds of Aleister Crowley and Gerald Gardner and shook out a fresh version of popular witchcraft. As a youngster, Alex Sanders had been introduced by his grandmother to Crowley, who gave him a ring. Yet, while he grew up magical, he did not grow up to be a Satanist. Instead, upon the death of the hereditary white witch Gardner (1964) he became, after a brief power struggle within the self-defining new religion of Wicca, the elected King of the Witches. His election occurred clairvoyantly when a rising of covens converged and named him king in 1965. Witchcraft teaches that power is what one pulls to oneself, and *that* Sanders did rather brilliantly. Equally skilled at pulling power, American witch Louise Huebner, who wrote *Power through Witchcraft* (1969), was in 1968 named "Official Witch of Los Angeles County" by order of the Los Angeles Board of County Supervisors. Known for her sense of humor in books such as *Never Strike a Happy Medium* (1970), Huebner in 2004, displaying her "Official Witch" proclamation affixed with the County Seal, explained her title and the wild decade that dubbed her by saying, "It was the sixties!"

Gerald Gardner was a tough act for Alex Sanders to follow. Gardner's popularity, and the political power he conjured, had grown after his famous July 31, 1940, ritual performed in the south of England to prevent Hitler from invading Britain. Folklorist Gardner wisely rooted Wicca in national history. He repeatedly reminded reporters that British witches had cast a spell that sank the Spanish armada when Spain tried to invade England in 1588. Gardner wrote the first nonfiction book on Wicca, *Witchcraft Today* (1954), as well as *The Meaning of Witchcraft* (1959).

Aleister Crowley was the first pop-culture Satanist. Gerald Gardner was the first pop-culture witch. Alex Sanders absorbed them both, and then took a step forward in the pop culture of witchcraft.

In 1966, the same year that Anton LaVey founded the Church of Satan in America, Alex Sanders in Britain was inching away from Gerald Gardner's premise that Wicca was an update of ancient pagan ritual. Like LaVey, Sanders engaged the McLuhanesque marriage of media and the occult. He wanted print, radio, and television coverage. So he adapted a whiter shade beyond the pale; his was a kinder, gentler, media-friendly Wicca. He pictured the dawning of the Age of Aquarius as the golden dawn of the "New Age." By 1967, he created his own Alexandrian Wicca tradition of ceremonial circles, and covens emphasizing ritual as well as instruction in Kabbalah and angel magic. Again, like LaVey hosting Magic Circle meetings out of his Black House, Sanders in his Notting Hill flat was supporting himself teaching class lessons that became his book, *The Alex Sanders Lectures* (1969). In the surge of 1960s pop culture, reporters caught a whiff of what was going on up at the Sanders place. Pop went the witch. Sanders, the healer and clairvoyant, became sensational. The papers splashed ink, printing photographs of him, long and lean in a white loincloth, surrounded by his naked coven. He was very *Mondo*, very *Cane*, very hip, very fun. He fully acknowledged the power of popular culture: "The people who come to Wicca usually do so through the public media such as books, television, and radio.[28] In 1969, June Johns, with her photographer husband, Jack Smith, wrote the sympathetic tell-all biography *King of the Witches*, which was later made into the film *The Legend of the Witches* (1970).

Alex Sanders (1926–88) was initiated into the craft at age seven, in 1933, by his grandmother, Mary Biddy, who scratched his scrotum with a knife, saying, "Now you are one of us." One wonders about the coincidence that this is actually the same sentence repeated over and over at the end of the 1932 film *Freaks*. His grandmother's statement gave Sanders the credential most witches would kill for: hereditary status. To carry on his magical lineage, in 1967 Sanders, who was divorced with two children, married the Catholic Maxine Morris, who became his Alexandrian high priestess and the mother of his third child. Alex, with Maxine—a blonde, twenty years younger—made quite a couple. As a hereditary witch and as a married man and father, Sanders, in the swinging 1960s of London, found the times amenable to bringing a bit of homosexual ritual out of the Wiccan closet that Gerald Gardner had kept tightly locked during the 1950s.

In the way that the bisexual Crowley used homosexual ritual to raise the Devil, Alex Sanders invoked sacred masturbation with another straight man to create a magical child who became his spirit guide. The provocative Sanders dramatized that polarity magic can, in fact, happen between humans of the same gender even when both are, in fact, straight. In the rede of who is authentic, genuine, and cool, if the full range of sexuality is too avant-garde for some practitioners, they are not as Wiccan or Satanic as they think they are.

Sanders also revealed that early on he had conjured on the ring given him by Aleister Crowley, and had practiced black sorcery for personal gain. He soon repented, trading darker Mephistophelean flair for the shimmer of an almost-Anglican routine. His conversion from black demonology to white magic gives him the evangelizing edge of a Saint Augustine who builds his personal sanctity on his past (and more interesting) record as a sinner. If the 1970s popularized the occult and put its mysteries on tabloid sale at suburban supermarkets everywhere, Alex Sanders helped point out the way.

Sanders dumped the black arts out of self-preservation; practitioners of the occult must be careful of how they use their powers. Magic is not for personal gain; otherwise all witches would be rich. Even when not invoked for personal reasons, black and white rituals can wither the witch. Gerald Gardner's rite to repel Hitler's attack so drained the coven who worked the spell that five members soon died. Gardner felt that his own physical health had been permanently impaired by the magic energy expended against Hitler.

In that same way, mass culture sometimes seems to drain the gravitas of witchcraft. Press coverage often sensationalizes—and changes the

subject—in the way some people believe a camera shrinks the soul or mag-
nifies the ego. The press has expectations that massage the message of
popular witchcraft. Reporters like to cast Anton LaVey as antagonist to
make headlines shocking to Christian readers. The media played Sanders
as a white witch whose Wicca was so co-Christian that he was ecumenical enough for Episcopalian tea parties. The Alexandrian tradition, according to Sanders, is "just another sect worshiping just another God." So the
readers feel a safe little thrill seeing discreet photos of Sanders' cult stripped
obligingly for naked sabbaths. Sanders has made white witchcraft once
again compatible with Christianity. His pagan movement is a restoration
of magic that tries to heal the cut caused when the Catholic Church published *Malleus Maleficarum* and invented the Inquisition.

"Membership is free," June Johns wrote in the November 1969 *Mensa
Bulletin*, "but before presenting himself for initiation the applicant must
be prepared to devote at least one, and possibly many more, evenings a
week to memorizing chants and learning procedure. After receiving the
first-grade initiation, witches are taught to develop clairvoyance (com-
pulsory) and to use magic in their normal lives."[29]

In the Puritan way Mrs. Hawthorne expurgated husband Nathaniel's personal journals to match the public persona she wanted for him, June Johns
managed Alex Sanders's image into a liberal, not lascivious, morality. Naked
witches meet, but only to conjure blessings for supplicants. As Johns noted,
"Every week hundreds of people, many of them non-witches, seek the
help of the four or five thousand witches who are scattered over Britain.
Some of the covens are of the traditional thirteen (eleven members with
a high priest and a high priestess), but for normal working meetings, *esbats*,
a quorum is two."[30] While one person alone can perform either gender or
polar magic, Sanders recommends two, because couples are what most people prefer. Even with Sanders's uncloseting homosexual magic, his Alexandrian tradition has never been very far from the Gardnerian tradition.
Courting acceptance, Alex Sanders left gay Wicca to the left three fingers
of the left hand. With his right hand, he gestured to the press, reassuringly
talking of heterosexual gender magic, which he conservatively limited to
married couples. In Catholicism, all sex acts must lead to the possibility of
conception. The Alexandrian tradition allows sex for recreation and magic.

June Johns has claimed that witches do not seek converts. However, all
religions proselytize. Christianity recruits individuals, and entire other cultures, with both cross and sword. In American witchcraft, Mistress Hibbins

tried to convert Hester Prynne into witchery. The Salem girls converted their peers. Anton LaVey sought suitable members. Alex Sanders regularly invited those on his mailing list "to come to England solely to become witches, with the intention of opening covens in their own countries." His heterosexual initiation of probationers enticed exhibitionistic married couples who might copulate in the coven circle. It excited singles who, instead of copulation, might be sensually whipped forty lashes on the naked buttocks with embroidery thread. He honored men with mutual masturbation spells; he honored women by placing them central to rituals.

Alex Sanders worked his magic typically. Respect for the female form is witchcraft's great appeal. The spell is cast on a fith-fath, a female figure, which can be molded from wax or formed from any material from mud to cornstalks to Barbie's body. Thomas Hardy's folk-occult novel, *The Return of the Native*, which originally appeared serialized monthly in the popular culture of British magazines in 1878, is mainstream literature that has integrated the fith-fath into its plot.

Hardy's process analysis of how to work a curse is as much detailed in *The Return of the Native* as any white or black magic book of ritual. In fact, Hardy is passing along practical witch lore protected behind the "mask" of his novel.

> She passed with her candle into an inner room, where, among other utensils, were two large brown pans, containing together perhaps a hundred-weight of liquid honey, the produce of the bees during the foregoing summer. On a shelf over the pans was a smooth and solid yellow mass of a hemispherical form, consisting of beeswax from the same take of honey. Susan took down the lump, and, cutting off several thin slices, heaped them in an iron ladle, with which she returned to the living-room, and placed the vessel in the hot ashes of the fireplace. As soon as the wax had softened to the plasticity of dough she kneaded the pieces together. And now her face became more intent. She began moulding the wax; and it was evident from her manner of manipulation that she was endeavouring to give it some preconceived form. The form was human.
>
> By warming and kneading, cutting and twisting, dismembering and rejoining the incipient image she had in about a quarter of an hour produced a shape which tolerably well resembled a woman, and was about six inches high. She laid it on the table to get cold and hard. Meanwhile she took the candle and went upstairs to where the little boy was lying.

"Did you notice, my dear, what Mrs. Eustacia wore this afternoon besides the dark dress?"

"A red ribbon round her neck."

"Anything else?"

"No—except sandal-shoes."

"A red ribbon and sandal-shoes," she said to herself.

Mrs. Nunsuch went and searched till she found a fragment of the narrowest red ribbon, which she took downstairs and tied round the neck of the image. Then fetching ink and a quill from the rickety bureau by the window, she blackened the feet of the image to the extent presumably covered by shoes; and on the instep of each foot marked cross-lines in the shape taken by the sandalstrings of those days. Finally she tied a bit of black thread round the upper part of the head, in faint resemblance to a snood worn for confining the hair.

Susan held the object at arm's length and contemplated it with a satisfaction in which there was no smile. To anybody acquainted with the inhabitants of Egdon Heath the image would have suggested Eustacia Yeobright.

From her workbasket in the window-seat the woman took a paper of pins, of the old long and yellow sort, whose heads were disposed to come off at their first usage. These she began to thrust into the image in all directions, with apparently excruciating energy. Probably as many as fifty were thus inserted, some into the head of the wax model, some into the shoulders, some into the trunk, some upwards through the soles of the feet, till the figure was completely permeated with pins.

She turned to the fire. It had been of turf; and though the high heap of ashes which turf fires produce was somewhat dark and dead on the outside, upon raking it abroad with the shovel the inside of the mass showed a glow of red heat. She took a few pieces of fresh turf from thc chimney-corner and built them together over the glow, upon which the fire brightened. Seizing with the tongs the image that she had made of Eustacia, she held it in the heat, and watched it as it began to waste slowly away. And while she stood thus engaged there came from between her lips a murmur of words.

It was a strange jargon—the Lord's Prayer repeated backwards—the incantation usual in proceedings for obtaining unhallowed assistance against an enemy. Susan uttered the lugubrious discourse three times slowly, and when it was completed the image had considerably diminished. As the wax dropped into the fire a long flame arose from the spot, and curling its tongue round the figure ate still further into its substance. A pin occasionally dropped with the wax, and the embers heated it red as it lay.[31]

Gender politics in witchcraft is a minefield akin to gender politics in religion, where women are rarely ordained even though they basically constitute the congregation. In the world of popular witchcraft, the feminine mystique still suffers from the slurs of the Inquisition. In *The Exorcist*, the person possessed by Satan is, of course, a young girl. This stereotype that Satan possesses females seems to fulfill a straight erotic fantasy that is no more accurate than the "red-blooded" American-male porno fantasy about lesbian sex. After Ira Levin wrote *Rosemary's Baby*, he authored *The Stepford Wives* (1972), a novel whose title has entered pop-culture language. Levin equates men's sexism with male Satanism in the story of a young feminist who moves with her husband to "Stepford, Connecticut," where the wives live under a spell. The best-selling novel was twice made into a film (1975 and 2004) with several television sequels, including *Revenge of the Stepford Wives* (1980) and *The Stepford Children* (1987).

Regarding the role of women in witchcraft, Kim Klein wrote in the *Washington Post: Potomac*, on May 10, 1970, "For today's radical women, witches represent the truly liberated females of an earlier age—the only ones who were neither wife, nun, nor mistress. 'They were the first Protestants, the first abortionists, and the first healers outside recognized medicine,' says Marilyn Webb, a member of WITCH, the Women's International Terrorist Conspiracy from Hell. In their fight to free women from the *Playboy* image, members of WITCH publicly hex such enslaving institutions as Bunny clubs and ladies' department stores."[32]

After winning a 1968 Tony Award for touring as the lead in the all-black *Hello, Dolly*, singer Pearl Bailey, whose astrologer was Maurice Woodruff, said on the *David Frost Show*, 600th broadcast, November 1, 1971, "You know, honey, I've been reincarnated . . . I've had four full lives before this one and I know all about the witches in Salem. I told David Merrick that a lot of them are still around today, but they're now called bitches."

If the role of the emancipated female is as difficult to define as that of the emancipated homosexual, so are the concepts of family and coven after the decade of the 1960s, which changed everything in American popular culture and politics. In the 1950s, Marlon Brando, in *The Wild One*, created a kind of alternative male family in a motorcycle gang that prefigured the Manson Family. In 1957, Sonny Barger founded the Hell's Angels, who incorporated in California in 1966. From their name to their actions, the Hell's Angels became archetype and stereotype of men living in sympathy with the Devil. But as a group they are not Wiccans—Gardnerian or Alexandrian. They seem more like Crowley and LaVey, although LaVey disavows crime and drugs. They rebel to break free of everything. Their tattoos, like ancient markings within secret circles of warriors, brag "Born to Lose" under an image of a Satan head smoking marijuana. Some may be hereditary witches; some may practice authentic witchcraft; but most, enlarging on the name Hell's Angels, seem to be pop-culture bad boys acting out Satanic styles, and playing the Satan card to intimidate people.

The media love, and hate, the Hell's Angels, who are as infamous as the Knights Templar for their sex rituals. Hunter Thompson, in his book *Hell's Angels: A Strange and Terrible Saga* (1967) reported as true the urban legend that a Hell's Angel earns his "Red Wing Patch" by performing cunnilingus on a menstruating woman, and his "Black Wing Patch" by having sex with an African-American woman. Through group rituals of oral sex, the Hell's Angels spontaneously continue pagan worship of females that some say masks their fraternal homomasculinity as heterosexual sophistication as much as it reinvents the central female-blood ritual of the fabled Black Mass. Through such oral worship, sexual outlaws ritualize the matriarchal communion of "eating the witch." In the underground sex-code of African-American and gay male grooming, a goatee, moustache, or triangular hair-tuft (called a "soul patch") beneath the lower lip signals the male's willingness to engage in whatever form of oral sex suits his preference.

Gershon Legman, in his Jungian book *Rationale of the Dirty Joke: An Analysis of Sexual Humor* (1968), mentions Aleister Crowley's rituals of cunnilingus as merely a sensational and "fawning imitation of Baudelaire and Swinburne," who were no literary slouches when it came to sex, drugs, and Satan. Legman calls Crowley a "pipsqueak . . . playing at perversion" and "other occulta and exotica." Legman prefers the Comte de Mirabeau, who presents cunnilingus "as a ritual act of worship of the mother goddess, combining the most utter oral submission to the woman" in a way that is not "masochistic or perverse" but rather "the sort of transcendental sexual rite that culminates the pre-patriarchal worship of woman now known as the Black Mass."[33]

The litany goes on. Insofar as urine is used worldwide for magical purposes, baptism into the Hell's Angels includes urination on the new member's jacket and jeans, as well as on the "colors" of his cut-off denim overlay that reads across his shoulders "Hell's Angels." Insofar as penetration equals bonding, ritual oral sodomy is increasingly reported in male-male initiations among bikers, fraternity boys, drumming circles, and Marines. Among straight men, same-sex anal sodomy is performed more often with objects, such as witchy broomsticks and hammer handles, than it is by an aggressive penis. In the 1970 camp movie of Gore Vidal's *Myra Breckinridge*, Myra, who has been surgically shape-shifted from Myron, is dressed as a witch who rides a phallic broom handle while s/he sodomizes a young all-American cowboy with a dildo.

The situation ethics of what is natural and what is violent depend on definitions and conditions. On December 6, 1969, when the Hell's Angels were hired as the security guards to keep order during a Rolling Stones rock concert at the Altamont Speedway outside San Francisco, the Angels, by their own nature, logic, and tribal morality, turned on the crowd, beating some and stabbing one to death. This Hell's Angels "natural sense of order" that civilians screamed was the disorder of mayhem was captured in a documentary film by David and Albert Maysles, *Gimme Shelter* (1970).

That same year, Mick Jagger starred in the magical-realist film *Performance*, a pop time-capsule of the 1960s written by Donald Cammell and directed by Nicolas Roeg, about the London gangster scene whose dynamic, minus the motorcycles, is rather like the Hell's Angels. Jagger played a fading rock star—an androgynous mandarin—hiding out with a handsome London gangster (James Fox) in an exchange of psychedelics, gender, bisexuality, sadomasochism, and—ultimately—personalities. In real life, Mick Jagger is a Rosetta Stone who when rolled over reads like a Rolodex of artists, projects, and events that are creative, dark, and magical. He was a longtime friend of *Performance* screenwriter Cammell, who played Osiris, the Egyptian God of Death, in their friend Kenneth Anger's *Lucifer Rising*. Cammell based his script for *Performance* on the works of magical realist Jorge Luis Borges. The *Performance* characters are shown reading Borges's book *A Personal Anthology* (1961; English version 1967), and Borges's face appears onscreen at the end of the film. The star-crossed Cammell was born in Scotland, not far from the mansion of Aleister Crowley whose books Cammell's father kept on his library shelves. As he lay dying at age sixty-two from a self-inflicted gunshot, Cammell said, "I cannot yet see Borges."

More gentle than the cunnilingual Angels, the hippie family commune represents the romantic return to an agrarian America where belief in the spiritual is still possible. Modeled after the New England transcendentalist projects at Brook Farm and Fruitlands, the hippie commune takes the urbanized individual back to nature. Transcendentalists like Ralph Waldo Emerson introduced American culture to Eastern concepts of Persian poetry, the *Bhagavad-Gita*, German idealism, and British romanticism.

These communes to urban muddled-class Americans are—besides loose in new sex, new drugs, and new nutrition—antiauthoritarian. Hippie liberation is equated, like witchcraft, with license.

After the Manson Family's Tate murders, the global media made *commune* synonymous with *cult*. The new gods worshiped by the drug visionaries, supplied "pharmaceutically" by the tarot knights of the Hell's Angels, seemed no longer the phenomena of an innocent astrology. Mature Christianity suddenly accorded the New Age gods of its children the same status primitive Christianity had given to the pagan gods: any god other than the Christian Jesus is no god at all but is, in fact, minion and facet of the Devil. Where before the Tate murders "love children" had wandered the Western world, suddenly more people than the customs police became suspicious of them and their gypsy ways, as well as of all alternative lifestyles. The bright 1960s gave way to the darker 1970s.

The fact is that while every coven is in a sense a commune, not every commune is a coven. The Manson Family became the popular press "coven of the decade." Manson's irresistible Rasputin-like image on the winter-solstice cover of *Life* magazine, December 19, 1969, enhanced the sado-masochistic sexuality, the mysticism and ritual, the drugs, and the slaying of a Hollywood star and her friends. The Manson cover of *Life* seemed to say "Is Satan Alive?" as much as *Life* magazine's sibling publication, *Time*, had asked on its Halloween cover (October 22, 1965), "Is God Dead?" Even more than the mainstream magazines, the supermarket tabloids headline the Manson Family as much as the Kennedy family.

Paul Watkins, Manson's second-in-command, in a *National Enquirer* article, is quoted as having said of his master Satan, "Manson was big on Scientology and black magic. He picked it all up in San Francisco. It was pretty powerful stuff. He was continually hypnotizing us . . . like mental thought transference." Watkins told of Charles Manson's desire for human sacrifice and the delight of the slaves in the torture-slaying of musician Gary Hinman, one of twenty-five supposed victims of the Manson Family. He added that Manson taught him a thing or two about sex:

> He would give us some of his philosophy at moonlight gatherings. For example. he once said, "Women must live for men, women must die for men, women must serve men. Women are like batteries. When they run down they must be discharged or disposed of." He told us that the only real way for happiness on earth was to serve him.
>
> As an example of his power, Charlie created a ritual which would start

with twelve girls and six men in a circle with Charlie in the middle. . . . On a signal, all the girls would grovel at his feet. They would lie there, kissing his toes and moaning their affection for him. Meanwhile we men would be lying back, getting out of our heads on acid and anything else that would send us crazy. When Charlie had enough of the moaning and feet-kissing he would end the ritual. . . . Now you are getting some idea of where Charlie's power stemmed from. You see, he controlled so much of our emotions, our food, our drink, our money, our drugs and our sex. . . . It was impossible to think of life without him.[34]

Understandably, law-and-order Satanist Anton LaVey immediately distanced himself from any real or perceived connection to Charles Manson. LaVey denied the rumor that the couple being wed by LaVey in a Satanic marriage ceremony captured on movie film were actually members of the Manson Family. He attributed Manson's multiple identity as Jesus, God, and Satan to instability caused by drug use. LaVey's summary of the Tate murders was emphatic:

It's a wonder there weren't *more* "occult" comparisons made. The fact that Manson pursued Scientology has frequently been mentioned. I don't think that Scientology can be blamed in any way, except as a means of adding substance to Manson's awareness that he was a loser. Scientology would use the technique of throwing his "bad pre-natal conditioning" up to him as another strike against him.

The hippie community is well-known for its obsession with any and all mystical devices and identities, so a smattering of ritualistic trappings was bound to enter the total picture of the murders.

As far as I'm concerned, the whole thing was a hippie killing. . . . This crime was perpetrated by irrational people, none of whom have a true conception of ANY God, let alone the Prince of Darkness![35]

In Chicago, as much as in trend-setting California, some adolescent gangs in the 1970s turned faddishly to witchcraft. As reporter David St. Albin Greene related, "I spent one sunny day in a Chicago neighborhood rife with teenage witches. My host and guide was 'Helios,' a gangly 18-year-old lad with long, brown hair who graduated from Kelvyn Park High last June and now attends junior college. He told his Polish-Catholic parents that he has adopted witchcraft as a religion, but they still are not sure what goes on nights when the gang takes over the basement and locks the doors. What Helios and his coven do down there, of course, is pay tribute to a phallic God and a fecund Goddess, scourge each other lightly with a home-made whip, and dig paganism in a variety of other undisclosed ways."[36]

Almost a year after Greene's gothic visit, an ex-Marine returned home to the same neighborhood. In his mid-twenties, he called himself simply LeJeunesse. In an interview over coffee, he remained typically noncommittal on rumors of intra-Marine rituals, both sexual and occult. He owned, however, to having stayed in Southern California several months after his discharge.

"Some coincidence," LeJeunesse said. "The night Sharon Tate was killed I was into a very humpy weekend with the Satan Trippers in L.A. I didn't know about it till Monday afternoon." LeJeunesse's theory explained the Tate murders as more Christian cult than Satanic. He continued,

> Manson called himself Jesus, right? It was all Jesus Manson's attempt to stop the birth of the Anti-Christ. Manson, you see, suspected that Polanski was way into Satanism as a result of *Rosemary's Baby*. He got vibrations that Polanski wanted to make sure his movie was a success, so he sold out to the Devil just like Rosemary's husband. Manson was a known prowler. He laid some heavy scouting on the Polanski house and found out that the Castavets were that supermarket couple, Leno and Rosemary LaBianca. They all met before Sharon got pregnant. Manson got it all together and ordered the deaths of the Polanski coven one night and the LaBianca's the next. He called himself Jesus, you know, and Polanski's wife was like carrying the Antichrist. I guess to him it all made sense. [Pulling up his shirt sleeve, LeJeunesse pointed to a Devil's Head tattooed over the initials USMC.] To me the whole witchcraft thing is a pretty good *in* to having some rough sex with chicks you wouldn't otherwise get without some kind of a scary it's-oh-so-spiritual gimmick.[37]

Coven can, of course, cover for sexual *orgy*: sweet young things submitting to the high priest and all that. Nevertheless, what some abuse, others use properly. Some witches find ritual nudity disgusting. Some find it necessary. Some, like Pontifex Maximus Frederic de Arechaga, who calls Ishtar "the original stripper," might approve of Cece Ingram billed in contemporary burlesque as "Satan's Angel." Others would call Cece's flaming tassels, spinning in opposite directions, a sacrilege. Anton LaVey would invite the burlesque artist to his altar.

Gardnerian witches, like Raymond Buckland (b. 1934), the high priest of a New York coven, find nudity necessary to release the body energy centered in the sex organs. Buckland's wife, Lady Rowen, is the center of their Long Island coven of white witchcraft. Naked but for a silver crown, some jewelry, and a leather garter, Lady Rowen leads the coven in chanting, spellbinding, and raising the "cone of power" in the half of their cellar that is not used for the Buckland Museum of Witchcraft and Magic. Their family coven numbers thirteen and centers on the high priestess. Mrs. Buckland says she turned to white witchery to find the spiritual meaning behind her physical motherhood.

Anthropologist Margaret Murray, in her classic pair of books *The Witch Cult in Western Europe* (1921) and *The God of the Witches* (1933), forged the engaging insight that witchery is a polytheism as old as the Stone Age. Gerald Gardner may have come closest to the truth, claiming that modern belief is hardly different from the Old Religion. Women's liberation may recognize how the ancient goddess religions come down, expressed in the Catholic devotion to "Mary, Mother of God," who in witch lore becomes the Goddess or "Rosemary, Mother of Satan." Gay liberation, which seems to some unnatural, may ultimately be nature's ironic way of calling all humans back to the joys of personal pleasure and recreational sex in an overpopulated world that hardly needs much more procreational sex. *The Gay Grimoire* states, "Homosexuality is nature's birth control."

Modern *Christianity* and modern *witchcraft*, for all their warring polarities, archetypes, and rituals, are reciprocal terms, like *mother* and *child*. A person really can't understand one term without understanding the other.

Perhaps *religion* and *witchcraft* are two sides of the same coin: both try to manage sex, power, and persona. Both try to comfort human nature. And both try to terrify human nature.

God knows, humans are caught between the Devil and the deep blue sea—or vice versa.

What does a solo soul cling to in the never-ending human dilemma?

When everybody shuts up, each person knows that the individual self, at least in body, and most likely in consciousness, will dissolve.

Both noble King Arthur and ignoble Adolf Hitler quested for the magical Christ's Holy Grail. Each person out of nature and nurture, projecting God, projecting Satan, projecting a sense of self, struggles between the dualities of animality and reason, body and soul, good and evil, light and dark, coming into being and fading into death.

The truth? You are God. You are Satan.

As men's prayers are a disease of the will,
so are their creeds a disease of the intellect.
—RALPH WALDO EMERSON, *Self-Reliance*

CHAPTER 4

Straight from the Witch's Mouth

PERSONAL INTERVIEWS WITH WITCHES

What you are looking for is looking for you.
                                —DAVID HURLES, OLD RELIABLE

S ABAEAN PONTIFEX MAXIMUS FREDERIC DE ARECHAGA;
   Dr. David Tronscoso; Charles J. Redmund; Adrian Kirch;
   Madame Yoland Savarini; Vern Overlee; Bishop West; Rita Norling;
   the Reform Tract Society; and Lilith St. John.

For twenty-first-century inquisitors, witchhunting is a .32-second chase by a search engine. In 1969 and 1970, I had to work harder than that. Witchcraft was secret territory.

In the ages before the Internet, witches had to hide in plain sight by advertising in code. In the twentieth century, seekers asked the owners of avant-garde or "retro-garde" bookstores questions about the "old books" or the "self-help" section. If the owners were not themselves witches, they often knew who was. Even with times changed, the old ways are still valid for searching out sorcery.

Check out incense boutiques with gemstones and crystal balls as well as the off-campus shops with window signs for "occult recordings." Become literate about the magic symbolism of jewelry, clothes, tattoos, and piercings. Interpret mystic insignia at coffee shops, concerts, and health fairs. To the diversified eye, young witches are as visible as crones, and gender is negotiable. Read the classifieds of local college or ethnic newspapers, as well as free local guides to arts, massage, hypnosis, and healing. Because sex is more "out" than witchcraft, a male or female witch can often be found hiding within the sex ads of the straight and gay underground press. As in classic "massage" listings, which did not offer actual massage because they were listings for coded "rub-and-tug" parlors, conventional wisdom knows that what people advertise is often a cover for what they are selling.

The Yellow Pages were once pop culture's best index. Listings included *astrologers, astrology schools, palmists, botanicas, metaphysical bookstores,* and *old curiosity shops.* There was no category for *witches,* who had to present themselves as "palmists" or "hypnotherapists." Because it's a principle of perception in popular culture that stereotype always trumps archetype, witches have always had to be self-protecting, because the stereotype is what gets burned at the stake.

Nothing can ruin the night more than looking out the windows of one's castle and seeing the villagers approaching with torches and pitchforks.

Geography also figures into how witches label themselves. California is always ten years ahead of the rest of American pop culture. On the West Coast, the Yellow Pages listed "hypnotherapy," which in the Midwest was listed under "relaxation techniques" or "stress reduction." As categories like *palmist, astrologer, numerologist,* and *midwife* have emerged, would it hurt to have a listing for *witch*?

I think it should be a rede of witchcraft that "what you are looking for is looking for you." In any group, ask, "Has anyone here any Native American blood?" There will almost always be someone. Ask also, "Does anyone here know a witch?"

Take advantage of the social possibilities of Silva Mind Institute groups, drumming circles, modern-primitive lectures, and psychic encounter groups like the Psychic Club of Dayton, Ohio. For ten dollars this club, which advertises itself as the place "where witches and warlocks abound," will match you to an astro-twin pen pal, a free location service for correspondence with others with the same interests, and a one-year subscription to the *Psychic Club Bulletin.* The more outrageous can join the Sisters of Perpetual Indulgence, who are men in comic nun-drag dedicated to charitable acts, as well as to running in high heels to dodge attacks from the Catholic Church which—itself having stolen so much from paganism—objects to the Sisters' dragging up the image of Catholic nuns.

In the last analysis, witches, like beauty and porno, are in the eye of the beholder. What people say about themselves, though "crafty," reveals way more than a Hallmark Halloween card. In the following interviews, popular practitioners in Wicca and witchcraft speak for themselves. In some of the shorter interviews, the question-and-answer format has been condensed to a statement.

Interviewed in 1969 and 1970, these practitioners provide a time capsule of the emerging American age of witchcraft liberation. Their points of view and predictions for witchcraft in the last quarter of the twentieth century have since increased in historical value.

The questions originally asked in 1970 of practitioners interviewed by mail were these:

Please respond to any of the following areas you feel pertinent to your realm. If these questions do not please you, write instead what you feel.

1. Please make a statement on witchcraft as you find it to be today.
2. Please make a statement on witchcraft as you think it ought to be today.
3. Why, do you believe, is the occult enjoying so much popularity?
4. What is your opinion of the laws for and against witchcraft? As a witch, have you experienced any discrimination?
5. Please make a statement concerning white witchery.
6. Please make a statement concerning the black arts.
7. Please make a statement on the role of the contemporary witch, male or female.
8. What do you think of the commercialization of witchcraft? For instance, *Rosemary's Baby*, TV's *Bewitched*. (Any comment on the Polanski-Tate-Manson affair?)
9. Please make a statement concerning the place of sexuality in the occult, black and/or white.
10. Please make a statement concerning the direction you think witchcraft will go in the coming *fin de siècle*. To greater or lesser acceptance? Any aspect of it that will become immensely popular?
11. List what in your opinion are ten of the most significant books or articles on witchcraft or the occult. (Anything from basic works to astrological cookbooks.)
12. If you would, please draw a word description of yourself or a friend as a practicing occultist. For instance, what your specific purpose is; what you find people consulting you for; what kind of people your clients are, etc.

FREDERIC DE ARECHAGA, SABAEAN PONTIFEX MAXIMUS, BISEXUAL, ASTROLOGY LECTURER, HEREDITARY WITCH, OWNER OF EL-SABARUM OCCULT SUPPLY STORE; CHICAGO

In Paris in May 1969, I first heard of the mysterious magician "Freddy." By the time I reached Amsterdam, I knew his last name—de Arechaga. In

London, I realized some of the mystic pedigree of Frederic de Arechaga. My friends on Lynette Avenue, Clapham Common, were the kind of artists and liberated sexualists who thrived in the Swinging '60s of London. They were sex magicians, and if they weren't witches themselves, they certainly knew who was Wiccan and wicked on the international sex circuit. After their introduction, I flew to Chicago, to meet the one and only Sabaean Pontifex Maximus Frederic de Arechaga.

That summer had been wild, erotic, and revolutionary. I flew to Europe on the Feast of Beltane, May Day; I received the contract for the first edition of this book on June 1; I turned thirty on June 20; the summer solstice was June 21; Judy Garland died in London June 22; the Stonewall Rebellion broke out in New York City's Greenwich Village the night of June 27–28 and ignited the gay liberation movement; the first men landed on the moon July 29; and I was hit in a horrible car crash, when a Checker cab drove through the rear window of my Volkswagen on August 9, the same night the Manson Family murdered everyone at the Polanski home and changed forever the worldview of cult and coven.

Riding this 143-day crest, I met with Freddy de Arechaga on Saturday afternoon, September 20, 1969. From my taxi, his storefront looked like a fun little head shop. The boys from Clapham Common had told me tales. The El-Sabarum facade hid something magic inside. First meetings are easy, unencumbered by baggage, and Freddy quickly closed up his tiny shop. The windows were darkened. Music played in the darkness. Incense burned on the glass counter where his sales pad lay. We were surrounded by artwork and books and "craft" ware for sale. While I gave his shop the once-over, he gave the same to me. "Would you like some tea?" he asked. "Would you like a joint?" Freddy drew back a curtain and ushered me into his Babylonian temple.

I'm such a child of the movies that everything looks like Hollywood to me: Freddy's temple, Anton LaVey's Black House, Andy Warhol's Factory, photographer Robert Mapplethorpe's apartment, painter George Dureau's French Quarter studio. It is a truism that homosexuality is a kind of "universal pass" that gets a person through doors and into private realities otherwise outside his caste and class. If I had been straight, I could not have written about witchcraft. I would not have known how to interpret Freddy, the former choreographer, or Freddy's Sabaeanist temple. I approached him with as much respect as I did my uncle the Catholic priest when he proudly showed me his new rectory and sanctuary. Rather than appointed with Roman Catholic regalia, Freddy's temple was everything Hollywood

Babylon should be. Doves cooed in cages hung in arches decorated with lights and palms.

That summer of 1969, everything was psychedelic.

We sat down on pillows and drank tea. The joint laid us back, sweet, but not out of it. We bonded in our mutual motives. I wanted his story as much as he was eager to share it. For four hours, we lay side by side, talking, with questions asked and answered. He marveled at my "fast magic" changing his spoken words to writing on my yellow legal pad. Freddy spoke with such conviction and intensity that my questions were hardly necessary to prompt his "take" on Sabaeanism, magic, witchcraft, and religion. Freddy was a handful—and then some.

JACK FRITSCHER: You are famously bisexual, almost as if gay isn't enough as we go into the seventies. In Europe, you are known as a hereditary witch. Do you practice white or black magic? And why a shop in Chicago?

FREDERIC DE ARECHAGA: Let me backtrack. In the sixth century before Christ, a Persian king in the area of Babylonia refused to attack Harran because it was a bastion of the Old Faith. Justinian, Caracalla, Alexander the Great—many historical personages—always went to the Oracles at Harran. I use Harran because Harran is responsible for the cloven-hoofed god which sensationalistic Christians think of as the goat-footed Devil. The word *warlock* is terribly profaned because it means liar.

FRITSCHER: Most witches don't use it. It's used by people who buy Hallmark cards.

DE ARECHAGA: Look *warlock* up in the dictionary. The word *witch* is a degeneracy from the Anglo-Saxon *wicca*, meaning "wise one." The essential value of a witch or wise one is they never have to admit that they are. They are simply acknowledged by the fact that in listening to them talk you know they're wise. What they were originally were *bab-ilu's* or *pontifexes*, that is, *bridges*. Both are the same word, the "gateway to the gods." *Bab* means "gate" and *ilu* means "god." In Chaldean Hebrew, *ilu* becomes *el*, giving you *Bab-el*, the gate to the gods and thus the Tower of Babel.

The gateway to the gods was architecturally a pyramidal structure which Sumerians, Egyptians, and Central Americans built to meet their gods, who were to return in fiery chariots.

FRITSCHER: You lean then toward *Chariots of the Gods* [Eric von Däniken, 1969].

DE ARECHAGA: Whether this leads to the ambiguity of UFOs, it's not my business to say. The point is that our august ancestors came from the heavens in fiery chariots, taught the hairy barbarians the way of the gods, taught them how to build structures, taught them to look at the heavens and calculate them, and then split after ruling several thousand years. This is true whether you're looking at the Vedas, Torah, Sacred Egyptian or Babylonian or Central American texts. The point is that Harran— mentioned in Genesis when Abraham decided to split from Ur—is where Abraham continually went. He went to Harran. Why? When he needed a wife for Isaac he went to Harran. Why? What's so precious in Harran? Ezekiel called it a great place of barter and exchange. I thought Babylon was supposed to be the great center. No matter. The fact still is that Harran is highly honored by everybody except for the Moslems who eventually took it over.

FRITSCHER: So what was the big mystery of Harran?

DE ARECHAGA: Study Harran and you'll find its religion was Sabaeanism, the Old Religion, the religion of earth. It is not a religion of hero worship and so it does not glorify any one god or any one people. It is not the monotheistic paranoia of Christians and Jews. It doesn't convert. It finds no need to display itself since the values in Sabaeanism are sufficient in themselves.

But what has happened? All the so-called crap of black magic is stuff stolen from the annals of the Sabaean temples. All the perfumes to the gods, the planetary deities, all come down through Harran. You can find in an old German book, the only book on Sabaeanism, that the perfumes, colors, shapes and all the things that eventually became occult lore were the things practiced long ago by the Pontifex of Saba.

In Harran, the most famous, but not the only, center of Sabaeanism, one god was favored. This early national god, predating Mardoch, was the god Sin, who is god of the moon. Sin, according to the ancients, was an old man whose symbol was the crescent moon. When you have a god, you put on his head the symbol of the planet he relates to. And if you put a crescent on top of somebody's head, it's going to very much look like horns. It was an ancient Sumerian and Babylonian practice to have antennae-looking things which eventually gave way to the placement of bull's horns, which you can see on the genii in ancient Babylonian temples. These are the symbols of Godhead, which only Michelangelo respected and understood enough to put on the head of Moses.

The fact is that Sin was the great god of the moon. Later, the moon became identified with the female matriarch through the Greeks who were hung up on matriarchy. Sabaeanism, I might add, is likewise a matriarchy.

FRITSCHER: You are, I was told, a matriarchal hereditary witch.

DE ARECHAGA: Very true. My mother related very much to the moon. As astronauts approached the moon, she sickened. When astronauts landed on the moon [July 20, 1969], she died. My hereditary position came through her. There's another lady, an ancient Egyptian frog goddess which very few people know about, Heka. The word *heka* in ancient Egyptian added to a word meant something magical. She was the goddess of magic. The roots of all this lie in remote antiquity.

FRITSCHER: The Greeks called her Hecate. I've studied quite a lot of the classics.

DE ARECHAGA: Unfortunately, reading books is not sufficient because most are secondary texts written by dusty Victorian archeologists who write in a profane, self-centered style as if the ancients were likewise Victorians. The philosophy of antiquity was much different from today. It was not hypocritical, nor materialistic, nor obsessed with rationalistic facts. We Sabaeans accept people and things as they are. We do not believe in converting people from or to anything. Because the main god—the embodiment of all Godhead—is truth, which exists independent and absolute; no one book is the authority.

FRITSCHER: So you have no Sabaean text like the absolute Bible of Jews and Christians?

DE ARECHAGA: Sabaeans have no one book. Therefore we extend truth through word of mouth. To categorize truth is impossible. It must be personal, and therefore word of mouth at the moment. So to say you have a *Book of Shadows* or a book of anything is bullshit. It's just down, around, unmitigated crap.

FRITSCHER: In England, Gerald Gardner was very much into the *Book of Shadows*.

DE ARECHAGA: Which he denied he wrote.

FRITSCHER: Which he suggested was constantly changing because of witches rewriting what they passed along by word of mouth.

DE ARECHAGA: I have been very much called down for opening my mouth against profane people. There are no temple-side philosophers today. Because I have a store here in Chicago, I have to face a lot of jerks who don't know their ass from an occult hole in the ground. The true pontifex does not have any need as do most of these children—like Aleister Crowley—to outdo each other. All the covens are fighting with each other. This shows their very lack of power. When you deal with the real thing, the infighting ceases because it is against your own philosophy.

One important thing that I don't think has been written in the occult or appreciated anywhere for that matter is that "value is sufficient unto itself." So if you as a novice create your very first thunderstorm in the middle of a sunny day, and then *don't* tell anybody, now. . . *that's* an accomplishment!

FRITSCHER: That's, literally, in the real sense of the word, *charming.*

DE ARECHAGA: It is an established tradition that when you put a spell on somebody and you go up and tell them, you break the spell. So in itself it works for its own value; this is the old, old school of values. This destroys any chance of self-glorification and all that Crowley nonsense about competing magicians.

FRITSCHER: Which Hollywood loves for its dramatic effect. Like *The Raven*, with Vincent Price battling Boris Karloff.

DE ARECHAGA: Not to glorify one's self. It's very difficult, but then a pontifex is not just an ordinary human being. He has to be above and beyond. This is the true Zarathusthra who has to metamorphize to a point of godlike qualities. Otherwise he is just a profane slob who enjoys an ego trip. The greatest ego-trippers these days are the Satanists. To begin with, to be a Satanist you must be a Catholic.

FRITSCHER: I am a Catholic. I believe in Satan. That is an underlying fact of my book. I believe Satan exists. That's why I'm talking to people who work with Satan.

DE ARECHAGA: You have your point of view. But you must know that Satanic rituals are all degenerate Catholic rituals. I've heard Anton LaVey's record and the Coven's record of the black mass and Louise Huebner or whatever her name is. They go off and they start rapping all this magical shit and they really don't know what the fuck they're talking about.

The Satanists—with all due respect to the Satanists—worship the god of the sun. Baal, Moloch. I can appreciate this. The sun god is the god of power. I can understand them relating to Saturn or Pluto. But then they turn around with all this crap on Satan, who is just the old Persian god *Saathan*, and start talking of him in terms of negation and hate and murder and carnage and crap. When they call him the Prince of Darkness and the Prince of Hell, they're talking Christian dogma. The Satanist was really created by the degenerate mind of witch finders, who were fascinated by the occult—but could not admit to it.

FRITSCHER: Over and over, I have heard it said that Satan is a fantasy created by Christians, but Satan is in both the Old and New Testaments.

DE ARECHAGA: There are thousands of existing old texts and old books
and old manuscripts that you can interpret to mean exactly what you
want. That's precisely why we Sabaenists have no one book to bind us.
The fact is, the Satanist symbols are a degeneration of the symbols of
ancient Harran. Satanists grossly misinterpret, for example, the Catholic
Mass into triteness, into parody in the Satanic Black Mass. Satanists are
sensationalizers who have read one, two, or three books—or even a
library—and then throw together an eclectic conglomeration of shit,
like Aleister Crowley. Take one of his books and you have so many errors
of names, herbs, and perfumes of ancient Egypt that he is a great mixture of nothing. But then, Crowley was a warped Christian's son.

FRITSCHER: Crowley remains very popular in England with many gay men
who like his bisexual magic, as well as with the Beatles and the Rolling
Stones. His Satanism, more than the white magic of the Old Religion,
appeals to those who like sex, drugs, and rock-and-roll.

DE ARECHAGA: Actually, the fact is, the Old Religion created what you'd
call the popular images of the occult. The Old Religion mothered the
palmist's hands, the idea of the seven planets, the idea of the ten powers, the idea of the five sacred numbers, the pentacle, the pentagram,
the six-pointed star, the snake, the symbols of the heavens. All this imagery that these style-conscious people degenerate and proselytize—all of
it is an adulteration of the Old Religion.

FRITSCHER: Are you saying this because your mother . . .

DE ARECHAGA: I don't say this because I am an hereditary pontifex of
the Old Religion, but simply because I have studied where these degen-
erations have come from. It's annoying. If people would just say this is
what this symbol means and let it go at that, I would have nothing to
say. But what pisses me is that these people have the nerve, the unmitigated gall to say that it's *their* idea. How *dare* they!

The fact is that the cross is an ancient, ancient symbol of the sun—
the god of the sun, which the Christians still worship on the sun's day.
Catholics use the sacred metal, which is gold. Catholics put halos on
their statues, which is typical of Gods like Apollo. Catholics still worship
in the same manner as the temple of Amun-Ra, the god of the sun,
because the whole idea of the tabernacle, and the Catholic priest genu-
flecting and throwing himself on the floor, is found in the ritual of the
divine sun cult.

FRITSCHER: Is any religion original?

DE ARECHAGA: Only the Old Religion. Today's people neglect their study
of genuine occult literature almost as much as their getting involved with
real magic. Everybody's hung up on being hung up. Everybody's in love
with love, but not with the reality of somebody else. That's because we
belong to a degenerate American society, brought up on false ideals and
false Gods who declare themselves the ultimate authority. These hippie
kids, young and old, who let their hair grow just to resist authority are
on a superficial ego trip. My hair is longish and I have facial hair, but
that doesn't make me a revolutionary. I'm not just regrooming myself
under a thatch of ego-tripping hair, the way they are regrooming the
values of our hypocritical society. These kids are as gullible as their establishment parents. If you really want to become a revolutionary, you simply have to stop being so gullible. You can't believe you are what other
people tell you that you are.

FRITSCHER: The government thrives on our gullibility.

DE ARECHAGA: But the truth is that the true philosopher's stone is found
within yourself. Believe your reality. The stone is not in some crummy
piece of metal which you must alchemize. True are the words from Harran identity to Delphic identity: *know thyself.*

FRITSCHER: *Gnothi sauton.* Inscribed on the Temple at Delphi.

DE ARECHAGA: The whole idea of destiny and divination is based on
knowing yourself so you can do something about it! All this nonsense
of heaven and hell is propaganda, because basically monotheistic cults,
whether Islamic, Buddhistic, or Christian, can be no more than self-
centered authoritarians, who are very class-conscious, and only interested in making outsiders into bloody peasants. Monotheism ignores
objective truth, knowledge, and wisdom. Monotheists become themselves subservient to their own authoritarianism. They program people
into being an audience, peasants fit only to work like animals, cretins who
do what is expected of them as it is so said by outside authority.

   We Old Religionists don't care about your sectarian squabbles, because
truth exists independently and in facets. We are about self-realization
of the person you are.

   If you want to worship the sun, you go to a Catholic church.

   If you want to worship Saturn, you go to a Synagogue.

   If you want to worship Venus, you go to a Mosque.

   If you want to worship the moon, you go to a Hare Krishna temple.

   If you want to worship Mercury, go to a Buddhist temple.

We Old Religionists don't have to build temples. There are enough people taking money for building funds. However, if you go to a church, synagogue, mosque, or temple, and you find their specific bag is something you really dig, then you deserve to be a Catholic, or one of the others. It's no skin off our back. The whole principle is based finding your self and on the art of change.

FRITSCHER: Perhaps religion and witchcraft, each with their various versions and sects, are both no more than projections of human personalities. Both change as we find our selves changing.

DE ARECHAGA: We never change. People never change. So we try to change things. That is the essence of magic. Changing things from one thing into another thing. Change is an art. That notion of change brings us to the hairy-assed question of black and white magic. First of all, black magic comes from a play on words which the ancients had the decorum to understand. Modern man is too damn stupid to allow himself the luxury of intelligent understanding of the play on words.

FRITSCHER: Because most moderns are fundamentalists who don't understand metaphor or that one thing can mean two things, like a double entendre. Most people are literalists. They'd be shocked to know the Bible wasn't written in English.

DE ARECHAGA: Most of what we have in English comes down from the ages, from other civilizations who delved into knowledge. Like [the] ancient Egypt that called itself *Khem*, which means black, the *black* land. Probably because the soil was at that time made very black by the Nile waters. The country of Khem, because of its advances, had attracted a great deal of respect. Through the Greeks, Romans, and Arabs we have come to use Egypt's *Kehm* terms. The art of the Greeks is *Khem*-istry, chemistry; al*Kehmy*, alchemy. But translate it with the Romans to *necro*, which means black, and you have the art of the black land: *necromancy*.

Because in magic you deal with unseen powers, necromancy implies dealing with dark spirits. And today—despite the fact that I could be crucified, stoned, and hanged for saying it—every spiritualist, every little old lady who plays in the séance parlor and tries to call the dead is a necromancer—and thus, a black magician. *Necromancy* means "divination through the dark, the black, the black land, meaning Egypt." Necropolis was the place of the dead, the netherworld. Finally the goody-goodies with Jesus Christ complexes identified the Satanists as black artists. Christians created the distinction between white and black magic. The truth of the matter is that the Satanist is not the self-indulgent libertine he thinks he is, because in doing what he's doing the way he's doing it he shows great uptightness in slavish reaction to specifics of Christianity. A libertine acts freely on his own. He is not compelled by reaction. Consequently, Satanists' initiations and orgies are very disappointing. They do not know the art. They're too hung up reacting to get into it.

FRITSCHER: Besides the Satanists, other spiritists have been wildly popular and made a lot of money in American pop culture. Money is a way of keeping score, because box-office receipts show what people want.

DE ARECHAGA: I run a shop and a religion. I agree. I am very aware of the very popular period of occult enlightenment brought about by Madame Blavatsky and the Theosophical Society. She meant well. However, what Besant did with theosophy stinks, because it's nothing more nowadays than Christianized ideas.[1] The goodie-goodies who are afraid to be real—they are the people who are afraid to be wrong. They won't go away, these people who are afraid of distinctions like heaven and hell. So they make distinctions between white and black magic. They distinguish ad nauseam. There is obviously no such thing as black magic or white magic; for I ask you, how many people have done evil while trying to do good? The art itself—and I'm sure that the notorious Merlin or any of the other Magi would stand behind me to admit—that white and black are both reciprocal part of one art, the most sublime art of all: the art which identifies itself with the real and the unreal, the art of metamorphosis.

FRITSCHER: Religion seems to be about "thou shalt keep everything the same." Magic seems to be about "the abracadabra of changing things."

DE ARECHAGA: That's one essential difference. The art of metamorphosis, of change, starts in yourself, so you can later change things outside yourself. This way you achieve a Godly thaumaturgic practice as the antique elders or prophets of biblical lore. But that takes one thing that most people haven't got the guts to do, and that is involve yourself in it *actively*. You can't stand off and be a shadow and an audience. You've got to *be* it. There is no *abracadabra*. There is no magical formula. It is an experience. Most people are afraid of experience, because they can be wrong, and most don't want to be proven wrong. The rub lies in Judeo-Christian ethics, which judge a man ridiculous to show his emotions. You don't feel. You just work. How can a person subsist on that?

FRITSCHER: How do ancient potions and modern drugs influence metamorphosis?

DE ARECHAGA: Hallucinogenics were never really used by the pontifex who wanted reality as it is. Drugs, when they were used, were used for very specific purposes and not by everybody for everything. The idea of drugs being used in sabbaths, making sabbaths wild orgies where people came flying in on brooms wearing conical hats and all that nonsense with weird unguents on their backsides and going up chimneys and all that is sheer imagination, degeneration of ideas of truth in the universe to ridiculously low terms.

FRITSCHER: What is the source of these stereotypes?

DE ARECHAGA: You must realize most of that lore grew up in an age of persecution where if you opened your mouth with an opinion about anything, such as "Hey, look the earth goes around the sun!" you were hanged or tortured. So why say anything to correct stereotypes? And if you did say something, why say the truth? This conundrum made the persecutors furious. Most of our stereotypes of witchcraft come from hysterical stories told by victims being tortured by the Inquisition.

FRITSCHER: Private interpretation of witchcraft leads to as much confusion as private interpretation of the Bible.

DE ARECHAGA: Or of any one book read slavishly. People under torture will always tell the torturer anything to get the torture to stop. All those individual stories about witches and Satan confused the inquisitors. They heard so many stories the Church figured there must be a "Great Book" of magic and sorcery. They wanted to destroy the evil book. That is why today we have only a fraction of the truths and glories of antiquity because of all those fundamentalist assholes who did nothing but burn down libraries and ruin all the books they could get their nasty hands on.

FRITSCHER: In Catholic tradition, the lore is that medieval monks saved all the ancient books by hiding them from marauding pagans, and by recopying them.

DE ARECHAGA: Did they save them all, or only the ones they approved of, and when they copied books, did they add and subtract information?

FRITSCHER: The Church defined information, perhaps the same as the Old Religion with its books. What is accurate?

DE ARECHAGA: The truth is that witches' sabbaths, their main festivals, were gatherings in which people ran around trees and rocks. These "dances," which some of the Shakers and more fervent Christian cultists still do, gave rise to the great superstition of the "fairy folk" in England.

FRITSCHER: Fairy folk are the free folk, the gay folk, who dance in a circle counterclockwise to the straight-line folks?

DE ARECHAGA: More bisexual than gay. Superstition is not part of the Old Religion, because *we know why* we do things. Superstition can only come from a society that does not know why it does what it does. They call what they do a superstition. Like the American soldiers wearing the ace of spades on their helmets in Vietnam. There is no superstition in our Old Religion because there is nothing you cannot explain. We do not believe in faith; we believe in reason. We do not believe in rationalization; we believe in trust. We have no fear. We can control man, beast, or spiritual entity when we want to. We can avoid confrontation when we feel that we're not physically or spiritually strong enough to deal with what is lurking there. We have an awareness. That's different than a gullible stupidity.

FRITSCHER: Religion teaches man has fallen. Your Old Religion doesn't recognize any fall from grace?

DE ARECHAGA: The fact is that we're not concerned with the Garden of Eden prior to the forbidden fruit, but rather afterwards. If more people actually read the Bible, they'd find it says in the third chapter of Genesis that God did not throw man out because man had disobeyed, but rather because man had become in *knowledge* like one of *them*, the gods. Man was thrown out of the garden lest he eat of the other tree. Very few people realize there was a second. This tree would make man *immortal*, like *them*. Therefore—and I might add that's an old pagan story stolen by the Hebrews—knowledge is the main purpose of our Old Religion. First, you must know yourself. Second, you must get above and beyond yourself. Love rests in the harmony of things, yes, but to be a Sabaean you must accept the understanding of all values of truth untarnished by the monotheisms of Christianity, Judaism, and Islam.

FRITSCHER: In Satanism, sadomasochism is ritually used to raise Satan. Paganism uses ritual endurance to increase bravery. White witches whip each other with silken threads. How kinky is the Old Religion?

DE ARECHAGA: In the sexual occult, sadomasochistic practices are a degeneracy like the Satanists are a degeneration of Christianity, and Christianity is a degeneracy of the Hebrew, and the Hebrew is a degeneracy of the Sumerian-Chaldean. Sadomasochistic practices are psychological trips where the individual suffers or lacks a certain thing. I mean these practices can be fun, because the best of people have these needs. Freud, and Jung, and psychiatrists who are not occultists, will go along with me. Sadomasochists have a need for authority, parenthood, a disciplinarian protector.

FRITSCHER: So sadomasochism fits tribes, religions, and societies centered on authority?

DE ARECHAGA: There is no central authority in the Old Religion. I don't care what the Satanists do. Sadomasochism has no direct place in the Old Religion. But it can play an indirect role.

FRITSCHER: In what way?

DE ARECHAGA: In sexuality. In sex rituals. You mentioned straight and gay. As far as homosexuality and heterosexuality are concerned, they're both queer, because to be a homosexual is one end of being heterosexual, which is the other end. They both lack each other. They are both equally degenerated and unpardonable.

FRITSCHER: Unpardonable?

DE ARECHAGA: They need no pardon. There is nothing wrong with either except both are incomplete without generating the other. I have had animals of all kinds here in my Temple. Right now I have two doves—both male. Nobody told them they're not to be having sex. I've had cats, dogs. The fact is—despite the heterosexual's arguments against it—that animals are by nature bisexual. As are also human beings, who I might remind you are animals as well. Bisexuality is no shame. The truth is that bisexuality is actually a better state of mind. It is a natural state of being. For instance, you will not find the peacocks with the peahens. You will not find lions with lionesses. Where the male has a family, he owns it like property. And it is the female who works. Woman is made for a great deal of work physiologically. She is consequently stronger than a man in every sense.

FRITSCHER: Which brings us to women in the occult.

DE ARECHAGA: But then I'm not going to get involved in that!

FRITSCHER: But your mother taught you . . .

DE ARECHAGA: What I am telling you. Everything. And the universe is ordered like this. From an ethical standpoint, bisexuality relates to the true value of things. When you love someone you do not love them because of their gender—which is the main sadness of many a relationship today.

FRITSCHER: You should love them because of their person, not their gender.

DE ARECHAGA: Confining oneself solely to the opposite gender is why there are so many divorces and disagreements. People have physical needs that can be satisfied only by both genders. Bisexuality is not a horrible thing. All kinds of sex are good, even though sex drives sometimes are ritualized into abuses like the murders of children.

FRITSCHER: Modern Satanists say they don't do that.

DE ARECHAGA: The fact is sex is important to humans. To deny it, the way Catholic priests embrace celibacy, is as degrading to a divine form as anything can be. The "aesthete" who lives totally for the spirit is as bad as a spirit which lives totally for the physical world. Anyone who knows spiritualism will tell you that. To be so enamored with that which you are not is the unhealthy mistake.

FRITSCHER: Such gender fluidity, such morphing sexuality, such access to knowledge and power. Are these why paganism, magic, and witchcraft have gained such popular appeal?

DE ARECHAGA: The same is true of the Old Religion, but we Sabaeans do it with balance. As Buddha said—which most Buddhists don't even follow—to become an ascetic esthete on one side or a self-indulgent libertine on the other, neither is good. Only by becoming both simultaneously do you negate the extremes and bring balance—that is, achieve Nirvana. This Nirvana is an ancient knowledge brought by the great illustrator Buddha, who was merely an incarnation of the ancient god Vishnu. You learn to know yourself in the equilibrium of things. Balanced, you—as Zarathusthra, also speak. This is a superhuman accomplishment. The purpose is one of intelligence.

FRITSCHER: White witches, pagans, and Satanists mention gods.

DE ARECHAGA: God is perfect. He is all that was, is, and shall be. God must, therefore, be both human and not human. We are the human aspect of God. We *are* God. The ultimate achievement is to become one in unity with that great intelligence of the divine order. We must remember that while we are God, God is not us. We do not have the right to become righteous or assume God's responsibilities. Like your hand is part of you, but you are not your hand. This is ancient cult.

FRITSCHER: Charles Manson claims to be God, Satan, and Jesus Christ.

DE ARECHAGA: Manson does not know his place in the order of things. He thinks he is the hand of God when God is not even in his hand. To know your place, consider how big you are in comparison to this house, and this house in comparison to this block, to this city, to this country, to this continent. You can pretty much see you can't see yourself already. Compare yourself to the world. You are nothing. A couple miles up you can't even look down and see the houses, let alone the people. Compare this solar system to the galaxies. How dare anyone presume to judge other men?

FRITSCHER: What about people finding God on drugs?

DE ARECHAGA: Drugs are the difference between searching for God truly and synthetically. In the cult of the Old Religion its ethical value lies, as I said earlier, in the value itself, in the reality of value. Since one of the by-products of value reality is power, which with the sense of intelligence is the main objective, I will ask a question of your reason. Which is the stronger power? That achieved through an hallucinogenic of any sort which is momentary and nonexistent once you come down from it? Or that which you achieve through your own power, from which you don't come down unless you wish to? This last stage you can always reach again and move to higher consciousness.

FRITSCHER: Aleister Crowley and others believe that drugs blaze the path to Satan and to God, so that later, without the drugs, the seeker can take the path beaten by drugs back to Satan or God.

DE ARECHAGA: That is not the reasoning of religion. That is the reasoning of drugs. The reasoning of Sabaeanism is singular. Sabaeanism is the only religion that can afford to have an atheist. Because you do not need God per se. First of all, God does not need you. And second, since you are God, you don't really need any further specification of God. And what is God? God is perfection. To use an ancient saying recorded by Plato from the words of Solon of Egypt, "I am all that is, was, and ever shall be. No mortal man has me unveiled. I am that I am and whatever so you wish to call me I am. For the fruit I brought forth is the sun."

FRITSCHER: The books you favor are ancient books.

DE ARECHAGA: That is the truth. I can say of the *Book of the Dead* that the sixty-fourth is considered to be the oldest chapter as well as the epitome of the *Book's* meaning. Originally called the *Book of the Coming Forth by Day*, the *Book of the Dead* in its first line of the sixty-fourth chapter says, "I am yesterday, today, and tomorrow. I have the power to be born a second time." *I have the power* is the important thing. People needn't get hung up with God. People *are* God. They should mind their own business and metamorphose themselves. That would be the end of war and arguments. Concerning yourself with your own deficiencies you achieve an awareness of yourself that is so deep you can't help but be cognizant of other people. You can't help but care and understand and when you have understanding and care, then you become like the ancient mariner: more sagacious, a little wiser but sadder. Sadder because you'll know.

FRITSCHER: How does Sabaeanism fit into the Old Religion?

DE ARECHAGA: *Saba* means "all." It's not to be confused with pantheism. This is a religion. It is not theology. It is not ritual or ceremony. Religion is not a church or a temple or a ground or a sky. Religion is nothing more than what you believe—namely, it is a philosophy of life. It is the way you become cognizant and aware of the world around you. *Saba*, meaning "all," is not monotheism, polytheism, or atheism. It is henotheism, in which God becomes a personal thing even if it means a denial of the existence of God. This doesn't necessarily make you an agnostic or an atheist. *Henotheism* means belief in one god and worship of that one god while acknowledging other gods exist for other people.

FRITSCHER: That toleration sounds democratic and not at all defensively tribal.

DE ARECHAGA: Henotheism is not about the exclusion of other gods. A pantheon is possible. In himself the atheist is as much a religious person as the agnostic, the monotheist. Though you may be temporarily a monotheist, you cannot remain so. A monotheist is an ass simply because he insists on making everybody else believe in his God. This shows his ignorance. My shop is called El-Sabarum, which means "of many gods." Our Illinois charter incorporates us as El Saba. We have incorporated, even legally, *everything*!

FRITSCHER: Here in your Temple, who does a Sabaeanist Old Religionist worship?

DE ARECHAGA: We can worship someone, anyone—perhaps you. We have occasions to burn incense for you as a guest, and make obeisance to you as a god. We can do this for a beloved friend. To do something is sufficient. To have done it is enough. We do not glorify it. If we achieve any title, it is relative to the person who asks. The only reason I've given you a title for me is because you ask a specific identity. But there are other times when I will not tell. I have worked in places where people have achieved titles, where they use their titles wrongly. I personally saw United States senators trying to make Jesus Christ a national savior. Now come on!

FRITSCHER: Isn't theocracy always the goal of most religions? Church not separated from the state. Church and state being the same.

DE ARECHAGA: Completely contrary to the Bill of Rights! Believe me. I know *reactionary* from *revolutionary!* I have served in this American government. I personally went out and *joined* the military service. I worked with journalism and I was deep inside the propaganda machine of this country. This is no different than any other country. But, hell, I also *made* myself an American citizen. I'm no chauvinistic patriot, but I am not stupid either.

FRITSCHER: Discussions of witchcraft always end up as discussions of politics, religion, and sex. The three things my parents said polite people never discuss.

DE ARECHAGA: That is why there is a silent majority in this country. Oh, I can tell you that I can see something valuable in America, but that worth is flying out the window because we have a bunch of bigoted slobs who can see nothing more than their own personal gain.

America's ability to change should be neither so readily dismissed nor should it be so readily advertised. Media advertisement makes things grow so terribly wild. There is a difference between informing people of something and sensationalizing it. There is a difference between printing facts and the competitive idea of selling newspapers.

In my store I cease to sell certain things when another shop begins to handle the item. I do this out of respect to the other person. I thank the gods that other people have done this in turn for me. Some, however, purposely imitate what I do because they've got to get in on the bandwagon. They have no respect. They usually don't know what they're doing and they usually close up quite suddenly and quite mysteriously— ha!—if you know what I mean. Did I say anything just now?

FRITSCHER: Never tell people you've created a thunderstorm.

DE ARECHAGA: Society's ethics are all screwed up. What is so shameful about a girl having a baby out of wedlock? In ancient times such girls were called *virgins*. That's what a virgin was: a woman who gave birth without a husband. Even Jesus Christ was a bastard in that respect. Because whether it was the Holy Ghost or some other holy person, the fact was he did not have a father. St. Joseph doesn't alleviate the fact Christ was a bastard. A monkey with a different hat is still a monkey. Christian sexual morality has programmed people into narrow-mindedness.

I mean, look at sixth-century Christianity. It was then that Christianity became solidified. It had very little to do with ancient Christianity.

FRITSCHER: You mean original Christianity was like the Old Religion of Christianity.

DE ARECHAGA: When Christianity was still in touch with its pagan folk roots in the Old Religion. Yes. But then in the sixth century, the Catholic Church said, "The people are not smart enough to understand reincarnation, so we will dump that doctrine." Those self-opinionated men decided that this was the people's capacity. They wanted to foster a group of peasants. Originally, Christianity was founded by the peasant Jesus for the peasants around him. Christianity has always been against patricians. Jesus warned the rich. The rich were told not only that they worshiped the wrong god, money, but no god at all. Christianity raided paganism and stole from the Ancients and adapted all the white magic of the Old Religion. That prayer of St. Francis of Assisi: "Lord, make me an instrument of your peace. Where there is hatred, let me sow love." And so on. Come on. I found it in an army chaplain's office, just like the Catholic Church found it in an old manuscript in the Vatican. It's the same wording as found in the prayer by Amenoteph IV of the eighteenth dynasty. I almost dropped dead.

FRITSCHER: If the Old Religion is so great, and if pagan rituals are so wonderful, and if Christianity folded all this greatness and goodness into itself, why does everyone scoff at Christianity? Maybe Jesus was an ultimate sorcerer. He was a miracle worker. Does that make him a magician? Houdini promised to come back from beyond the grave. He didn't. Jesus did. Maybe the magician Jesus who faced Satan has been lost in reactions to the institutionalization of Christianity in things like the Inquisition and the Vatican.

DE ARECHAGA: I'll tell you modern witch hunters something. When you go out looking for witches or warlocks or whatever you want to call them, ask them a couple of questions. Most witches are full of crap. Make them put it on the line.

Ask them if they're bisexual. If they're not, it's a giveaway.

Ask them if they really know astrology.

A true pontifex must know his astronomy and astrology. They're both the same; astronomy is astrology without occult delineation. You'll find that most people today are profane astrologers. Sacred astrology, however, continues with a procession of the equinoxes, which the profane do not observe. Consequently profane charts are off about 28 degrees. That means that hippie Haight Street in San Francisco is off about 28 degrees. This coupled with the fact that there are thirteen, and not just twelve, zodiac signs—check it out in any planetarium!—makes most people drop back one sign from what they think they are. There goes the great pickup line, "What's your sign?" You've always thought you're a Gemini. You're really a Taurus. This is not to say one can't find some consolation in profane astrology. Its principles are basically sound.

You just lay those two questions about bisexuality and astrology on anybody who claims to be a witch and see what happens.

Don't be too ready to accept everyone who tells you that they are a witch or that they have psychic power or that they worship Satan so you can quiver and get scared.

FRITSCHER: Like the Manson Family believed Charles Manson.

DE ARECHAGA: Remember the Mayans. They were visited by the Old People who established the Mayan culture and then went back up into space. The abandoned Mayans waited and looked for those old gods to come back. They waited thousands of years, and not being discriminating, they accepted the first strangers who showed up: priests wearing symbols of the sun and soldiers whose crescent helmets were symbols of the moon.

Good old gullible America ought to learn from what happened to the uncritical Mayans!

In the end, in the way many movements grow beyond their leaders, the Sabaean Religious Order at 3221 Sheffield, Chicago, distanced itself from the teachings and person of Frederic de Arechaga, who in the 1970s converted to Santaria, renamed himself Odun, and dedicated himself to the god Obatala.

Dr. David Tronscoso, B.A., D.D., ESP Reader, Love Counselor, Psychoanalyst; Hollywood

I am a spiritual psychoanalyst and reader of the occult, as well as a marriage and love counselor. The occult is popular because people are tired of the same old drags. Sex is necessary to the occult, but, like narcotics, sex can be taken to extremes.

Witchcraft, in general, is an important catharsis, relieving our society's pressures. The hands-off attitude of the courts these days is beautiful, as it leaves the field wide open and lush. The more commercialization of the occult, the better. I prefer the clean-cut look of witches much more than the filthy hag look.

I make no distinction between white and black witches. Essentially, white and black magic? What's the difference? The power is neutral, colorless, and works under spiritual laws man yet does not understand, much less control. Have you ever heard of "black" or "white" electricity?

As time goes by, witchcraft will achieve a greater scientific acceptance, and be used for healing in areas like marriage counseling.

Charles J. Redmund, Psychic Consultant; Los Angeles

My clients are from all walks of life, but they all have the same problems, which are in this order: money, love affairs, problems at work, health, and sex.

I would like to see some direction in the witchcraft movement. And I would really like to see federal laws that not only allow the practice of witchcraft but ensure our privacy as well.

Witchcraft should be used for the highest philosophical and healing purposes and not as a superstitious activity to offset personal emotional stress. Witchcraft is the bringing back of old philosophies, old practice, and old religion. Practitioners must be discreet so as not to arouse once again the hostile forces. I mean this in regard to the bad press surrounding the mysteries of the Polanski-Tate-Manson affair.

To my mind, white witchery is the only kind to practice.

The black arts, however, represent a very powerful force. This force is the same used by the Catholic Church and the white witches. The power is the same; the use is different. I believe that the role of the contemporary witch or warlock should be that of self-sacrifice for self-enlightenment, fulfillment, and positive aid to one's fellows.

Thousands are today going mad under emotional stress and strain. Our psychiatrists and psychologists may not be able to handle this great load alone. The contemporary witch can help to ease this load through dedicated patience and research. This will bring witchcraft to greater acceptance, and it will become more closely aligned with popular metaphysical practices as men, dissatisfied with the present ways of modern life, go back to the old philosophies.

My list of significant books includes *The Golden Dawn, The Book of Black Magic and Pacts* [A. E. Waite (1898)], and *Riches within Your Reach* [Robert Collier (1947)].

Christians, I think, will find in witchcraft certain elements that are not readily available in Christianity, such as the essential part that sexuality plays in occult practice. Sexuality is an essential part of occult practice. It seems a pity that so many religions have ruled out sexuality except in "marital bliss." Sex is a key note of the only great human symphony.

ADRIAN KIRCH, MAIL-ORDER OCCULT BOTANICA OPERATOR AND
BOOKSELLER; SHELTON, CONNECTICUT

Sex is overrated in both white and black magic, although many believe
a homosexual is granted special powers.

The pulse of witchcraft is stronger than ever. I run a small business
called The House of Kirch. We sell through mail order: white magic rituals, spells, charm bags, herbs, and whatever you can imagine. Our items
are merchandised as curios. Quite frankly, I commercialize by selling
white magic. I don't see why not. Isn't commercial TV's *Bewitched* an
enjoyable program that shows a witch as an everyday person? Elizabeth
Montgomery is no hag. She's a charming young housewife. She makes
white witchcraft more acceptable. Because of television and movies like
Rosemary's Baby, I think Americans by the end of this century will accept
white witchcraft. The majority, however, will never accept black magic.
After all, white witchcraft cannot be bad because it helps others. Help-
ing others is a form of love. Most white witches and warlocks endeavor
to help rid man of problems like the facing of death and illness. Many
old white-witch remedies, in fact, have helped modern medicine.

Because I believe in freedom of religion and the right of any individual to explore the mysteries of this universe, I oppose any repression
of the religion of witchcraft. Laws should govern black, not white, magic
to save churches and cemeteries from desecration. We white witches
and warlocks believe in a law of retribution whereby if you harm, you
will be harmed. I do not harm others, and do not worship Satan in
any way.

One of my favorite books is the *Encyclopedia of Witchcraft and Demonology* [Rossell Hope Robbins (1969)].

MADAME YOLAND SAVARINI, *Midnight* TABLOID COLUMNIST,
RESIDENT ASTROLOGER, NUMEROLOGIST; MONTREAL, QUEBEC

The coming of the Aquarian Age has greatly appealed to the young who
are dissatisfied both with old established religions and the new establishment religion of technology. In general, my feelings about witchcraft
are divided because I am an astrologer and numerologist. I fear most
of all the damage done by amateur adventurers into the occult. These
people often do not have the best interests of their fellow men at heart.
Responsible study of witchcraft could beneficially add to man's store

of knowledge about himself and his work. Consideration of witchcraft could greatly aid scientists studying the human mind.

The witch or warlock in tapping the powers of the occult becomes something more than the average human being. He must learn to use his powers for good. I think the black arts are best left alone by those who wish to begin a career of practicing witchcraft. I would suggest a study of black magic merely to be protected against its evil influence.

There are dangers involved in demonic witchcraft, but one should know enough of the enemy's methods to fight him. Something like the Manson-Tate affair, for instance, is detrimental to the cause of witchcraft. As I said, tapping the occult can bring forth strange power that gets loose in a room, a house, a body.

I believe the commercialization of witchcraft to be inevitable. As a phenomenon, witchcraft contains all the necessary elements for popular appeal. However, the crassly commercialized media often give an erroneous impression of the art. Why create new misleading ideas just when the old historical fears of witchcraft are dying out? Witches are now tolerated, and with no more fear of persecution they can finally help mankind. It's true that certain occult sects have attached great importance to sexuality, but in white witchery its role has never been particularly important. In my area of the occult—astrology, numerology, palmistry—sex has little significance. Bizarre sexual rites generally accompany the black arts.

It's a truism that—barring any regrettable incidents—witchcraft will become more popular. For some people, it will replace currently established religion.

The books most significant to me as a person and a columnist are Sir James Frazer's *The Golden Bough*; Dr. Margaret Murray's *The Witch Cult in Modern Europe*; R. H. Robbins's *Encyclopedia of Witchcraft and Demonology*; Reginald Scot's *Discoverie of Witchcraft*; and Reverend Montague Summers's translation of Jacob Sprenger's *Malleus Maleficarum*, or *The Hammer of Witches*.

VERN OVERLEE, EDITOR OF *Power Publications*, AUTHOR OF THE BOOK OF AUTOMATIC WRITING *Let the Dead Speak of Their Life*; SPARTA, WISCONSIN; www.vernoverlee.com

Witchcraft is as misunderstood as ever. It is not glamorous. It is not what authors of commercialized versions think will sell. Witchcraft is not meant to be what it has become today: men attempting to control others.

What is witchcraft? I'll tell you: it's man being controlled by unseen forces. It is man being controlled to serve or harm mankind. It is not the laws, you see, which do harm in the world of witchcraft; it is the holding back of truths, allowing distorted truths and imagined tales to be publicized.

To associate people like Charles Manson with witchcraft is to make witchcraft appeal to the wrong kind of people. It doesn't matter if white and black magicians are male or female, as long as they use their gifts. For instance, sex in marriage consumates harmony. Any other use of sex is carnal.

White witchcraft exists so that men can ask the powers that be to bring good, healing, and peace of mind to man. The powers that be behind black arts bring evil to humans. We must serve the Father. Everyone of us must attempt to benefit mankind, as this force when used or mis-used is magnified a hundredfold. If it were not for this, I would not have answered the questions you asked.

The books I recommend are all the words of Jesus, the teachings of Swedenborg, the Bab of the Bahai Faith, *Psychic Surgery* by Jesse Thomas, and *Thirty Years among the Dead* by Einar Nelson [alternate author, Carl Wickland (1924)].

BISHOP WEST, AFRICAN-AMERICAN SPIRITUAL ADVISOR.
SEATTLE, WASHINGTON

Witchcraft is very real and possibly dangerous when worked by both born witches and fakes. I am not a warlock or a spiritualist, but I am a born spiritual person who has God-given power to remove any spell or curse put on a person. I believe in the occult, because I have Bible proof in chapter and verse. For twenty-one years I have been a popular per-sonality removing spells, curses, and snakes out of people. Mr. Hubert H. Humphrey, vice president of the United States, sent me a letter on January 14, 1969, thanking me for my spiritual advice on his political life and the future of politics.

Some television commercials of witchcraft are very good imitations of the real thing. The black arts? They consist of some candles, not all; some soils, not all; some roots of various kinds—not all roots—and of many spirits, but not all spirits. Witchcraft is African, like civilization,

with a lot of voodoo. It is impossible for laws to stop witchcraft which
has been everywhere for all time.

What white witchery is is witchery practiced by some white persons
who began learning the art of witchcraft years ago from some black
people who they had watched practice it; and the white people have
practiced white witchery ever since. As for sex in the occult, according
to very much study, that got the most attention with the Inquisition
about 1484 in Rome, Italy.

My practice is to consult with people to bring them luck, remove
spells and curses, and predict the future. The books of great significance
are the Holy Bible, the sixth through tenth books of Moses, and *Legends of Incense, Herb and Oil Magic* [Lewis de Claremont (1936)].

Rita Norling, White Witch, Chic Aromatherapist, Owner of Mail-Order Botanica; Los Angeles

You must well know that not all things are permitted to be revealed and
consequently I will not break the ancient tradition, although I am appearing regularly on television. The shortest and best observation I can make
on our craft is that we witches have suddenly become acceptable to the
media of America. I am constantly in the news because of reporters
who seek me out. I appear on TV and radio through the Associated
Press. I give lectures. I am an Old Religionist whom the president of the
Foundation of the Junior Blind has asked to speak to sightless children.
I don't believe in Satanism or evil spells, and I have been interviewed
by *Reader's Digest*.

All the candles, oils, and associated animal parts which I sell mail-order have special meaning in good witchcraft. I am a white witch, like
my grandmother, and I follow nature. My son is like me; he sees the
spirit world in what he calls "Technicolor." If an earthquake is to make
California fall into the ocean, keep my number, because I will feel the
vibrations with enough warning to let you know!

Black witches follow the ethic of the Seven Deadly Sins. Evil deeds
are repaid in evil multiplied three times. I don't believe in Satanic ritual like inverting the crucifix and saying the Lord's Prayer backwards.

Faith can work miracles. I make no supernatural claims, but there
are people all over the world who honestly believe in good-luck candles
and love packets of black cat bone or heart of swallow. Aromatic oils
and incense help elevate a person's vibrations that raise their personal

magnetism to draw to themselves love, wealth, and power. A person must know how to manipulate such forces, so I have devotion to Venus, Diana, and Pan, but Zeus is my favorite.

REFORM TRACT SOCIETY; MILLVILLE, CALIFORNIA [LETTER TO THE AUTHOR]

Look magazine calls California "A Window into the Future." It is indeed that. In all reality the End has come here. The cycle is full. This State can truly be called The "UPPER ROOM" of BABYLON. Here thinking is one mass mind. ONE No. 6 [worst possible] MAN MIND. . . . [This is] the WITCHCRAFT OF MODERN MAN. . . . I know I sound pessimistic, and I am. But I'm here to tell these modern coneys I CAN BEAT THE DEVIL. I can beat him at his own game. . . . God's Anointed will not give these damnable bastard coney Gentile dog black devil Purple People Eaters Fathers a free branch to hang from. That's for sure. . . . The people in the U.S. are sick beyond thinking in GOD'S BOOK.

LILITH ST. JOHN, SORCERER, ALCHEMIST, LECTURER; BURLINGAME, CALIFORNIA

There are many witchcraft groups popping up. A lot of them read a few "occult" books and think all they have to do is draw a circle of salt around themselves and they're witches. Consequently, the 1970s occult explosion has both encouraged and disappointed me. I'm encouraged because the great interest in witchcraft would seem to indicate a growing awareness—however confused—of the very real power of magic. I'm disappointed because of all the confusion and misconceptions propagated by so-called white witches.

Distinctions between white and black magic are euphemistic. All *real* magic is black—that is, selfish, sensual, and materialistic. Black magicians must become organized into the religion which they are and be respected as such. After all, one hopes that a knowledge of black magic would make an individual self-reliant, confident, and honest. White witchcraft does none of these things for its adherents, who are typically weak, confused, and self-deceivers. These "white witches" play at the Devil's game, don't they? They use the Devil's tools in their quest for crumbs of power. These white heretics must be called to task for using in vain the names of all those who suffered and died as agents of the Devil in ages past.

My personal satisfaction in the occult is great. The competent witch must do much study in the fields of psychology, anthropology, and sociology. I find that my practice of real magic—black magic—has contributed enormously to my self-realization. I have come to know the power that is within me, learned to revel in the indulgence of my ego, and known greater fulfillment of my desires than at any previous time in my life. My only complaint is that we witches are barely tolerated. My sixteen-year-old son was denied entrance into a social club because I am a witch. They've made a hard time for him in school. I finally had to throw a few curses on certain teachers to get him some peace.

All the voguish nonsense of witchcraft disturbs me. However, the existence of such growing groups as Anton LaVey's Church of Satan, with its vigorous and honest approach, tend to balance the picture and encourage some optimism. Now that we are above ground, we will grow and become a world power. Anton LaVey is our leader. White witchcraft will die out.

I use my powers to help people for my own monetary gain. Most people consult me on love, sexual, and money problems. My private clientele includes laborers, businessmen, a few tycoons, and some of the "creep" element. I make talismans and charms, so people can carry something with them.

In short, I'm a black witch.

What white witches do is something else. I can't keep track of their foibles.

NOTES

PREFACE

1. As a participant in Mapplethorpe's life and in the aftermath of the scandal, I
have little doubt that his many famous photographs of himself as Satan, particularly
with a bullwhip tailing out of his anus, were the last straw for his apocalyptic abusers
who fantasized that they were wrestling the Devil, his pomps, and his works. This fundamentalist perception grew also among the Manhattan Art Reich. On June 5, 1995,
the cover of *The New Yorker* dubbed him "Prince of Dark Rooms" for a piece by
grotesque writer Peter Conrad. On June 25, 1995, in the *New York Times* review "Fallen
Angel," Grace Glueck wrote in the way typical of Puritans made lubricious by homosexuality, sadomasochism, and Satan. She demonized him as a black magician with a
cape, and featured a 1985 self-portrait of Mapplethorpe with horns on his head. Printing the same irresistible portrait, the July 1995 *Vanity Fair* characterized Mapplethorpe
in the sleazy Patricia Morrisroe reportage "The Demon Romantics" using code like
"Dionysian" and clucking over his mantra to his sex partners and some of his models:
"Do it for Satan."

INTRODUCTORY INTERVIEW

1. This interview is so often referenced, quoted, and reprinted, that specific notice
is here posted that the entire question-and-answer interview is, with all rights reserved,
© 1971, 2004 Jack Fritscher. Beware that no part of this interview, either questions or
answers, may be reproduced in any form without written permission from the author.

2. George Wallace, segregationist governor of Alabama, ran for president of the United States on a third-party ticket in 1968, causing the defection of southern Democrats from the Democratic Party, which thus made possible the election of Republican Richard Nixon (who was, years later, forced to resign the presidency for his political crimes). The Green Party's Ralph Nader repeated this political ritual in 2000, taking votes from Democrat Al Gore, and thus making possible the presidency of George W. Bush—who has, incidentally, said that witchcraft is not a religion.

3. Buxom blonde movie star Mansfield, alleged lover of President John F. Kennedy, was decapitated in a car crash while driving out of New Orleans on the foggy night of June 29, 1967.

4. Roman Polanski won the Academy Award 2003 as best director for his film *The Pianist* (2002). He has directed more than twenty-two films including *Repulsion* (1965), *Fearless Vampire Killers* (1967), *Rosemary's Baby* (1968), *Macbeth* (1971), *Chinatown* (1974), and the satanic-themed *The Ninth Gate* (2000). Five times nominated as best director, he was prevented by law from attending the March 23, 2003, Oscar telecast in Hollywood as he remained a fugitive from America because of his conviction for statutory rape of a thirteen-year-old girl in 1979.

5. Montague Summers, 1880–1948, was the author of *The Vampire—His Kith and Kin: The Philosophy of Vampirism* (1928), and *Witchcraft and Black Magic* (1946).

6. In the thirteenth century, writer and bishop Saint Albertus Magnus (Albert the Great, ca. 1200–80) was the teacher of Saint Thomas Aquinas (1225–74), the premiere theologian of the Catholic Church. Even during his life Albertus was rumored to have been an alchemist who found the "Philosopher's Stone," which according to legend he gave to Thomas Aquinas.

7. See Jack Fritscher, *Mapplethorpe: Assault with a Deadly Camera* (New York: Hastings House, 1994).

8. Blanche Barton, *The Secret Life of a Satanist: The Authorized Biography of Anton LaVey* (Los Angeles: Feral House, 1992); Blanche Barton, *The Church of Satan: A History of the World's Most Notorious Religion* (New York: Hells Kitchen Productions, 1990); Blanche Barton, *The Cloven Hoof*, P.O. Box 210666, Chula Vista, Calif. Available online at http://www.ChurchofSatan.com.

1. THE MEDIUM AS MEDIUM

1. Rossell Hope Robbins, *The Encyclopedia of Witchcraft and Demonology* (New York: Crown, 1969), 338.

2. Edward Lucie-Smith, *Joan of Arc* (London: Penguin, 2000), 213, 260, 261.

3. Robbins, 340, quoting George Burr in *Johnson's Encyclopedia*.

4. See John Fritscher, "The Sensibility and Conscious Style of William Bradford's *Of Plymouth Plantation*," *Bucknell Review*, no. 17, December 1969, 80–90.

5. Two other founders of the GAA were *Village Voice* columnist Arthur Bell and the antipatriarchist Arthur Evans. In 1978 when I was editor in chief of *International*

Drummer magazine, I published Arthur Evan's San Francisco debut article as the "Red Queen." His new book *Witchcraft and the Gay Counterculture* (1978), following my own witchcraft book by six years, had made him a radical faerie of interest to me—precisely because he was the polar opposite of the masculine-identified readers whom the cultural force of *Drummer* represented. (See "Are You Butch Enough?" *Drummer*, no. 25, December 1978.) The GAA inspired the Gay and Lesbian Alliance against Defamation (GLAAD), founded in 1985.

6. Dr. Leo Louis Martello, *Gay*, December 31, 1969, 4.

7. Martello, *Gay*, April 27, 1970, 4.

8. Martello, *Gay*, January 19, 1970, 4.

9. Jack Fritscher, "Chasing Danny Boy," in *Chasing Danny Boy: Powerful Stories of Celtic Eros*, ed. Mark Hemry (San Francisco: Palm Drive, 2000), 79–98.

10. Martello, *Gay*, April 27, 1970.

11. Joshua Trachtenberg, *The Devil and the Jews* (New York: Meridian, 1961), 215, 216.

12. See Arkon Daraul, *Secret Societies: A History* (New York: MJF Books/Fine Creative Media/Carol, 1989), 168.

13. Thom Gunn, interview with the author, Western Michigan University, 1970.

14. Marc Ambinder, "'You Helped This Happen': Falwell's Controversial Comments Draw Fire," ABC News, September 14, 2001. Available online at http://www.ABCnews.com.

15. In many ways, Anger was the pop-culture recruiter for the "Gay Magic Mafia" that circled the "Crowley Connection" to art and music in the 1960s and 1970s. Without Crowley via Anger, the U.S. Senate would never have disbanded the National Endowment for the Arts. Satanism connects the dots in this way. As Crowley influenced Anger, Anger influenced Andy Warhol. Without Warhol, New York photographer Robert Mapplethorpe would never have bothered posing himself in the signature self-portraits as an urban Satanist, replete with horns and a tail made from a leather whip, that he used to illustrate *A Season in Hell* by poet Arthur Rimbaud (1986). The splendid Mapplethorpe—"The Prince of Darkrooms"—was demonized on the floor of the U.S. Senate, as had earlier pop-culture icons Charlie Chaplin, Ingrid Bergman (for not living up to the pure woman she played in the movie *Saint Joan of Arc*), and Elizabeth Taylor. Mapplethorpe's perfect, pure, and formal photographs of flowers, faces, and fetishes were deemed Satanic. In the mother of all fundamentalist hissy-fits, Republican senator Jesse Helms, equating art and pornography, single-handedly used the cause célèbre that was Mapplethorpe to destroy federal funding for any but the most censored of artists supported by the National Endowment for the Arts.

16. Betty Comden and Adolph Green, *The New York Musicals of Comden and Green: On the Town, Wonderful Town, Bells Are Ringing* (New York; Applause Books, 1997), 189.

2. THE SELLING OF THE AGE OF AQUARIUS

1. See Peter Bart, "A Black Eye for Old Blue Eyes: A Book Review of George Jacobs' *My Life with Frank Sinatra*," *Variety*, June 16–22, 2003, 4.

2. Eden Ahbez, "Nature Boy," Crestview Music/Edwin H. Morris and Company, 1947.

3. See John Fritscher, "Some Attitudes and a Posture: Religious Metaphor and Ritual in Tennessee Williams' Query of the American God," *Modern Drama* 13 (1970), 201–15.

4. In the more recent television series *The Sopranos*, the astrological theme song performed by the techno-group Alabama 3 (A3) at the opening of each episode, "Woke Up This Morning: Chosen One Mix," warns the predestined Italian-American Mafia characters about both the moon and *malocchio* (the evil eye). Paraphrased, the lyric warns that to "shine" they must "burn," because astrologically their birth was "under a bad sign" with their eyes reflecting "a blue moon."

5. Aureus display advertisement, *In Touch for Men*, November 1986, 17.

6. Anton LaVey, album cover "Notes for *The Satanic Mass*," *The Satanic Mass Ceremony* (Murgenstrumm Records, 1968).

7. Everett Henderson, "What Makes Mick Mighty? Can He Be All Sexes to All People?" *Gay*, December 15, 1969, 6.

8. See John Fritscher, "Malory's *Morte d'Arthur:* Sex and Magic in King Arthur's Camelot; the Search for King Arthur, the Grail, Magic, Women, Family, Courtly Love, and Grace," Master of Arts Thesis, Loyola University, 1967. Available online at http://www.jackfritscher.com.

9. As witchcraft, magic, and sorcery continue to refold themselves, presenting everything old as new again, *The Others* (2001), starring Nicole Kidman, was yet another version of *The Turn of the Screw*. Witchcraft, sorcery, and magic continue to recombine themselves. The musical *Dance of the Vampires* (2003)—based on the Roman Polanski film *The Fearless Vampire Killers* (1967)—flopped on Broadway, but continued as a hit in Europe, where *Vampires* had opened in Vienna in 1997.

10. John Nevin, "Orgasmic Theater of the Supernatural," *National Close-Up Magazine*, April 27, 1970.

11. Sam Steward, interview with the author, June 1972.

12. The young filmmakers who shot the box office phenomenon *The Blair Witch Project* (1999) named their production company "Haxan." *The Blair Witch Project* spawned sequels (*Blair Witch 2*), a parody (in *Mad* magazine), and lesbian porn (*The Erotic Witch Project*).

13. In 1986, Larry Harvey, on a beach in San Francisco burnt a large effigy that, by the way of alternative-culture momentum, has escalated into the epic Burning Man festival occurring annually on Labor Day in Nevada. Harvey denies any connection of Burning Man to witchcraft or Wicca. However, many practitioners scoff at his denial the way Anton LaVey scoffed at white witches who claim they never use black magic. Whatever conceptual-artist Harvey originally intended, the fact is that Burning Man has been co-opted by all kinds of "trad" and "rad" party-goers, artists, gay and straight fornicators, witches, new-age hipsters, Wiccans, nudists, and eco-worshiping pagans. Burning Man is to American fundamentalism what the French resistance was to Nazis. Burning Man is a modern primitive resurrection of sacred dance, music, tattooing, piercing, shamanism, witchcraft, drugs, sex, and iconoclastic Satanism—as typified at

the hamburger tent called "McSatan's." Rising up once a year—more often than Brigadoon, Burning Man is quite simply the rebellious Luciferian decade of the 1960s revived. And not in vain. In the first decade of the twenty-first century, Burning Man is the only party happening on a numb planet.

14. Edward Lucie-Smith, *Eroticism in Western Art* (New York: Oxford University Press, 1972), 227, 239.

15. Herbert Brean, "Hidden Sell Technique Is Almost Here," *Life*, March 31, 1958, 102–14.

16. Frederic de Arechaga, interview with the author, September 20, 1969.

17. Joseph R. Rosenberger, *The Demon Lovers* (Atlanta: Pendulum, 1969), 205.

18. Tennessee Williams, "Preface, *The Slapstick Comedy*," *Esquire*, August 1965, 95.

19. Catherine Yronwode, advertising brochure, Lucky Mojo Company. Available online at http://luckymojo.com.

3. SEX AND WITCHCRAFT

1. See Joe Hyams, "A Revealing Look into the Mysterious Mind of Charles 'Satan' Manson," *National Enquirer*, February 15, 1970.

2. Anton LaVey, *National Insider*, February 22, 1970.

3. Frederic de Arechaga, interview with the author, September 20, 1969.

4. Adrian Kirch, interview with the author, February 8, 1970.

5. Gerald Gardner, *The Book of Shadows*, quoted from pages purportedly hand-copied by Gardner, and shown to the author in a private office at the East End Public Bath and Wash House across the street from the Bethnal Green Museum of Childhood, London, May 17, 1969. Within cult, no codified and copyrighted true *Book of Shadows* exists because copies of this ever-adapting document are typically hand-written by covens and witches; on the internet, the very mutable (and some say tampered-with) content of *The Book of Shadows* is reflected in the thousands of files posted. Commercially, Robin B. May and Gerald Brosseau have created a book titled *Gardner's Book of Shadows* (New York: Allisone Press, 2000).

6. Tom Burke, "Princess Leda's Castle in the Air," *Esquire*, March 1970, 107.

7. Edward Lucie-Smith, *Race, Sex, and Gender in Contemporary Art* (New York: Harry N. Abrams, 1994), 95.

8. Brothers of Blasphemy, internet party invitation, collection of the author, November 7, 2003.

9. Sons of Satan personal ad, *Drummer*, April 1989, 92.

10. William Carney, *The Real Thing* (New York: Putnam, 1968), 49, 50, 119, 122.

11. Ibid., 43.

12. Ibid., 47.

13. Jack Fritscher, *Some Dance to Remember* (Stamford, Conn.: Knights Press, 1990), 276–78.

14. In June 1993, *Esquire* revisited Lois's Ali cover, and brought it out of the closet,

by shooting the very reluctant gay icon "Marky Mark" Wahlberg stripped to the waist, bound to a stake with ropes, groping his crotch and screaming. Peggy Sirota shot the photo of Wahlberg as a kind of postmodern Saint Sebastian, to illustrate the feature article "The Penitent Marky Mark and the Fabulous New Straight Camp."

15. Edward Lucie-Smith, *Eroticism in Western Art* (New York: Oxford University Press, 1972), 265.

16. Fritscher, *Some Dance*, 253.

17. Ibid.,161.

18. Ibid., 173.

19. Marco Vassi, *The Metasex Manifesto* (New York: Bantam Books, Penthouse Press, Ltd, 1976), 89–94.

20. Fritscher, *Some Dance*, 239.

21. Mark Thompson, introduction to *Leatherfolk: Radical Sex, People, Politics, and Practice* (Boston: Alyson, 1991), xiii.

22. Carney, *The Real Thing*, 47.

23. Anton LaVey, private conversation with the author, August 3, 1971.

24. Heribert Jone and Urban Adelman, *Moral Theology*, additional translation and editing by Jack Fritscher (Westminster, Md.: Newman Press, 1961).

25. Michelle Carr and Elvia Lahman, *Velvet Hammer* e-zine, souvenir program of the Velvet Hammer Burlesque Company, "Interview with Anton LaVey," September 11, 1997. Available online at http://www.velvethammerburlesque.com.

26. Anton LaVey, private conversation with the author, August 3, 1971.

27. Anton LaVey, informational brochure for the Church of Satan, 1969.

28. Alex Sanders, *Alex Sanders Lectures* (New York: Magickal Childe, 1984), 29.

29. June Johns, *Mensa Bulletin*, October–November, 1969.

30. Ibid.

31. Thomas Hardy, *The Return of the Native* (New York: Signet Classic, 1959), 355–57.

32. Kim Klein, *The Washington Post: Potomac*, May 10, 1970.

33. Gershon Legman, *Rationale of the Dirty Joke: An Analysis of Sexual Humor* (New York: Grove Press, 1968), 575.

34. Steve Dunleavy, "The Incredible Story of Satan and His Fanatic Followers," *National Enquirer,* January 11, 1970.

35. Anton LaVey, *National Insider*, January 4, 1970.

36. Daniel St. Albin Greene, "There May Be a Witch Next Door," *National Observer*, October 13, 1969, 24.

37. LeJeunesse, interview with the author, May 15, 1970.

4. STRAIGHT FROM THE WITCH'S MOUTH

1. Free-thinking feminist Annie Besant (1847–1933) met Madame Blavatsky in 1887 and converted from Christianity to Blavatsky's theosophy. When Blavatsky died in 1891, the Theosophical Society split in two, with Besant as head of one branch.

INDEX

Trumbo, Dalton, 63
Truzzi, Marcello, 70
Tuatha de Danaan, 59, 60
Turing, Alan, 144, 145
Turn of the Screw (film), 97, 110, 228
Twain, Mark, 114
"Twelve Musical Albums of the Zodiac"
  (album series), 88
Twice Told Tales (book), 137
Twilight Zone (TV series), 116
*Typical Day's Torture of Woman Accused
  of Witchcraft* (book), 171

UFO, 126, 201
Uncle Tom's Cabin (book), xi
Unholy Three (film), 112
United States Chaplain's Manual (book), x
United States Constitution, 3, 44, 55, 123,
  136, 181
United States postal laws on frontal
  nudity, 52, 168
United States Postal Service, 181
United States Supreme Court, 52
United States vs. Fay (court case), 51
Unitrol: The Healing Magic of the Mind
  (book), 56
Universe Book Club, 71
University of Alabama, 49
University of Goettingen, 69
University of Michigan, 76
University of South Carolina, 49
*Urban Aboriginals: A Celebration of
  Leathersexuality* (book), 151
urine, 59, 146, 158, 159, 181, 190
USA Trilogy (book), 107

Vadim, Roger, 84
vagina dentata, 107
Vagina Monologs (play), 108
Vampira, 116
vampire, xv, 21, 31, 41, 77, 98, 99, 101, 107,
  108, 111, 112, 117, 127, 158, 226, 228

Vampire: His Kith and Kin (book), 226
Vampyr (film), 99, 157, 158
Van Druten, John, 36, 96
Vandals, 35
vanishing creme, 125
Vanity Fair (magazine), 225
Vassi, Marco, 164, 230
Vatican, 10, 81, 216
Vatican Council II, ix, 143, 163
Vaughan, Sarah, 81
Velvet Hammer (Burlesque Company,
  and e-zine), 178, 230
Venus (Goddess), 91, 93, 96, 206, 223
Veterans of the Spanish Civil War, 14
Via Veneto, 81
Vidal, Gore, 96, 191
Vietnam, 15, 157, 210
Village Voice (newspaper), 226
Vincent de Paul, Saint, 169
Violent Bear It Away (book), 64
virgin sacrifice, 29, 48
Virgin Spring (film), 103, 105
Visigoths, 35
Viva la Muerte (film), 111
volcano God, 49
von Däniken, Erich, xi, 201
von Krafft-Ebing, Richard Feiherr, 57,
  108, 112
von Sternberg, Joseph, 107
von Sydow, Max, 103
voodoo, 86, 120, 122, 123, 129, 135, 153,
  170, 222
"Voodoo Chile" (song), 86

Waggner, George, 100
Wahlberg, (Marky) Mark, 230
Walden: or Life in the Woods (book), xi,
  xii
Wallace, George, 15, 61, 181, 226
Walpurgisnacht, 3, 27
Waltari, Mika, 108
Wanda the Witch, 124

A Ray and Pat Browne Book

Murder on the Reservation: American Indian Crime Fiction
Ray B. Browne

ﹰ

Goddesses and Monsters: Women, Myth, Power, and Popular Culture
Jane Caputi

ﹰ

Mystery, Violence, and Popular Culture
John G. Cawelti

ﹰ

Baseball and Country Music
Don Cusic

ﹰ

Popular Witchcraft: Straight from the Witch's Mouth, 2nd edition
Jack Fritscher

ﹰ

The Essential Guide to Werewolf Literature
Brian J. Frost

ﹰ

Images of the Corpse: From the Renaissance to Cyberspace
Edited by Elizabeth Klaver

ﹰ

Walking Shadows: Orson Welles, William Randolph Hearst, and Citizen Kane
John Evangelist Walsh

ﹰ

Spectral America: Phantoms and the National Imagination
Edited by Jeffrey Andrew Weinstock